AF580590

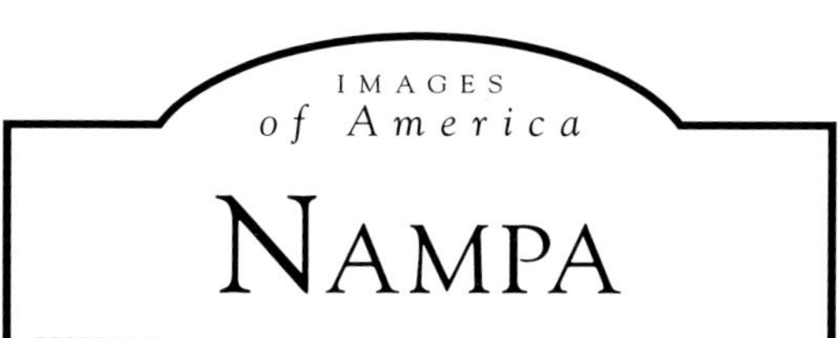
IMAGES
of America
NAMPA

On the Cover: Taken in 1949, this image shows Nampa's Main Street looking northwest. The presence of new cars and bicycles illustrates that the city was recovering economically from World War II. (Courtesy of the Canyon County Historical Society.)

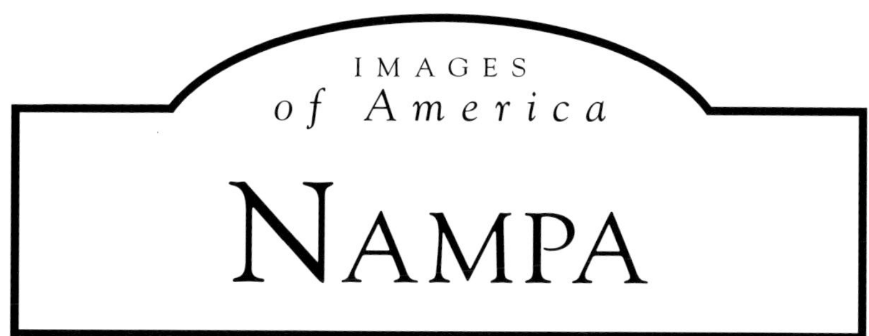

Larry Cain

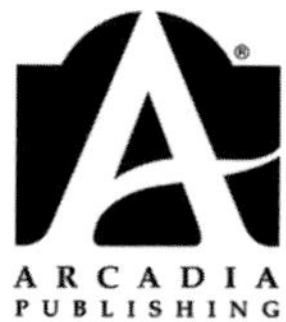

ISBN 978-1-4671-3212-1

Published by Arcadia Publishing
Charleston, South Carolina

Printed in the United States of America

Library of Congress Control Number: 2014931003

For all general information, please contact Arcadia Publishing:
Telephone 843-853-2070
Fax 843-853-0044
E-mail sales@arcadiapublishing.com
For customer service and orders:
Toll-Free 1-888-313-2665

Visit us on the Internet at www.arcadiapublishing.com

Dedicated to my son Kevin Cain, who would have loved the history and pictures presented in this book.

Contents

Acknowledgments		6
Introduction		7
1.	Transportation	9
2.	Business and Industry	25
3.	Restaurants, Hotels, and Entertainment	41
4.	Churches, Schools, and Public Buildings	53
5.	Downtown and Neighborhoods	63
6.	Radio	75
7.	Events	87
8.	Sports	105

Acknowledgments

Special thanks go to Tom Mark and the Canyon County Historical Society for their help with most of the photographs in this book. I would also like to thank Bob Quinly for his editing help on this and other books. My wife, Bonnie Jean Cain, gave constant encouragement and suggestions along the way. I should mention my high school history teacher, Annie Laurie Bird, who gave me a love of history and an ongoing curiosity about my hometown's past. Unless otherwise noted, all photographs are courtesy of the Canyon County Historical Society.

Introduction

When plans for the Boise & Central Idaho railway were approved, the tracks were to cross Alexander Duffes's Indian Creek Ranch. Duffes started the Nampa Townsite Company, which was incorporated on September 6, 1886. Within a year, the town had grown from 15 houses to 50. Daniel Bacon moved his newspaper from Boise to Nampa in 1888 and renamed it the *Nampa Progress*; this helped develop the town, and its population grew to 347 by 1890. In a few more months, irrigated farming became possible close to Nampa, and a year later, a municipal government was organized.

By 1900, Nampa had a good representation of church denominations and an adequate school system. About 66,000 acres of irrigated farms were in production near the town, and another branch railway—the Boise, Nampa & Owyhee—had reached Murphy in 1899. With the Idaho Central being purchased by the Oregon Short Line, the Boise branch line retained the name while the rest of the railroad became part of the Oregon Short Line. These two railroads merged in Nampa along with the Idaho Northern and the Boise, Nampa & Owyhee. Four railroads meeting in Nampa gave it the nickname of the "Junction City."

By 1900, the town had an aggressive home-building industry, a number of churches, and a good school system, which graduated its first high school class (nine girls) in 1903. The first boy to graduate was Adin Fox in 1904. These things made it an attractive place to settle. Nearly 66,000 acres of irrigated farmland now surrounded the town, and it was becoming a trade center for the agricultural area, which created a friendly atmosphere for the growth of business.

The travel book *Over the Range to the Golden Gate*, published in 1904, describes Nampa: "Population 1500, industries, fine agriculture and fruit and exceptional stock raising facilities. Iron foundry, canning and evaporating establishments, creamery. One hundred and fifty thousand acres of fine land now under water; forty thousand acres under cultivation, balance will be irrigated upon completion of present irrigation plants."

In 1907, the completion of the Deer Flat Reservoir (or Lake Lowell) brought thousands of additional acres under cultivation. The most important industry that year was the opening of the Western Idaho Sugar factory. It flourished until 1909, when blight corrupted the beet crop. The farmers thought the company had given them bad seed, and the beet crop fell off so drastically that the factory was dismantled in 1912. But the growth in other areas of agriculture led to more expansion in Nampa. In 1926, Pacific Fruit Express opened, which contributed to more growth. The company operated refrigerated railcars so produce could be shipped all over the United States and Canada. It was a joint venture between the Union Pacific and Southern Pacific Railroads.

Business growth brought the formation of the chamber of commerce in 1905. It put out advertising and publications that extolled the virtues of Nampa, the Junction City. These promotions brought people to settle in the town and attracted new businesses to Nampa.

Social life blossomed by 1900 and continued to grow through the 20th century. Many clubs were formed. They sponsored all kinds of entertainment to raise money for noble causes, and improvements for the citizens of the city flowed forth. The Women's Century Club was the most prominent in the early years, and the group is still a force today. It was the driving force in obtaining a library for the city's readers, and it also formed the first kindergarten. Other clubs and organizations that brought improvement to Nampa include the Lions, with their glasses program; and Kiwanis, which funded a track for the high school athletic program, to name just two. All of the service clubs were dedicated to the improvement of life for Nampa's citizens.

Dances were a favorite pastime of the town's populace from the beginning. Some of the dance halls that were very popular were Yorgason's, the Lake Lowell Pavilion, Moonbeam, and the Eagles in the 1920s, as well as Shadowland and El Patio in the ensuing years. The movies were always a huge draw. The most popular theater was the Majestic, with its fantastic decoration. Others were the Liberty (later the Adelaide) and the Pix. Sports were also popular. High school sports like football and basketball started in 1909, and both were still being played over 100 years later. Fans came to old Rodeo Park and, later, Bulldog Bowl for football, and after 1937, they gathered at the Central Assembly Building for basketball. Local town teams in basketball, baseball, and softball brought the faithful to the parks on warm summer evenings.

Education improved, and the schools multiplied. In 1929, Central Junior High School was opened, and 1937 saw the Central Assembly Building and Eastside and Roosevelt Grade Schools put into service. Lincoln Elementary School began in 1949, and a new high school was established in 1955, showing that the city was dedicated to education. Northwest Nazarene College opened in 1913 and continued to grow with the town. The Nazarene Academy evolved into Nampa Christian High School. As of today, two more public high schools and a number of charter schools have been added to the mix.

Nampa saw its share of disasters and bad times, such as the fire of 1909, the Drake Drug fire in 1937, the explosion of the Forbidden Palace in 1947, and, of course, the Great Depression, but they also had good times and enjoyed special events like Chautauqua, Harvest Festival, rodeos, sports, and business promotions that brought in special entertainment and low prices.

As the century matured, Nampa grew and became a typical American small town. A national publication, *Parade Magazine*, featured Nampa as just that, devoting parts of two issues to the community. The *Idaho Free Press* and KFXD started a publicity campaign a full month before the big event. There was a full week of activities in the town, including a Hollywood premiere at the Majestic. Additionally, Mutual Broadcasting System produced their daily show "The Better Half" from Central Auditorium, and the well-known local group the Eight Piano Symphony performed. The magazine tabbed Nampa as "Main Street America," and a new sign proclaimed the distinction over the Eleventh Avenue subway. The merchants' business during that week broke all records by a landslide.

Nampa's history is rich, and this book will give readers a flavor of the community's growth, activities, and life in general, with photographs that illustrate the years and the interests of the people.

One

Transportation

Transportation was Nampa's finest asset, but there has to be something to ship to the markets of the nation and the world. Agriculture was the product, a commodity that found its way to the gleaming rails leading out of the Junction City. The Pacific Fruit Express, with its refrigerator cars, supplied the means to ship fresh produce across the nation. In the early days, silver came down to Murphy, Idaho, from Silver City, then to Nampa and the Oregon Short Line, and later, the Union Pacific Railroad. Cattle followed the valuable mineral from Murphy. Cattle and lumber found their way to the Idaho Northern from McCall to Nampa. Passengers boarded the trains in Junction City being funneled in by the connecting railroads. Many others were brought to the depot by the interurban light rail line that covered the valley. It made a complete circle, traveling from Boise to Caldwell to Nampa. The smaller towns of Middleton, Star, Eagle, and Meridian were just a few of the stops on the way. The railroad cars did not lack for something to fill them.

Buses carried people around the valley starting in the early 1920s, but they really became a factor when the interurban ceased operations in May 1925. Each day, 30 stages passed through Nampa going east and west; that number soon increased to 36 a day. Union Pacific Stages started operating a line between Nampa, Boise, Gooding, Jerome, Hagerman, and Twin Falls. Greyhound and Trailways followed, and a person could go just about anywhere in the nation on a bus.

The automobile cannot be overlooked, as it added personal transportation to the mix. By the 1930s, Nampa's transportation outlets were the most comprehensive in Idaho.

Nampa continued to see freight shipped in abundance during World War II. Produce, cattle, and lumber continued with the addition of soldiers and materials to aid the war effort. Products are still shipped today by rail and truck out of Nampa, a process that will continue into the future.

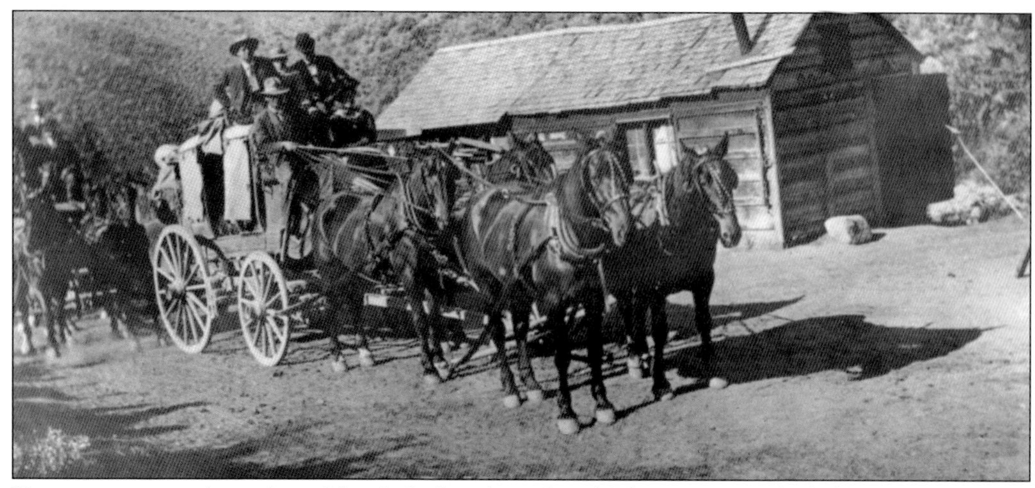

Horsepower moved people and freight before the railroad. This stage is at the halfway stop between Murphy and Silver City. Later, when the Boise, Nampa & Owyhee Railroad was completed, horses were still used to carry passengers and freight from Murphy to Silver City (as the railroad ended at Murphy).

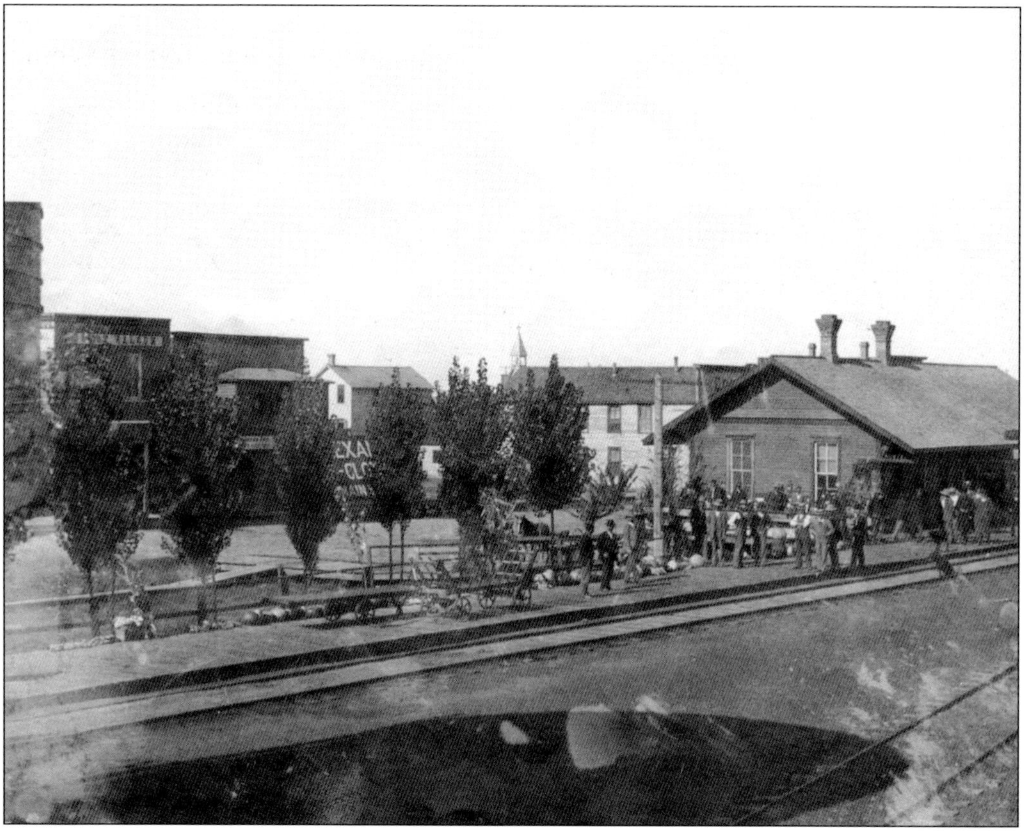

Nampa's first depot, located on Front Street, is pictured around 1900. It served as both a passenger and freight depot. The building had been moved from King Hill and was in service until 1903, when a new depot was erected. It was still used as a freight depot for a number of years.

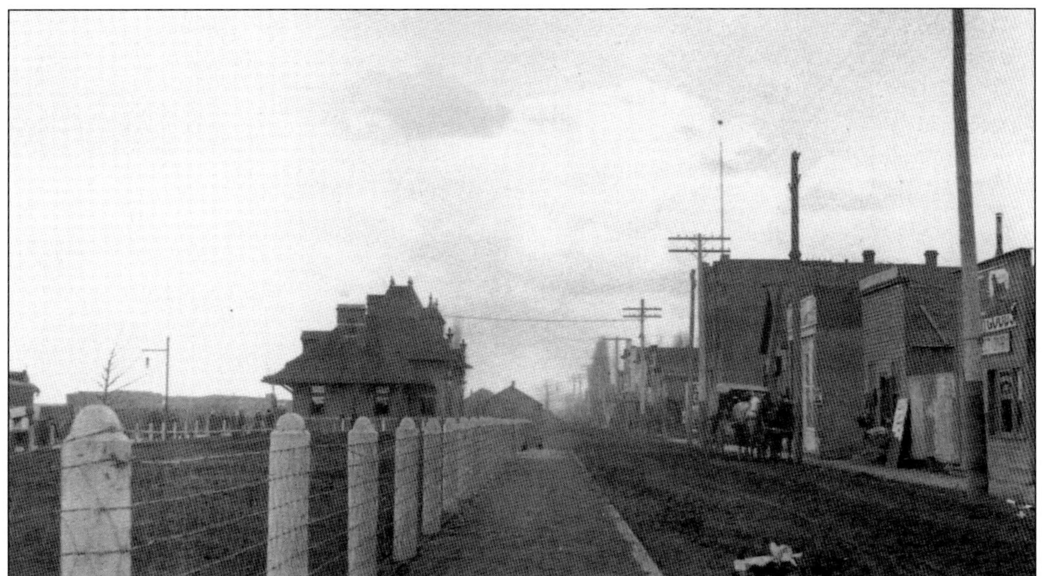

The new Oregon Short Line (OSL) depot located on Front Street opened in 1903. Barely visible just left of center, people are waiting for the next train as a horse-and-buggy traverses the muddy street on the right. Travel by horse was about to be put out to pasture as the first automobile appeared in Nampa in 1903, when Horatio Jackson passed through on his coast-to-coast drive. The old depot can be seen in the distance.

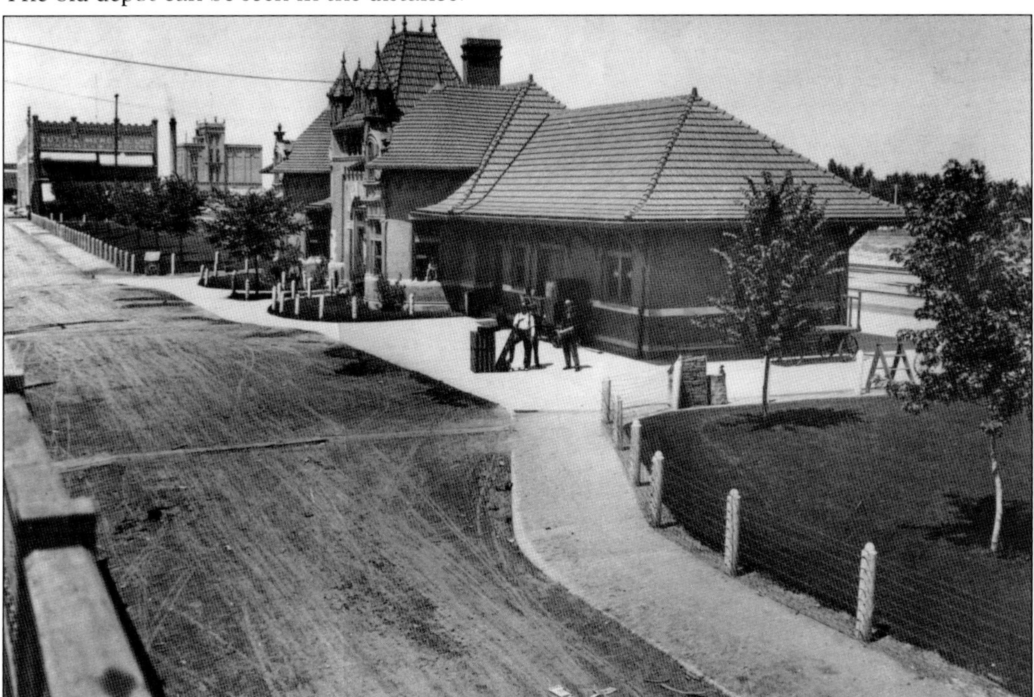

In 1908, the street is smoother but still dirt. The OSL Depot is seen here from the balcony of the Commercial Hotel. The Tuttle Mercantile Company and the new brewery can be seen in the background. The image can be dated to sometime between 1907 (when the brewery was built) and 1909 (when the Commercial Hotel burned).

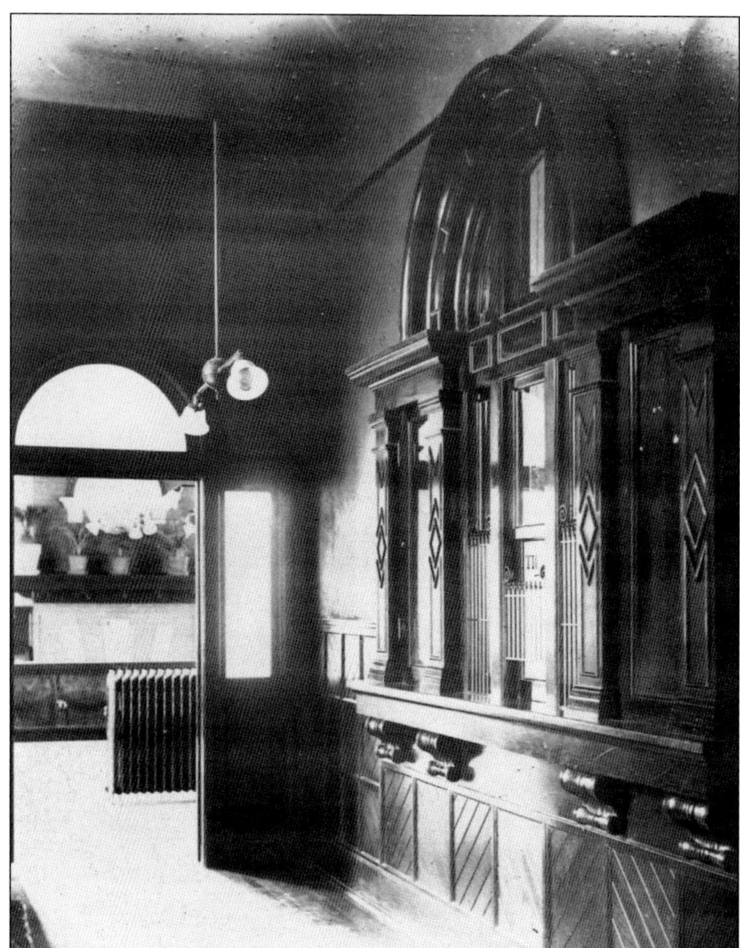

In this interior view of the Oregon Short Line depot, the ticket window, where departing passengers purchased their tickets, is in the foreground. The ladies' waiting room is in the background. There were separate waiting rooms for men and women; the women's had a fireplace, however, and the men's did not. Each side had a door to the loading platform.

This is a c. 1907 front view of the depot, located at the end of G Street (later Twelfth Avenue South) on the south side of the tracks. It houses the Canyon County Historical Society's Depot Museum today. The corner at left where the men are standing was the entrance to the Cosmopolitan Saloon.

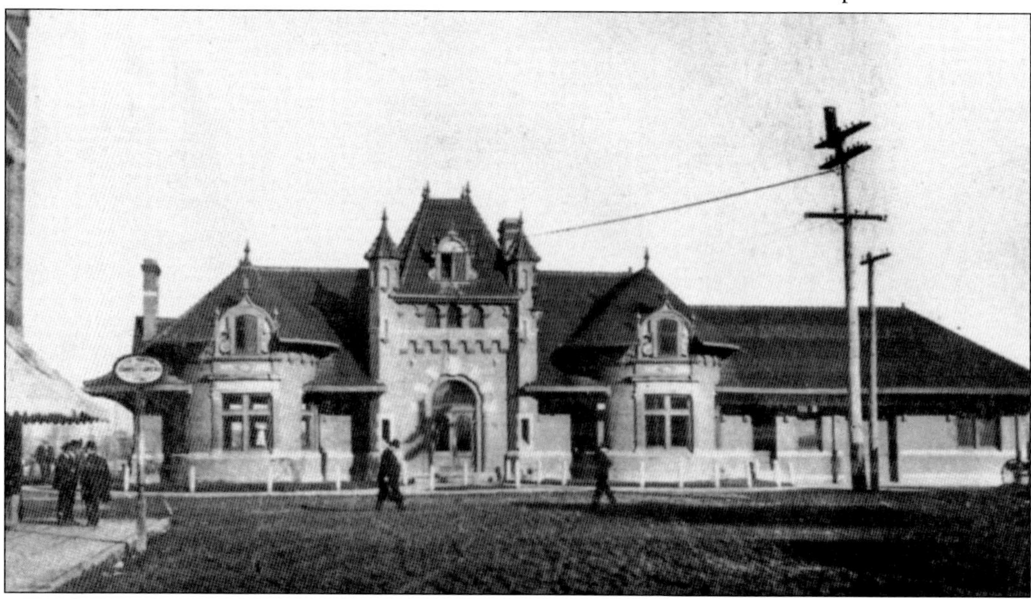

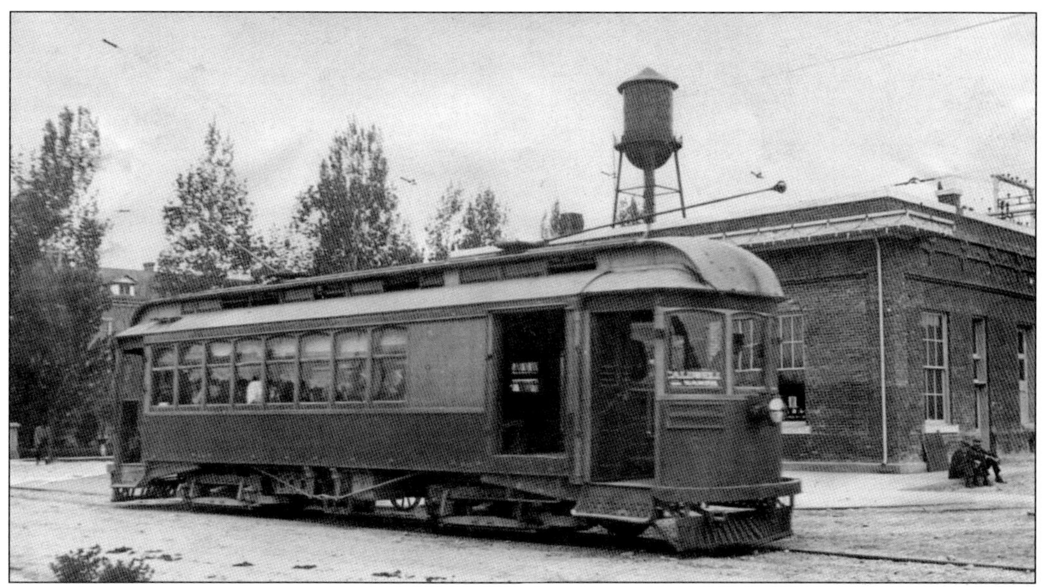

This interurban car is leaving the depot at Eleventh Avenue and Second Street South. The sign in the window of the car is announcing Caldwell as the next stop. The interurban was purchased by the Idaho Power Company, and when the line ceased operations, the depot was used as office space by the company.

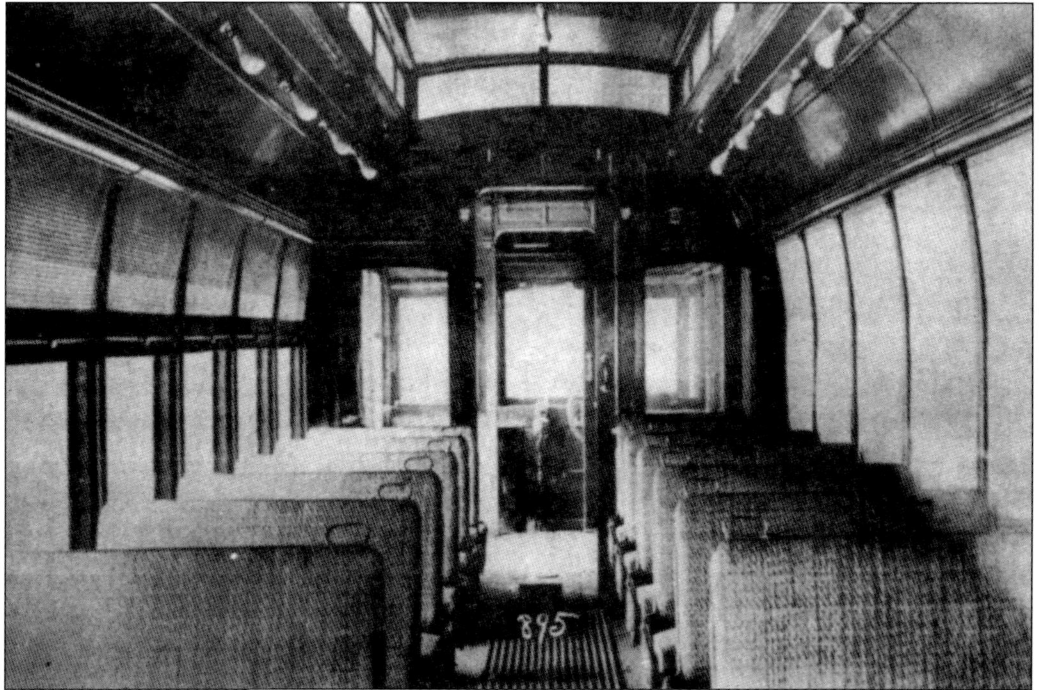

This is the interior of an interurban car around 1908. It had upholstered seats and windows that opened; everything one could want. These cars stopped many, many times before making the full circle. Not only did they stop at Nampa, Boise, and Caldwell, they also paused at every little town on the line, in addition to stops in rural areas.

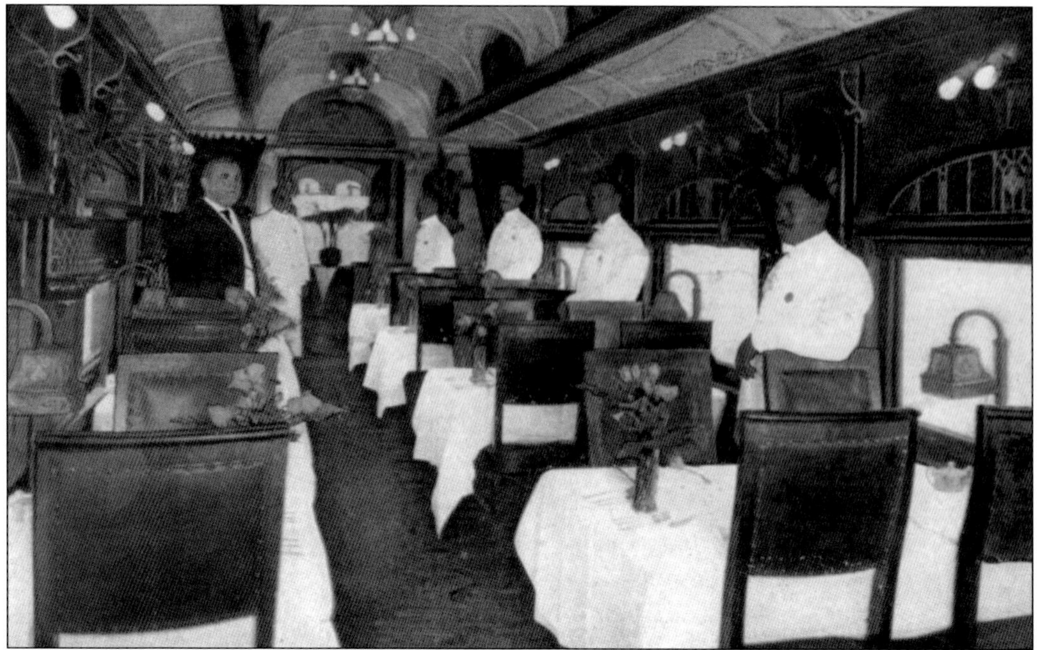

Even though the interurban car was comfortable, the OSL dining car was nothing but luxury, as shown here. It had full service with waiters, busboys, and multicourse meals. Every railroad advertised its food and service and competed with each other for the top spot. In the 1800s, the Pullman Hotel car offered 133 food items.

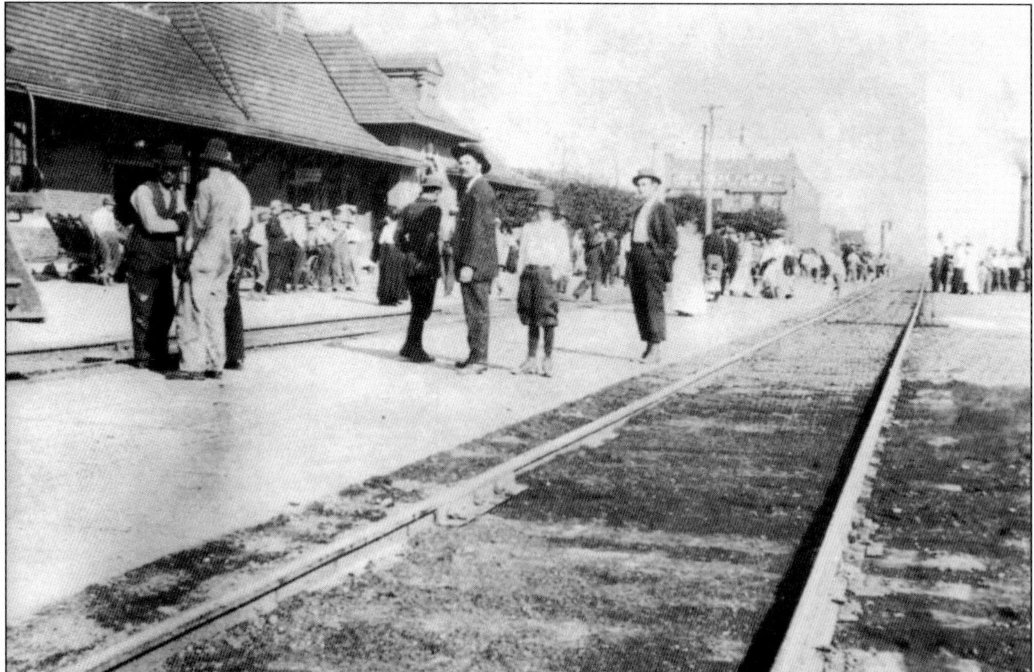

It looks like a train will be arriving soon, as people are waiting on both sides of the tracks at the OSL depot around 1915. The fashions of the day are well represented, including the short pants worn by young boys. Smoke is coming from the Crescent Brewery's chimney on the right.

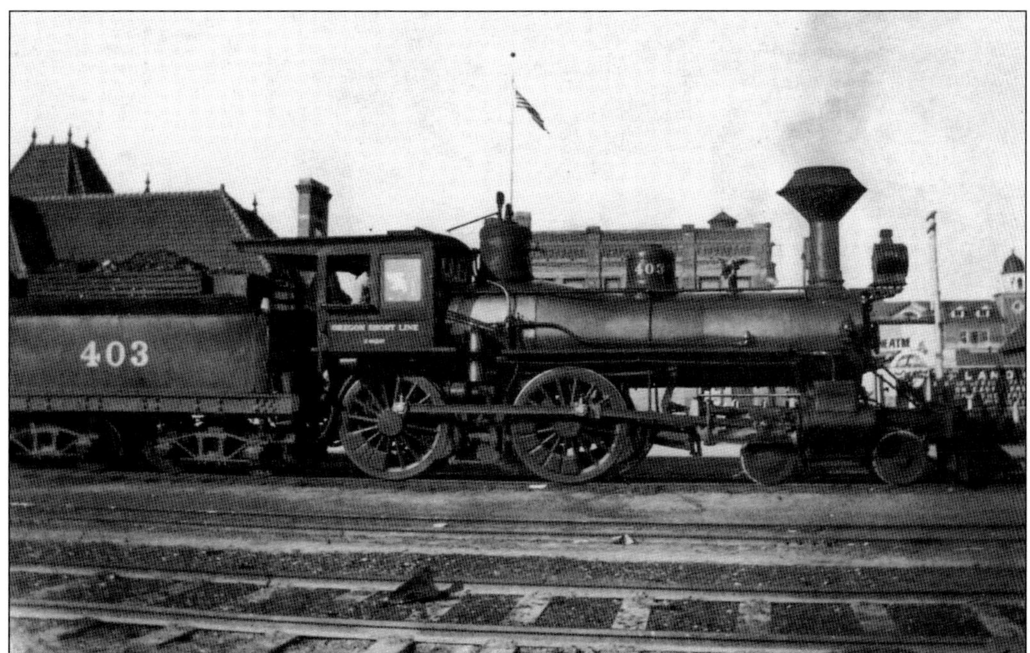

The pony engine, a small locomotive, was used mainly on the branch line between Nampa and Boise. The number of cars pulled was much less than on a train on the main line; thus, the smaller engine. The trains that made up the Boise local carried freight and passengers. The engine has "Oregon Short Line" written under the window where the engineer is seen.

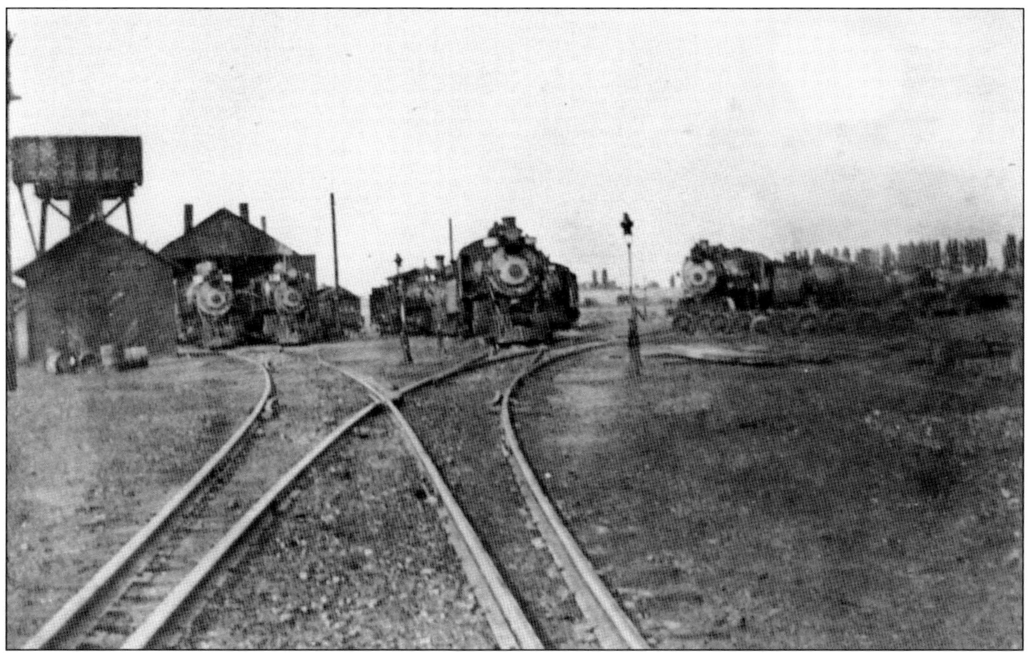

Pictured here around 1916 is the first roundhouse in Nampa. Much of the work was done outdoors, as evidenced by the trucks on the right. It would grow over the years as service needs increased. New buildings of greater size allowed the work to move inside. The engines were serviced and repaired in the facility.

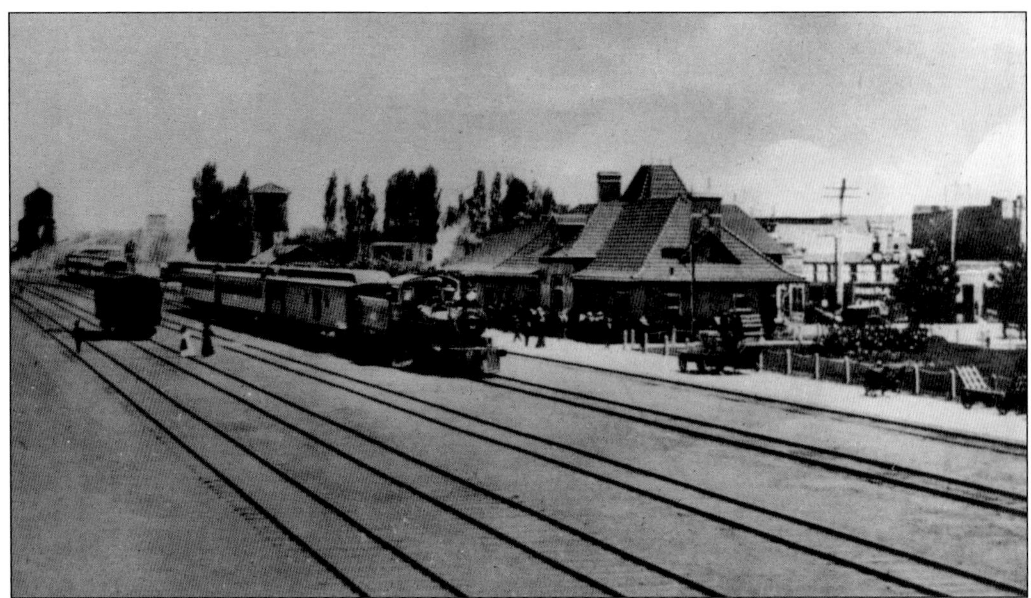

The pony engine is pulling a mail and freight car and two passenger cars for the trip to Boise on the local in about 1915. The coaling station (the tall, dark building) can be seen in the yard south of the train. Note that the platform is filled with people, while the streets seem to be empty.

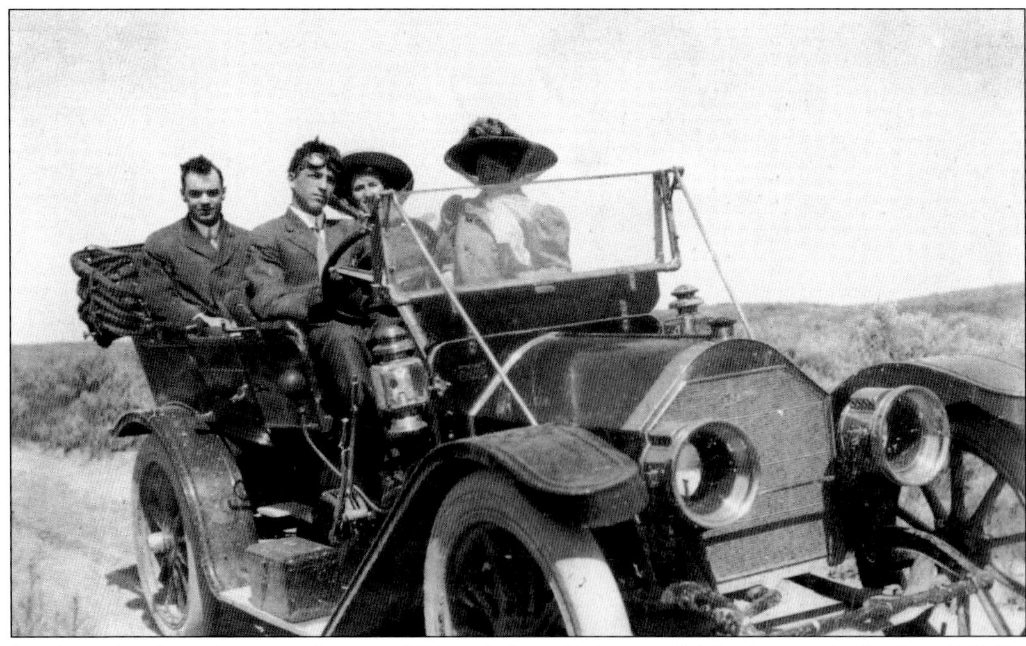

Joe Partridge drives Emmett Road in 1910 with Jesse Colvin and Ada Artz in the back and Nellie Williamson beside him. This was an adventurous trip over the pockmarked roads of the time. Partridge was an outstanding athlete and student at Nampa High School. He served as a fighter pilot in World War I and went on to become a lawyer.

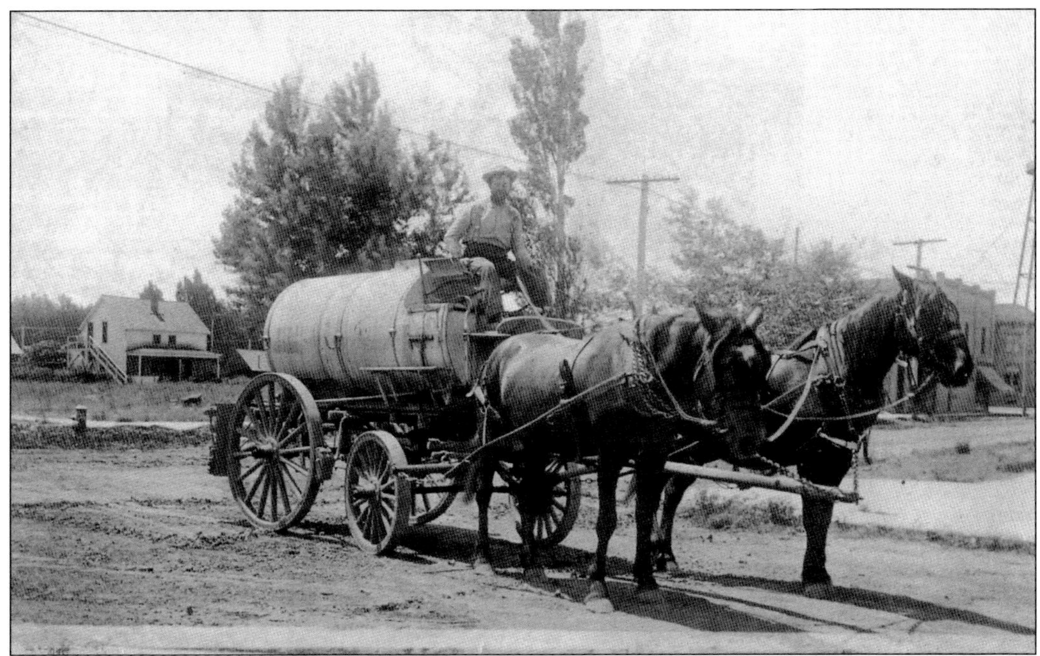

Mr. Park is pictured here driving the city water wagon in about 1908. Water was applied to the roads in the dry months to keep the dust down. Horses and buggies could raise the dust, but automobiles increased it. The photograph was taken at the corner of Thirteenth Avenue and Second Street South. The Odd Fellows Hall is a block down on the left.

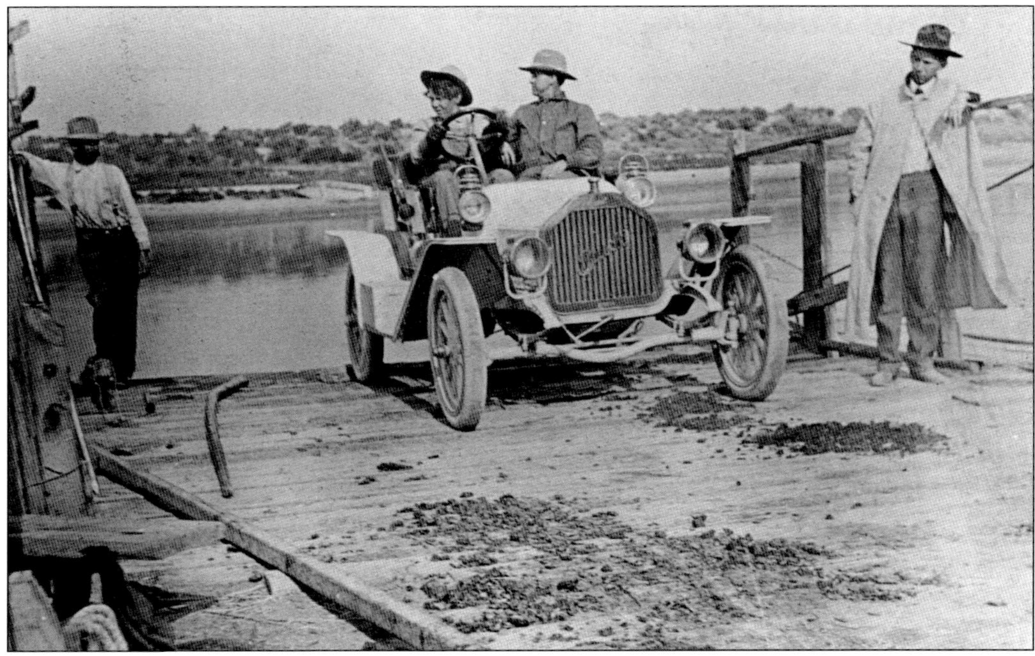

Frank Joyner drives the family's new Buick—with his father, Dr J.C. Joyner, in the passenger seat—onto the barge at Walters Ferry in about 1915. Ed Meek is the ferryman at left, and Mon Schumate looks on. Ferries were common then; they were used to get to Homedale and Marsing, as there were no bridges at those locations.

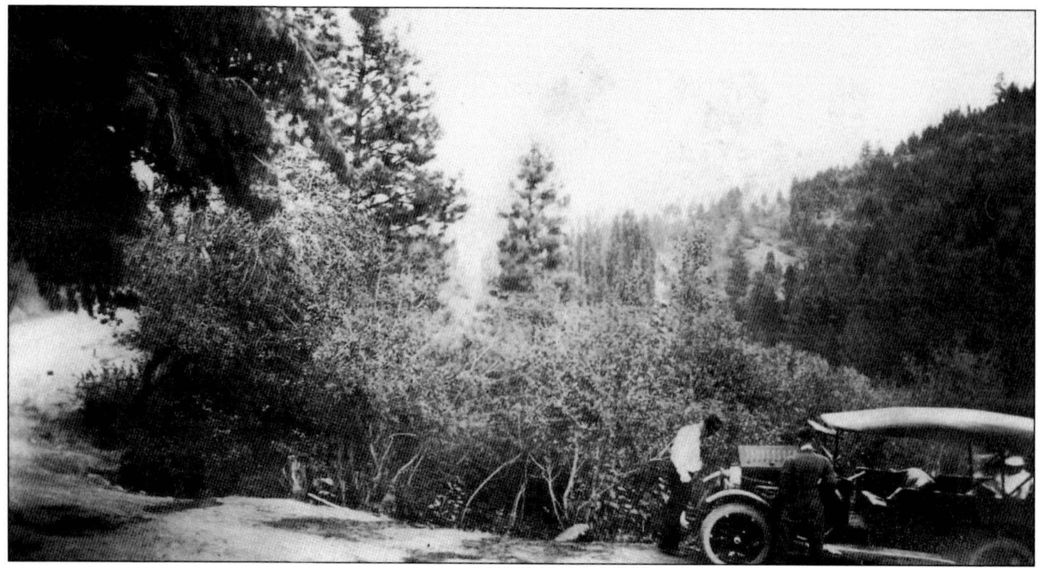

The Idaho City road is seen here around 1922. It was not unusual for a trip to be interrupted by a faulty carburetor or a flat tire. Roadside repairs were commonplace in that era, when cars and tires were not as reliable as they are today. A full tool kit and the knowledge of how to use it were as important as a driver's license.

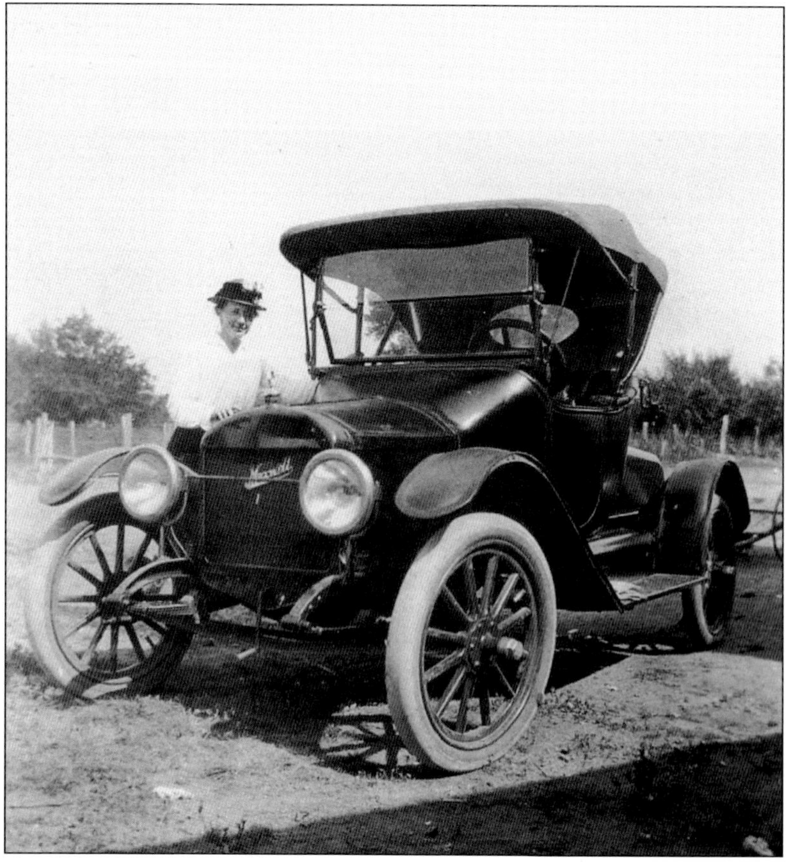

Clara Bauman proudly poses by her new Maxwell in about 1925. She and her husband, Oscar, ran the Bon Ton Candy Kitchen in downtown Nampa. The Maxwell was Jack Benny's old car that Rochester drove on his radio show. Like most automobiles of the 1920s, it provided little shelter from the elements.

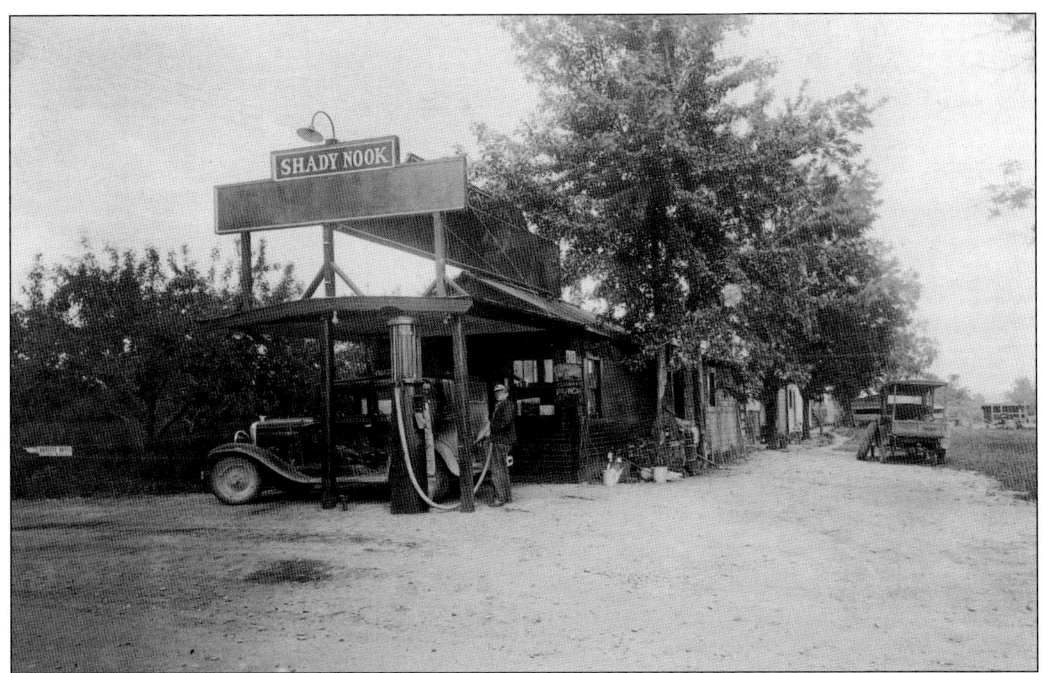

Al Waldrat pumps gas at his Shady Nook service station around 1923. This was the first gas station between Nampa and Caldwell. The sign on the fence at right is for the Payette Hotel. Not only cars got a "drink;" the sign on the wall of the station is for punch.

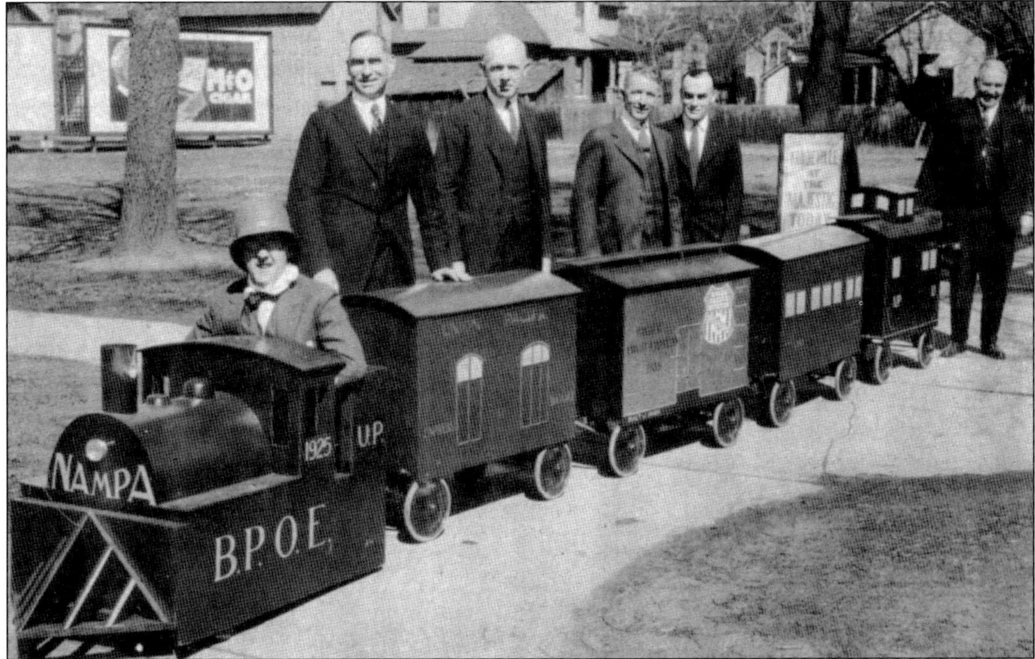

Members of the Nampa Elks Club proudly show off their contribution to Boise's 1925 celebration of the railroad's main line coming through the Capital City for the first time. From left to right are Julius Jacobson (the driver), Jess Hawley, Edgar Graham, Elbert Delana, P.G. Flack, and Erv Johnson (secretary of the lodge).

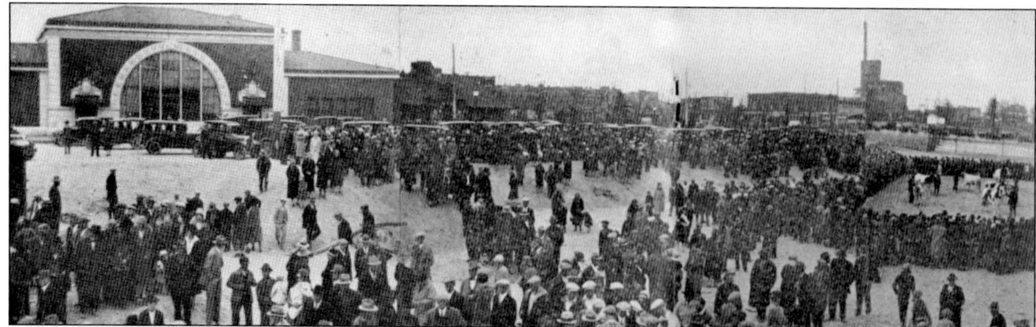

In 1925, Union Pacific replaced the old depot with this new version. Located on the opposite side of the tracks from the 1903 building, it served the city for a number of years. This photograph shows a cattle auction underway on the grounds. The old depot was then used for offices.

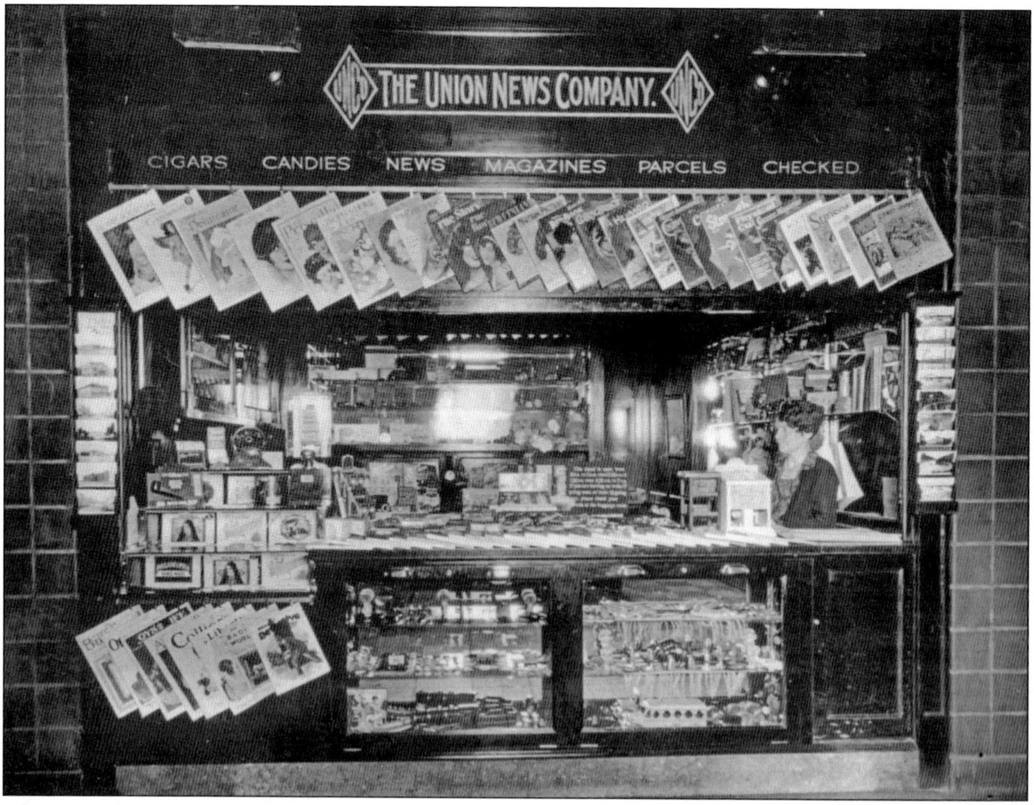

The 1925 depot contained the Union News Company, which sold a huge selection of magazines, newspapers, candy, and cigars and even checked customers' parcels. A traveler needed diversion from the monotony of the road and those hours waiting in the depot for the next train.

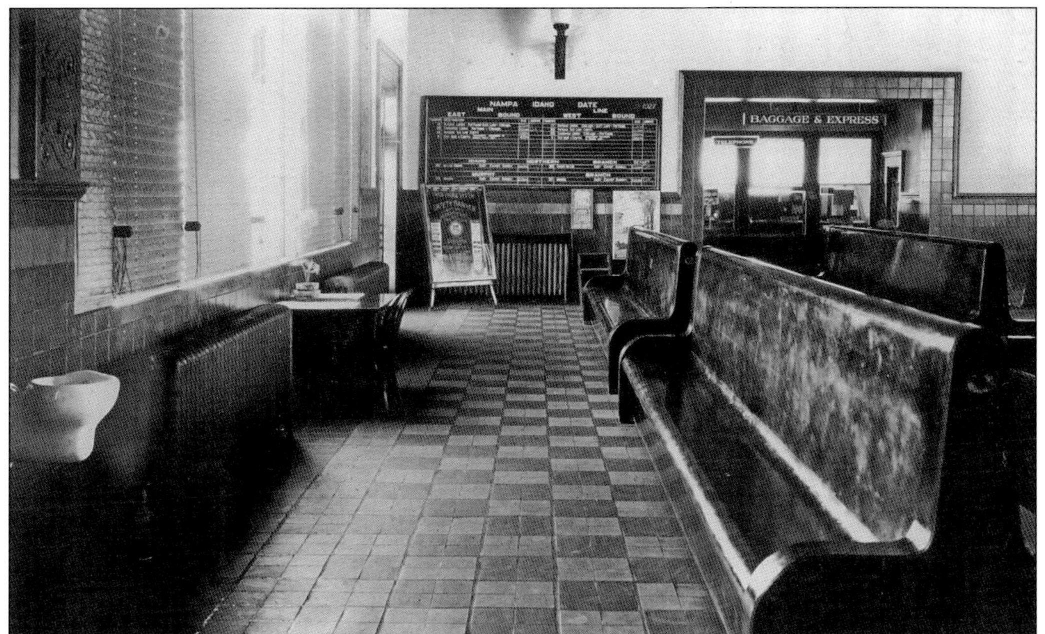

The interior of the new depot is pictured here in 1925. The big board on the wall gives the departure times for various trains. The top shows four going west and four going east on Union Pacific. The next group down shows one arriving and one leaving on the Idaho Northern. The last shows two trains on the Boise, Nampa & Owyhee line.

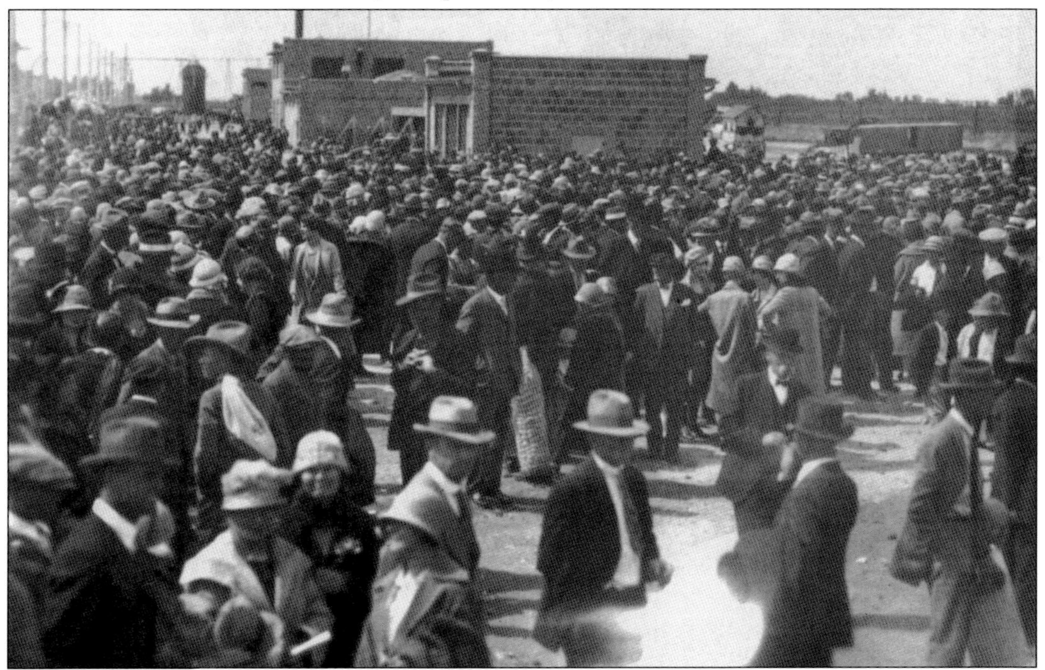

This is the opening-day celebration of Pacific Fruit Express in Nampa on May 4, 1926. As can be seen, the town really turned out for the event. The facility, a joint venture between Union Pacific and Southern Pacific, supplied jobs to men in the area, helping to soften the impact of the Great Depression on Nampa.

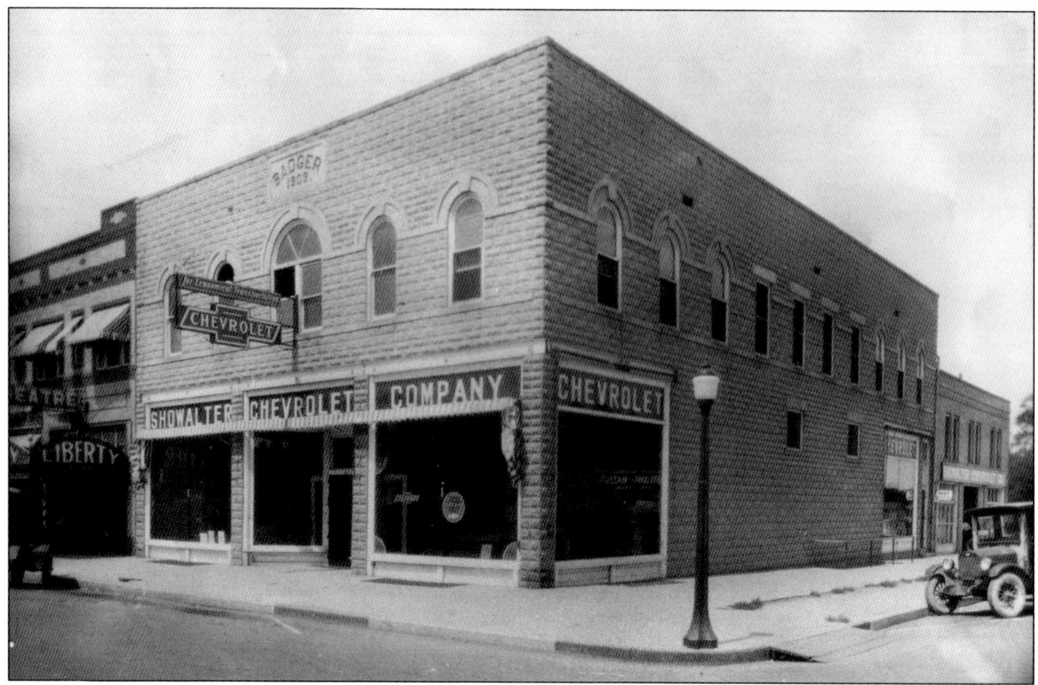

This is the Showalter Chevrolet showroom and shop at First Street and Fourteenth Avenue South in 1930. It was owned by Bill Showalter, who started the business in 1925. Showalter expanded his operation, building at Second Street and Tenth Avenue South in the 1930s. He also expanded his automobile line to include Chevrolet, Oldsmobile, and Cadillac.

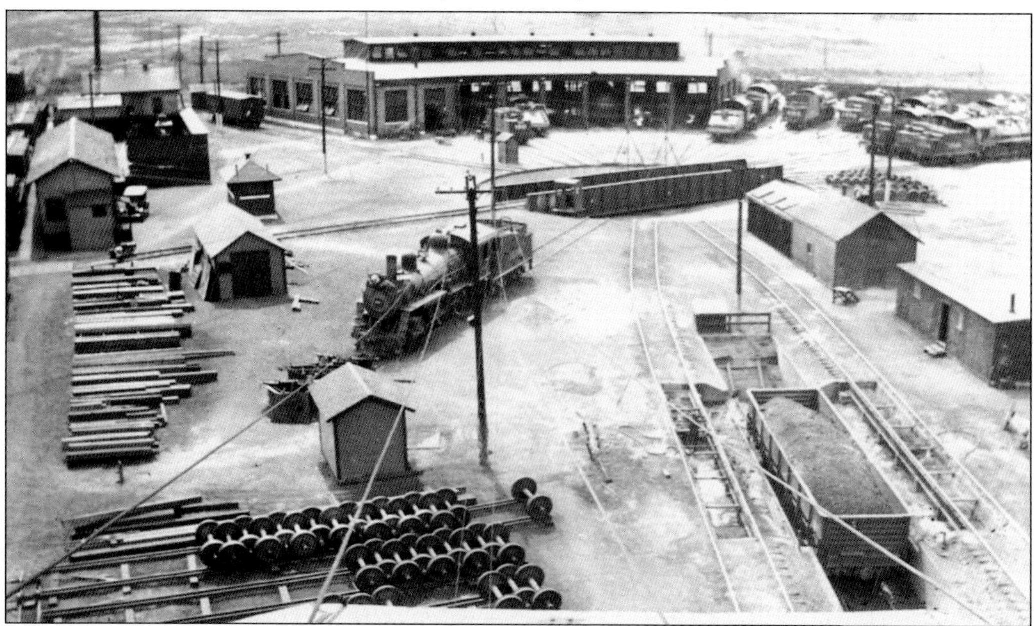

The Nampa roundhouse is seen here in a 1924 photograph by C.H. Peake. Both engines and railcars were serviced and repaired at the facility. During the 1920s, when Union Pacific was developing a sports program for its employees, a baseball field with bleachers and fencing was built on the grounds beside the roundhouse.

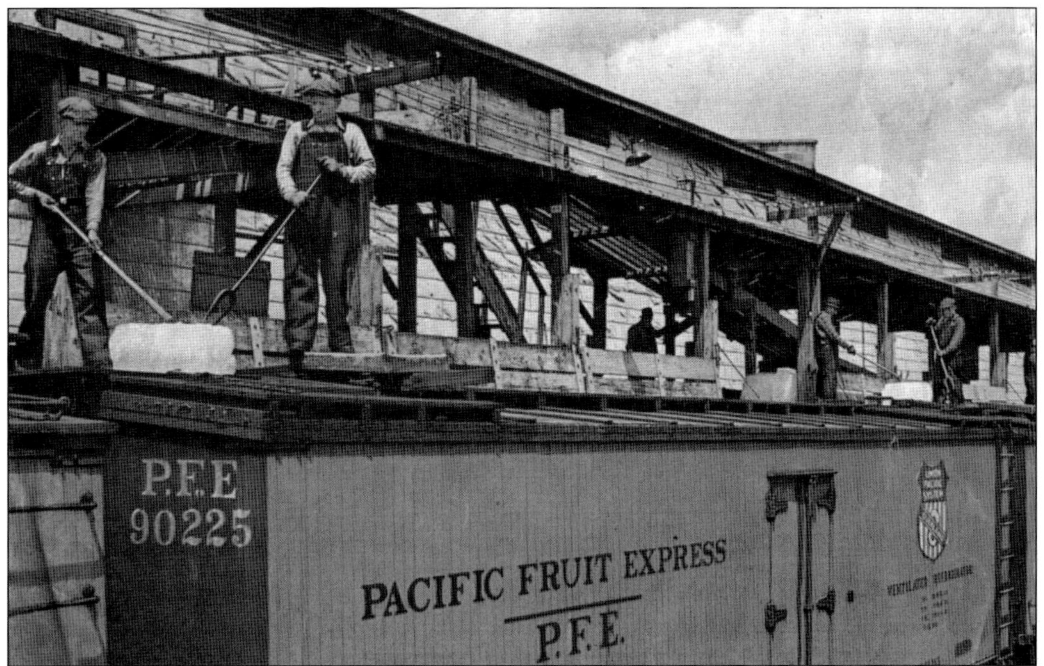

These cars are being iced at Pacific Fruit Express (PFE) in 1960. The facility built, repaired, and refurbished refrigerator cars that carried local produce to the markets of America. In 1941, a football game between the College of Idaho and Gonzaga University, named the "Lettuce Bowl," promoted the crop that was carried on the cars from PFE.

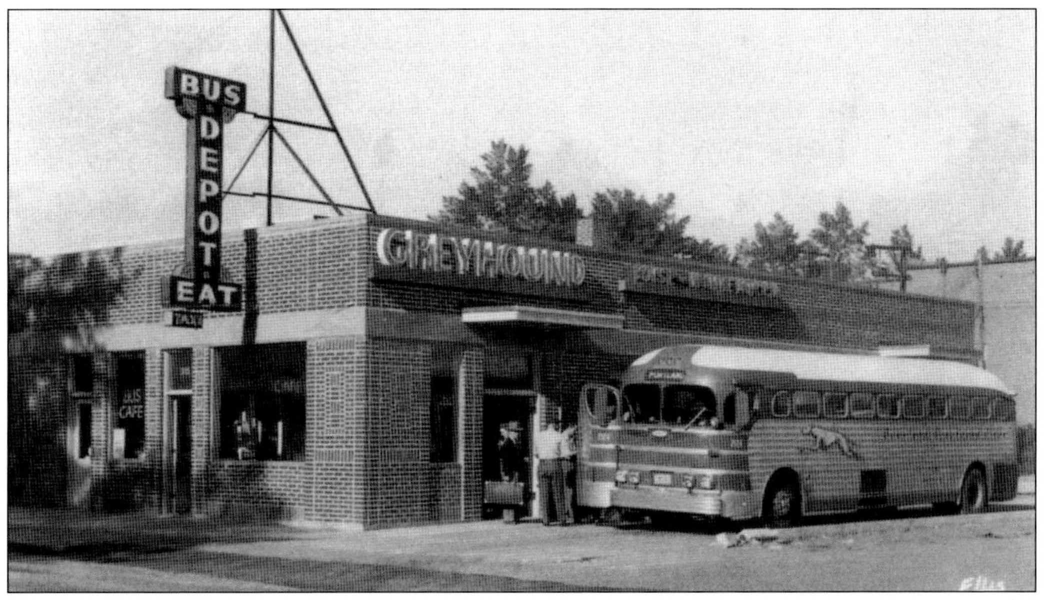

In this image by Ellis Photography, a Greyhound bus is being loaded with passengers at the depot on Twelfth Avenue South between Third and Fourth Streets in 1950. From the size of the gentleman's suitcase, one might guess he was going a long way. The Trailways Depot was on the corner of Second Street and Thirteenth Avenue South.

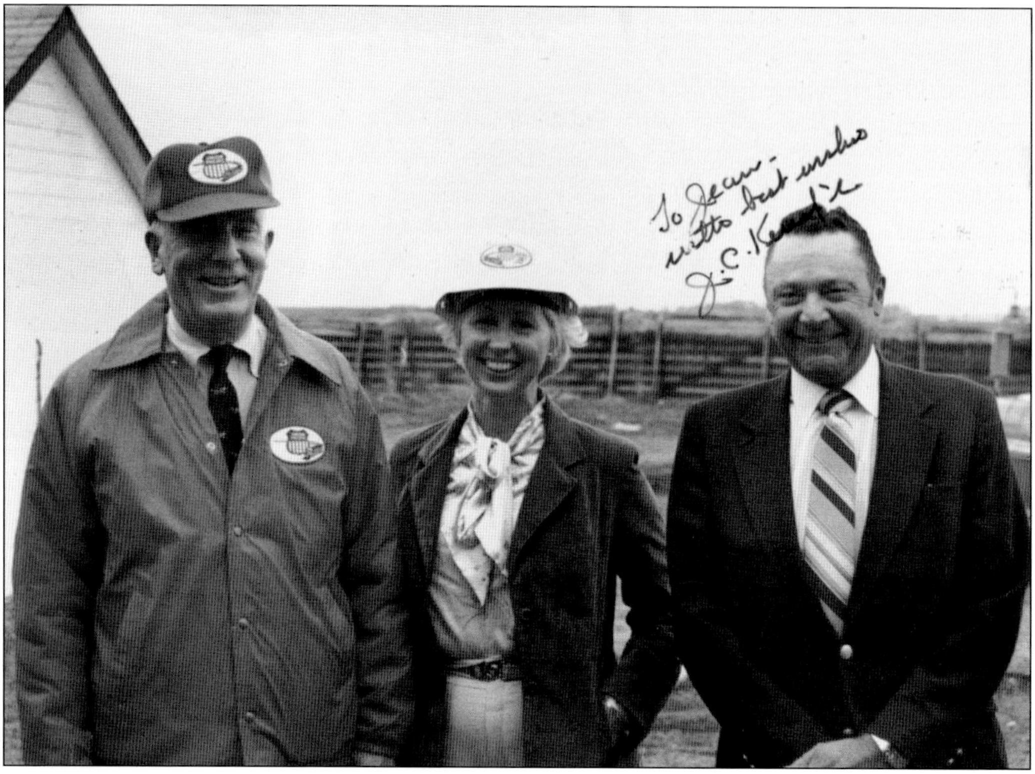

From left to right, this 1980 photograph shows J.C. Kinnifick, president and chief operating officer of the Union Pacific Railroad; Jean Cain of Nampa, the first woman mainline trainmaster in the United States; and Robert Holland, vice president of Maintenance of Way. Cain served as trainmaster for 10 years out of Salt Lake City to McCammon, Idaho. Later, she was safety manager over six states.

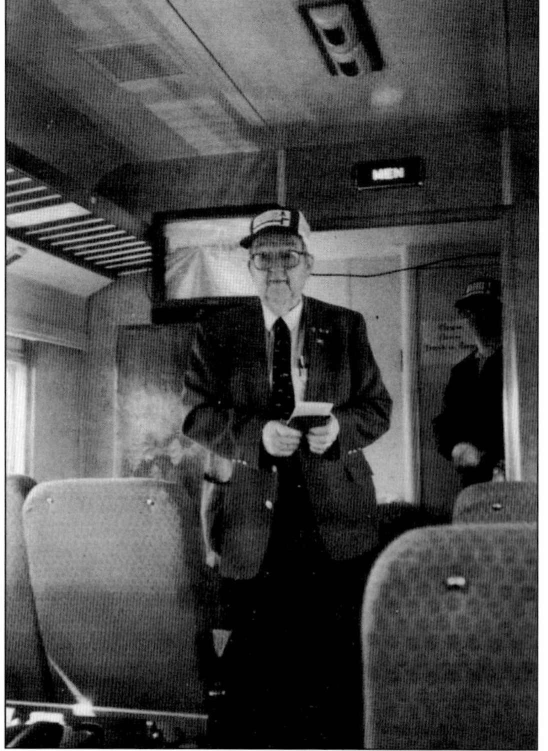

Paul Shira was working with Operation Lifesaver on the Union Pacific Railroad in 1990. This was a program started in 1972 by Union Pacific, Gov. Cecil Andrus, and the Idaho Peace Officers Association to reduce automobile accidents at rail crossings. It was originally to last six weeks, but the program reduced accidents by 43 percent and continued on through the years.

Two

Business and Industry

Nampa started its growth when Alexander Duffes platted the town and began to sell lots. However, the town's future was in doubt when Duffes and his partners encountered financial problems. Many have called Duffes the "father of Nampa," but it could also be said that it was Col. William E. Dewey who was responsible for the town's future growth. Dewey bought out Duffes and his partners and built the magnificent Dewey Palace Hotel. He and his son E.H. (Ed) Dewey made insightful business decisions, building two railroads: the route to the Thunder Mountain mining district, the Idaho Northern; and the Boise, Nampa, & Owyhee Railroad.

When Colonel Dewey died in May 1903, Ed took over direction of the family's business, continuing his foresight on the need for growth of the town. He started the electric company and the telephone company in Nampa, later selling the electric concern to the Idaho Power Company and serving on its board until his death in January 1943.

Industry included the first sugar factory, which was built in 1906 at a cost of $1.25 million and had the capacity to handle 750 tons of beets per day. However, beet blight caused its closure, and it was dismantled and reconstructed in Spanish Fork, Utah. Crescent Brewery and Idaho White Pine Milling Company were entries into business in 1907.

Farms and dairies surrounded Nampa, and agriculture provided grist for Carnation Milk Company, the new sugar factory, many produce houses, the egg cannery, Greenleaf Creamery, Jensma Creamery, and Idaho Equity Exchange, among others.

Retail stores sprang up to supply people's needs. Automobile companies, machine shops, barbershops, and more filled the demand by the public. Restaurants, hotels, theaters, dance halls, and—after 1933 and the repeal of Prohibition—bars and nightclubs, supplied entertainment and diversion for workers in their off-time. The economy grew in every direction. As soon as a need was anticipated, someone filled the void.

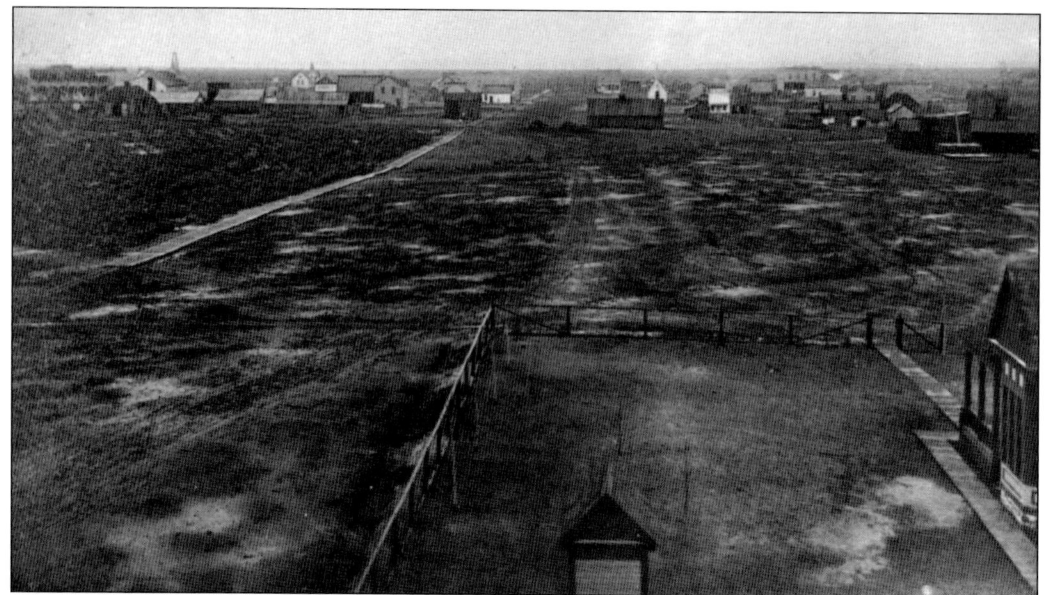

Nampa businesses were sparse in 1890, as this photograph shows. This is the corner of Sixteenth Avenue and Second Street South (looking to the northwest down Second). The town was only four years old, but the Deweys and the railroads would soon bring a boom to the business community.

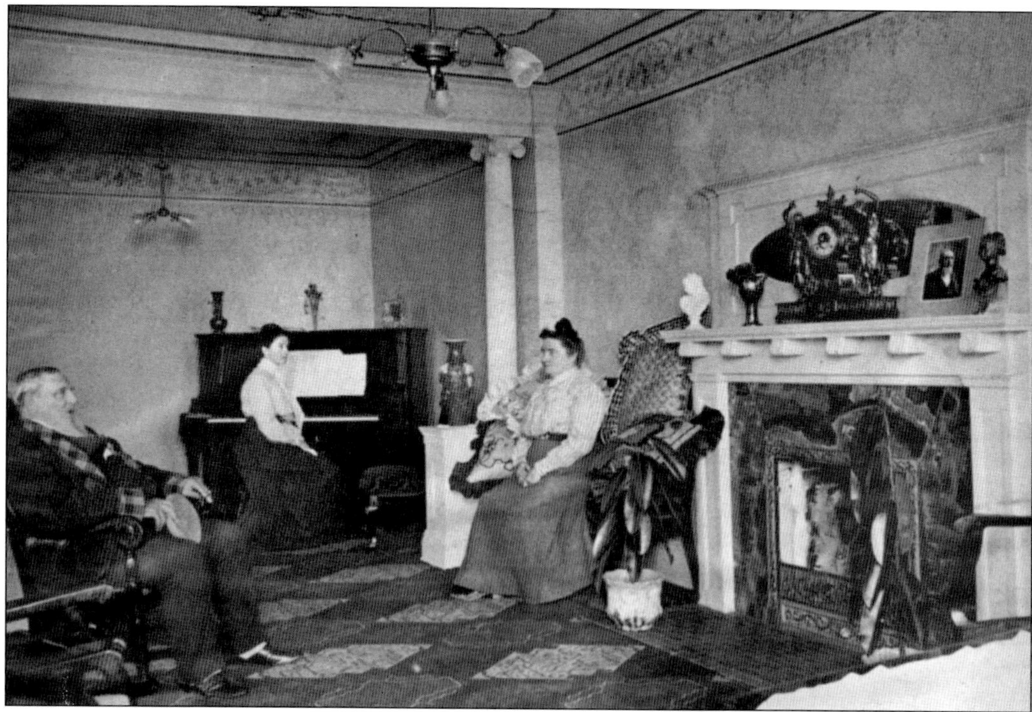

William Dewey, his wife, Belle, and her niece are pictured in their private suite in the new Dewey Palace Hotel. The hotel was opened in January 1903, and Dewey died in May of that year. Belle continued to live in the suite and was a force in the family businesses. She owned several houses that she rented out. She and her daughter took over the hotel when the colonel's estate was settled.

Edward H. Dewey brought railroads, electricity, and telephones to the Junction City. He was involved in numerous business ventures, all of which were successful, and was the driving force behind the Boise, Nampa & Owyhee and Idaho Northern Railroads. He served on the Idaho Power board until his death in 1943.

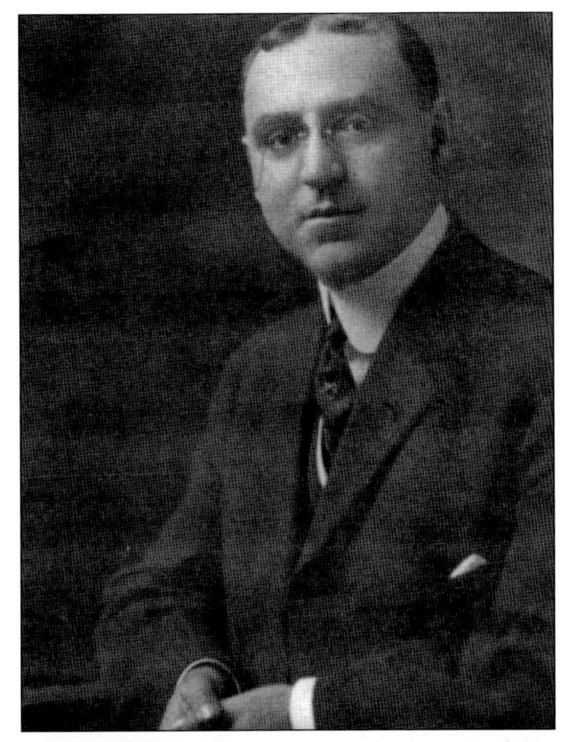

Fred Mock is pictured in front of one of his businesses in 1900. Mock and his partner surveyed the Boise, Nampa & Owyhee Railroad to Murphy for the Deweys. Mock was also a successful author, newspaperman, builder, and world traveler. He lectured all over the world about his travels. He lived to his 90s and, up until his death, was always noted as a snappy dresser.

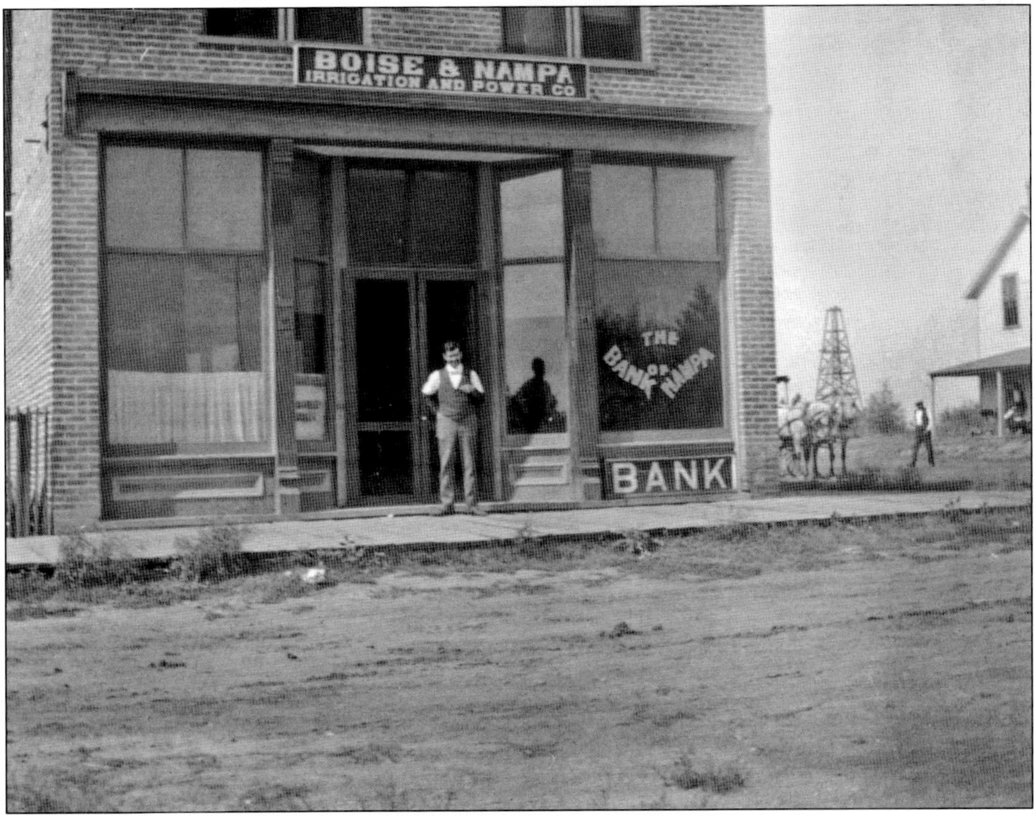

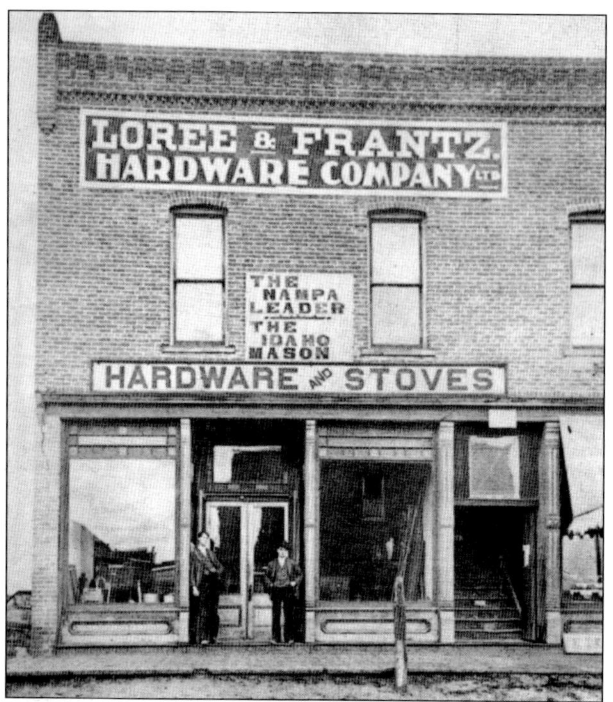

Pictured around 1900 is the Loree & Frantz Hardware Company. The *Idaho Leader* newspaper was upstairs. The paper became the *Nampa Leader* and, finally, the *Leader Herald*, publishing continually until the late 1930s when it was bought out by the *Idaho Free Press*. The *Leader* also published the *Idaho Mason* newspaper, as seen on the sign attached to the building.

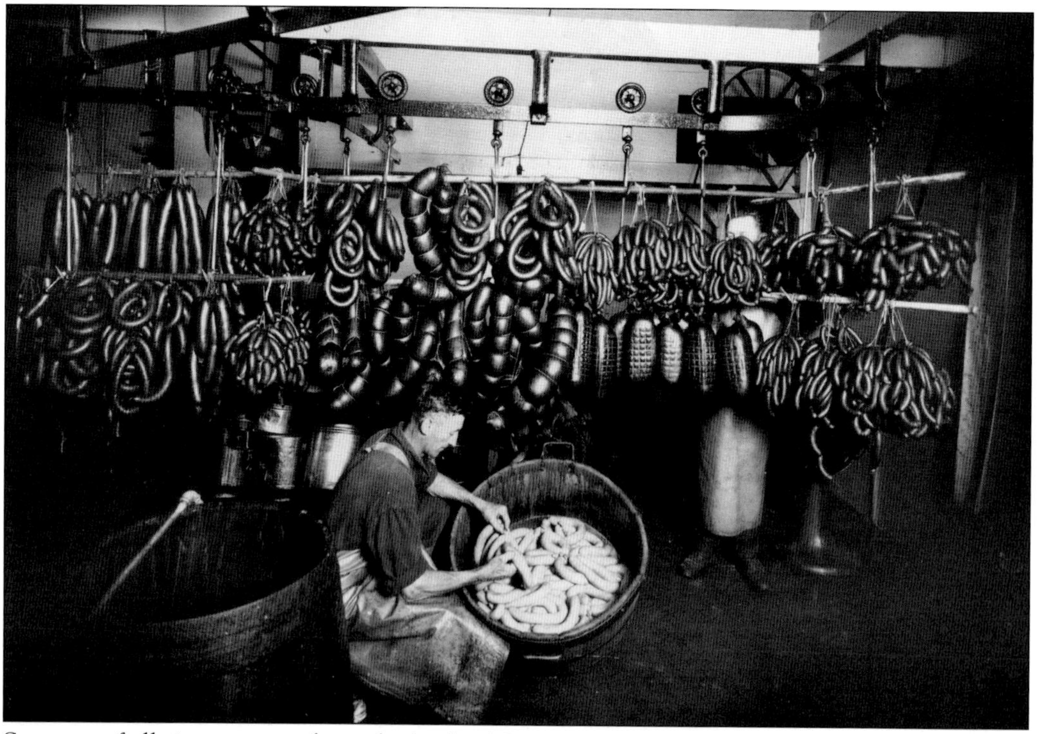

Sausages of all sizes were made in the back of George King's meat market, as seen here with an unidentified man around 1909. The large number of different sausages makes one wonder what they all were. King grew his meat market into a large meatpacking concern. His home was on the corner of Twelfth Avenue and Tenth Street.

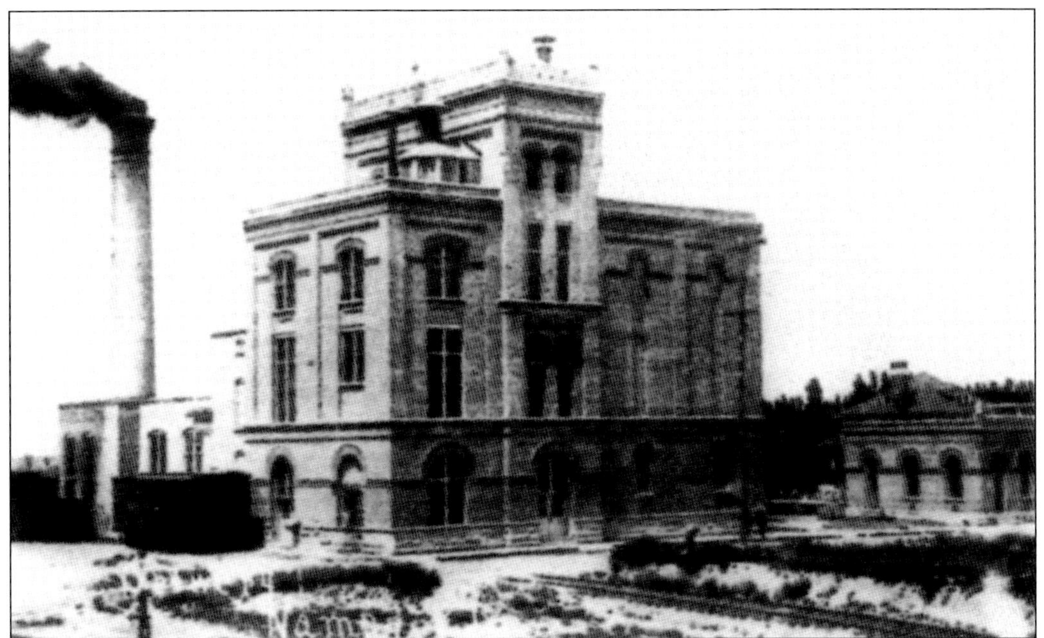

Jacob Lockman's Crescent Brewing Company opened in 1907. The main building was where the beer was made, and the building on the right was the bottling plant. The golden nectar was pumped from the main plant to the bottling facility through brass pipes. The facility had a beautiful hospitality room. Lockman held a contest to name his beer, and Fred Mock took the $50 prize with *Overland Beer.*

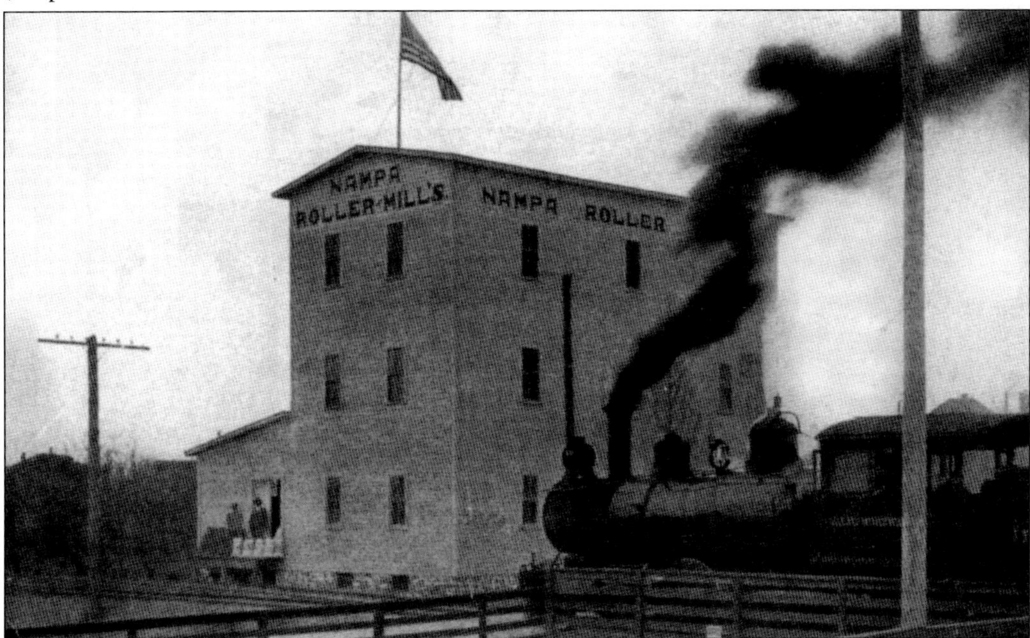

Nampa Roller Mills processed grain and other products from the agriculture producers surrounding the town. It was located right on the tracks, where its product could be loaded and shipped easily. The mill was just another example of the businesses that grew out of the crops grown in the surrounding area.

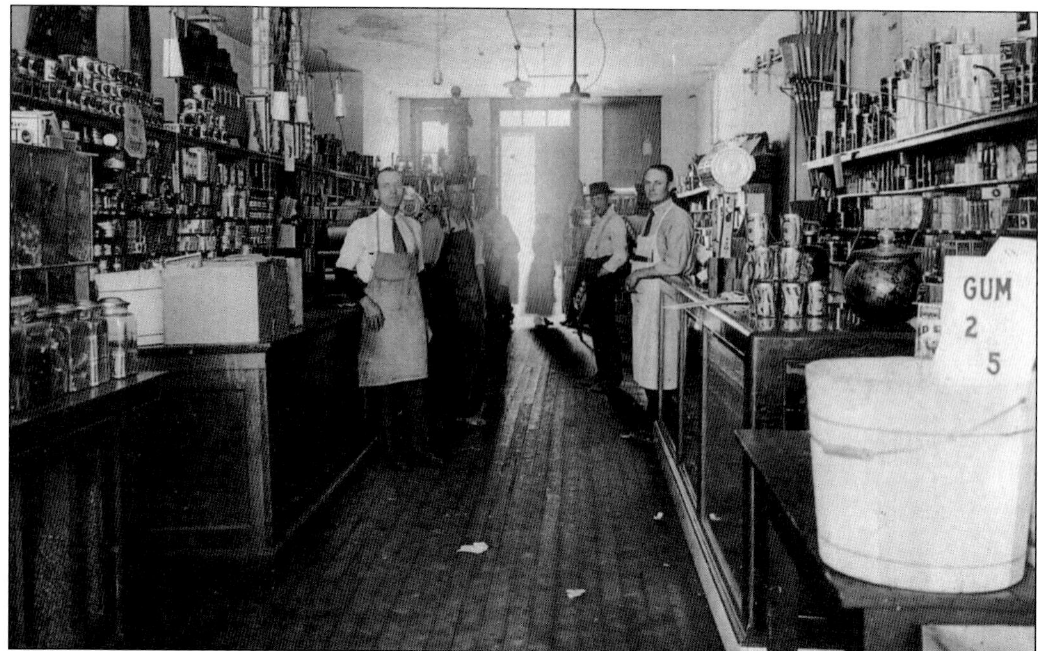

The grocery department of Falk's Nampa D, Nampa's largest department store, is seen here in the 1920s. There was a door opening into the main sales floor of the department store at that time. Later, the door was closed up, and it became Storey Hatchery's outlet in town. Finally, it was remodeled and made over into the Nafziger-Banks clothing store, which opened its doors in 1946 and is still in business today.

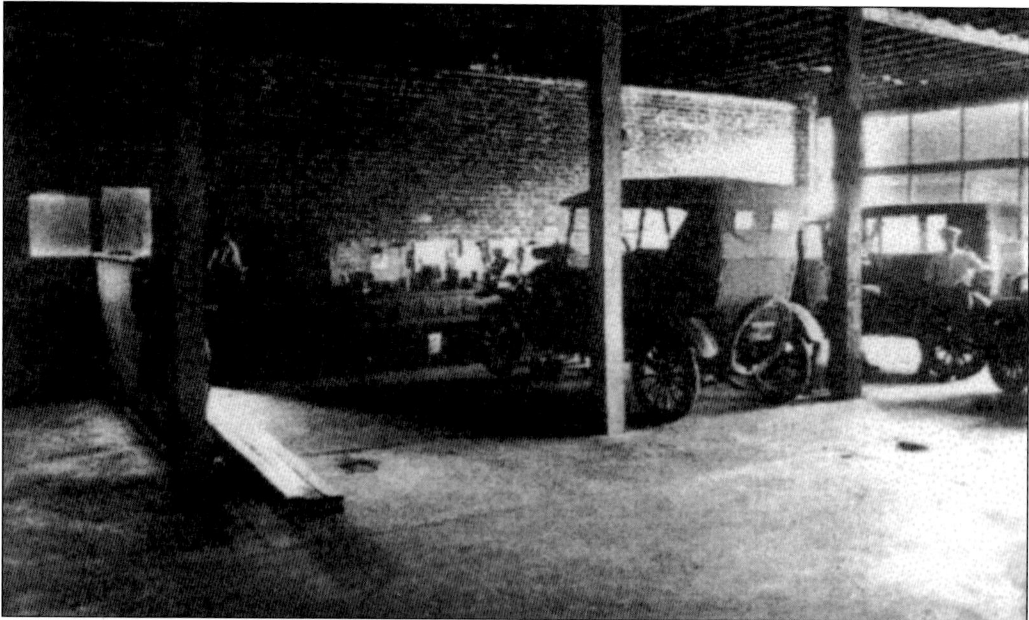
Lindsey Ford's shop was located on the corner of Eleventh Avenue (US Highway 30 at that time) and Third Street South. It was a service that all car dealers had to have. Hugh Nichols, a Nampa policeman, was murdered at the dealership, being shot through the showroom window. The crime has never been solved.

Mr. and Mrs. Al Lindsey are pictured here around 1934. Lindsey was Idaho's first Ford dealer. His biggest competition in Nampa was Bill Showalter's Chevrolet dealership. Both men added to their automobile lines—Lindsey with Mercury and Lincoln, and Showalter with Oldsmobile and Cadillac. Lindsey's sons joined the business, and the name was changed to Lindsey & Sons.

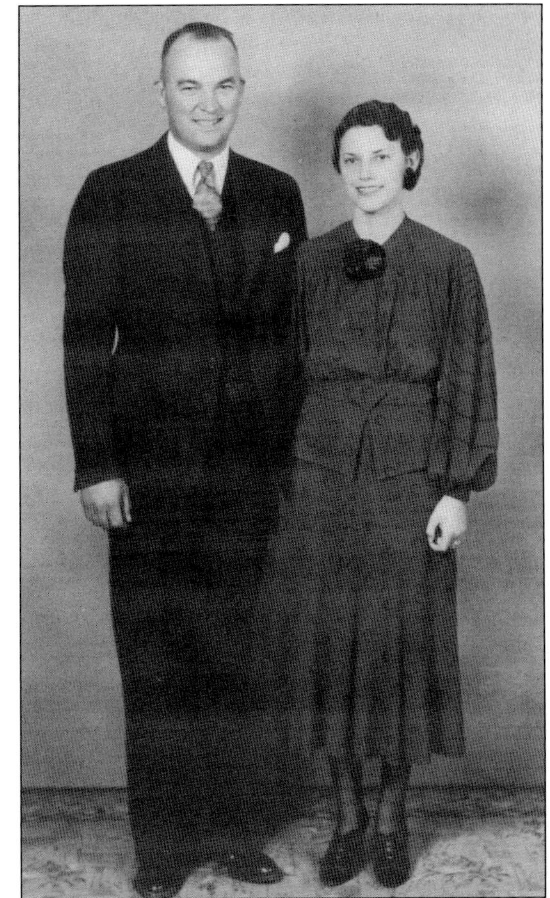

The Nampa State Bank was located on the corner of First Street and Twelfth Avenue South and was affiliated with the Boise First National Bank. C.R. Hickey's insurance business was upstairs. Hickey was also the head cashier for the bank. His mother homesteaded in Nampa in 1886 when there were only two other families in the area.

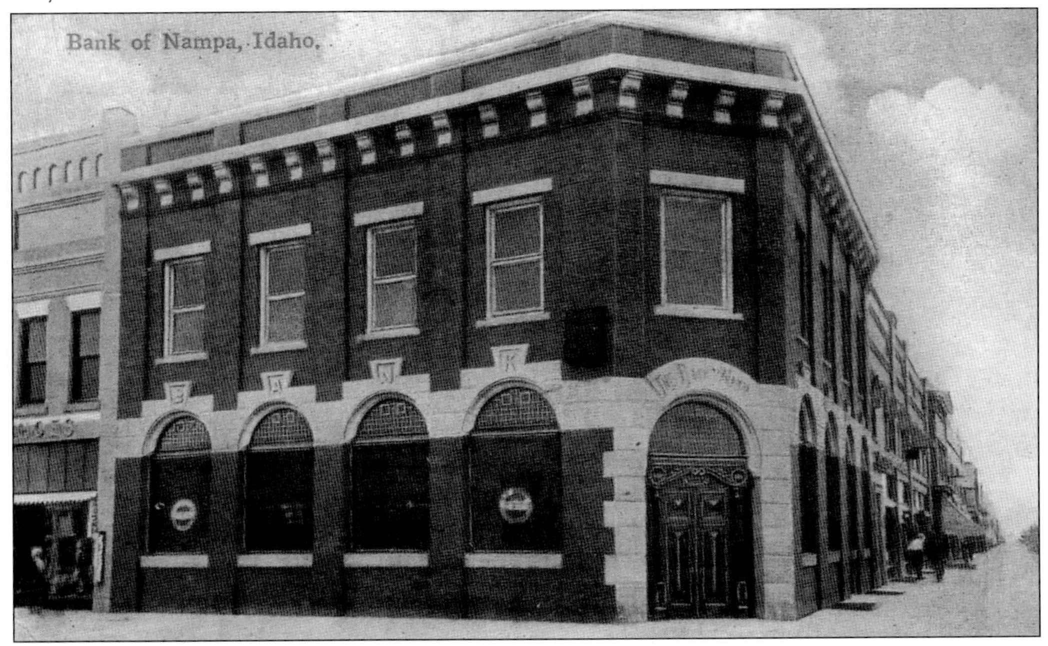

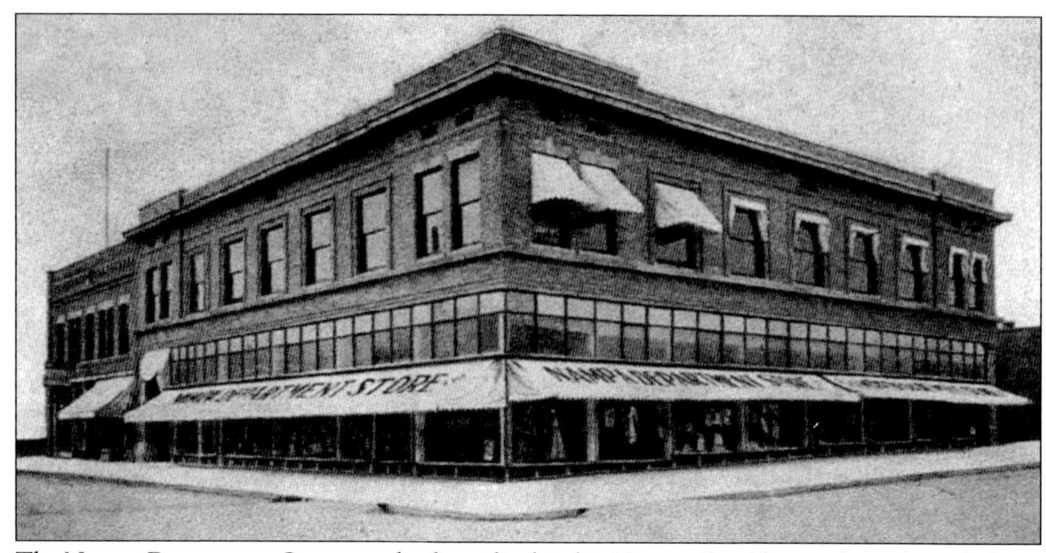

The Nampa Department Store was the first of its kind in Nampa. It sold everything from clothing to groceries. The store was later purchased by Nathan Falk and renamed Falk's Nampa D. John Wengert's Golden Rule Store was its biggest competition in the 1930s and 1940s. The store's last name before it closed was Van Englen's.

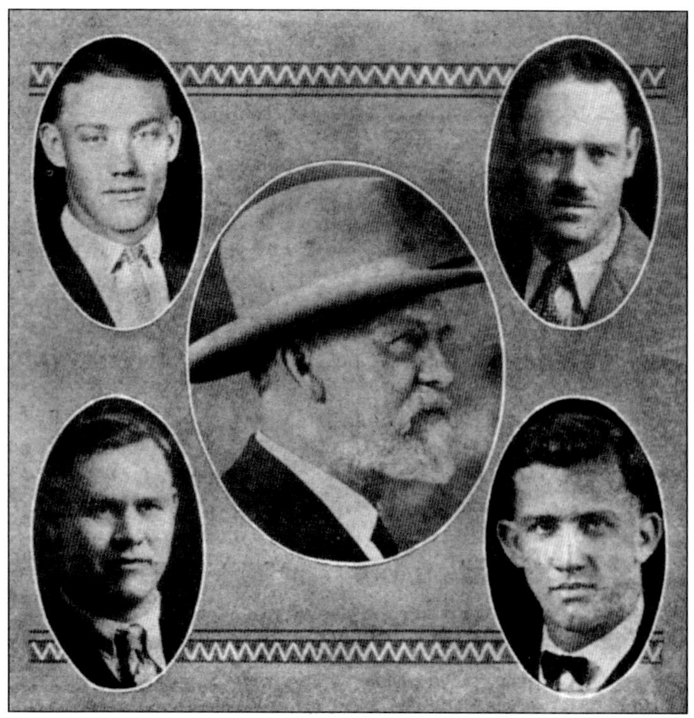

These Keim Packing executives are, clockwise from top left, Stan Keim (secretary-treasurer), Wallace Keim (vice president of the retail department), Richard Keim (manager of the slaughter plant, W.H. Keim (vice president of purchasing), and in the center, H.H. Keim (president and chief executive officer). The company supplied meat to the western United States for over 50 years. H.H. Keim served as mayor of Nampa in the 1910s.

Jacob Lockman is pictured overseeing the retooling of the brewery after Prohibition. Lockman had sold most of the equipment to a brewery in South America because Canyon County went dry before the whole nation. He was forced to stop selling his beer in 1916. The retooling was completed and new equipment installed in order for the beer to begin flowing in April 1934.

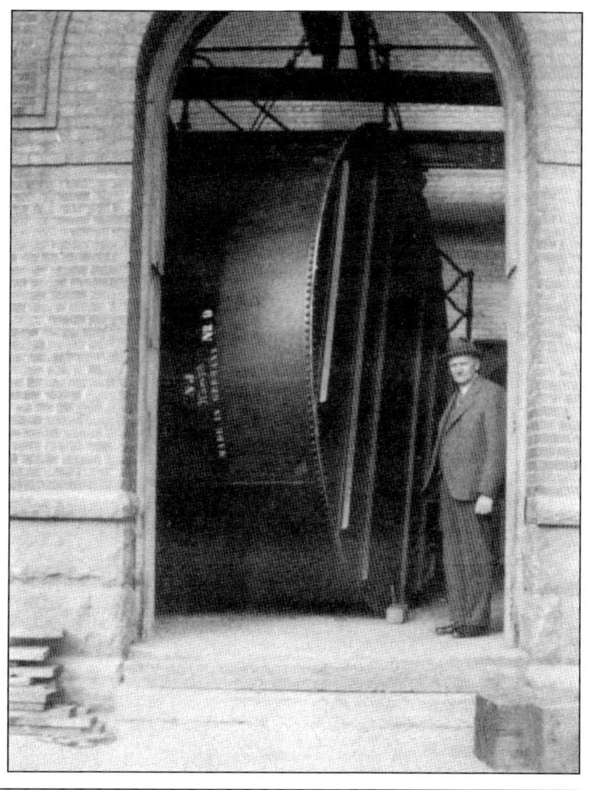

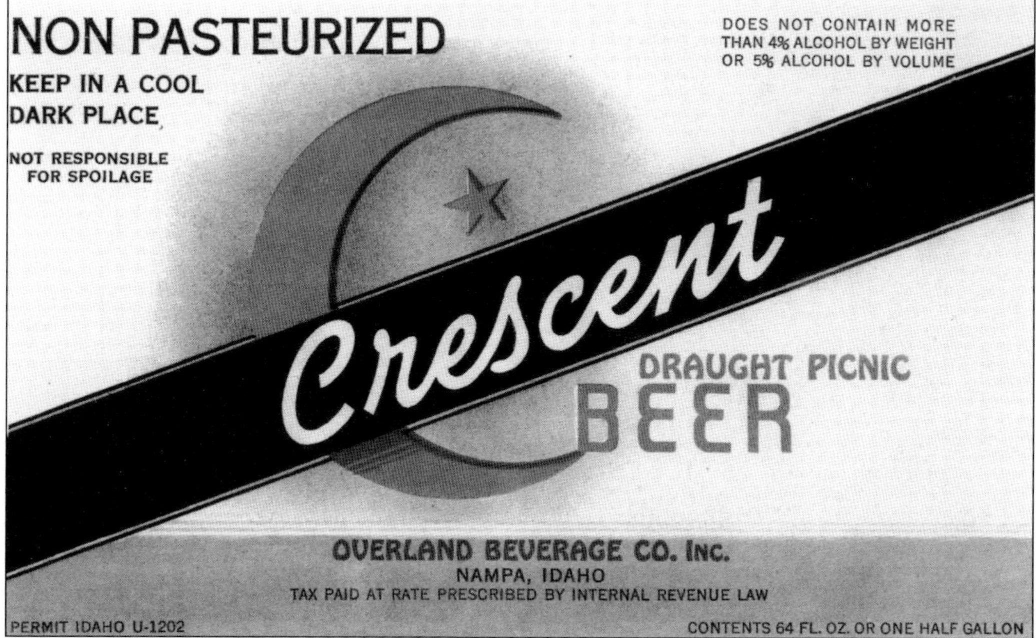

One of Lockman's products was Crescent Draught Picnic Beer, shown here. The most popular was Overland Beer, named by Fred Mock. The company brought out an additional brand in 1939 called Stutz. During Prohibition, Lockman stored onions and made soft drinks at the brewery. He threw a huge party on its reopening, serving beer, bread, sausages, and other food.

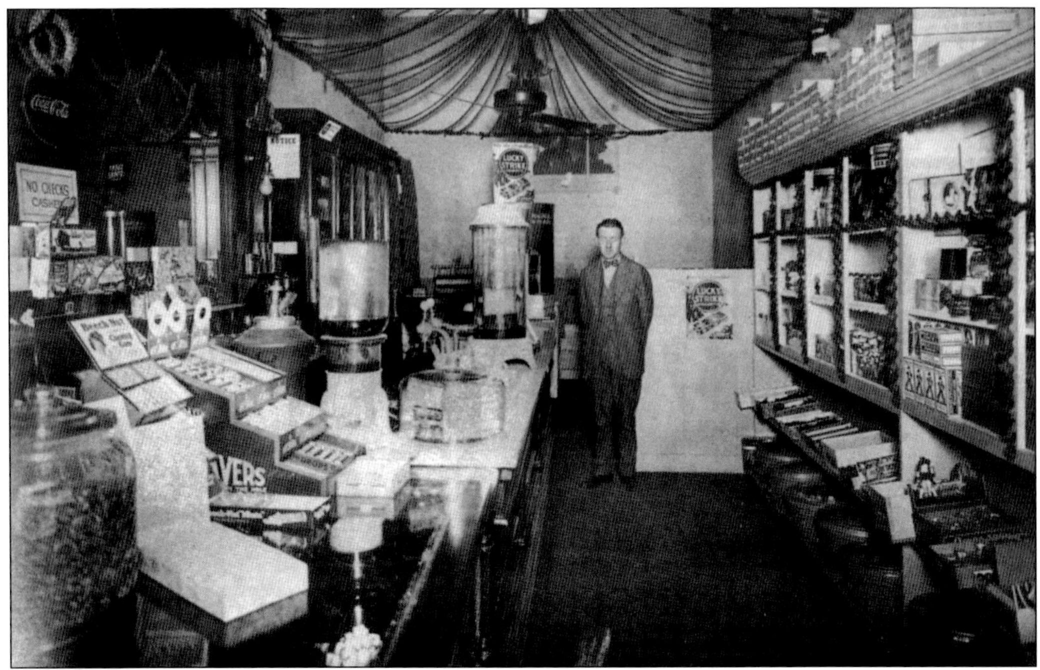

Oscar Clements is seen in his Liberty Sweetshop around 1935. Later, the right side was filled with magazines, and candy was the featured item. It was right next door to the Adelaide Theater and was one of the most popular hangouts for children in Nampa. The shop was in the Waddell Building, which contained apartments, the Liberty Theater (Adelaide), the sweetshop, and the Liberty Tavern.

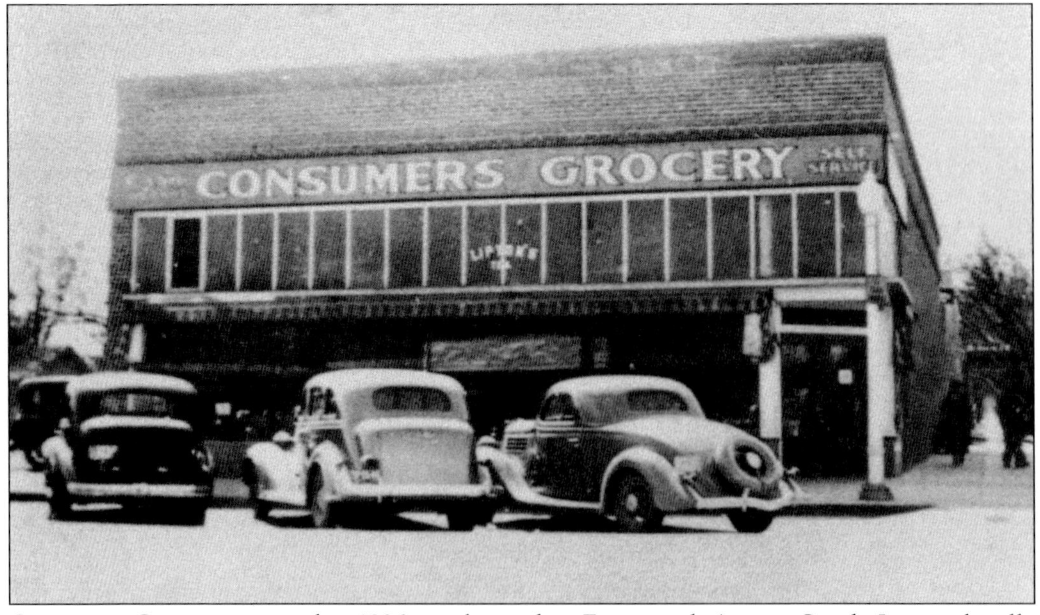

Consumers Grocery, pictured in 1936, was located on Fourteenth Avenue South. It was a locally owned concern started by Herman Tiller, and competed with Albertsons and Safeway for housewives' grocery dollars. The store expanded in later years to include multiple locations, but, along with Safeway, it is no longer in business in Nampa.

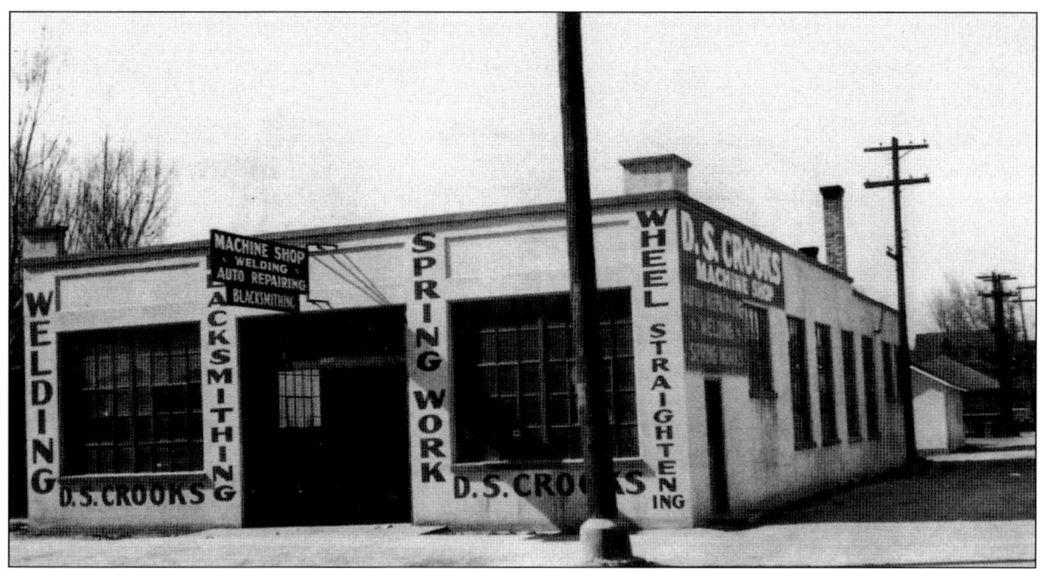

Crooks Machine Shop is pictured here in 1938, with signage advertising welding, auto repair, spring work, and blacksmithing. The shop competed with Gowen's and Hughes for the same market. Gowen's was probably the most successful, although all three did a good business. Gowen's was located on Eleventh Avenue North at the subway.

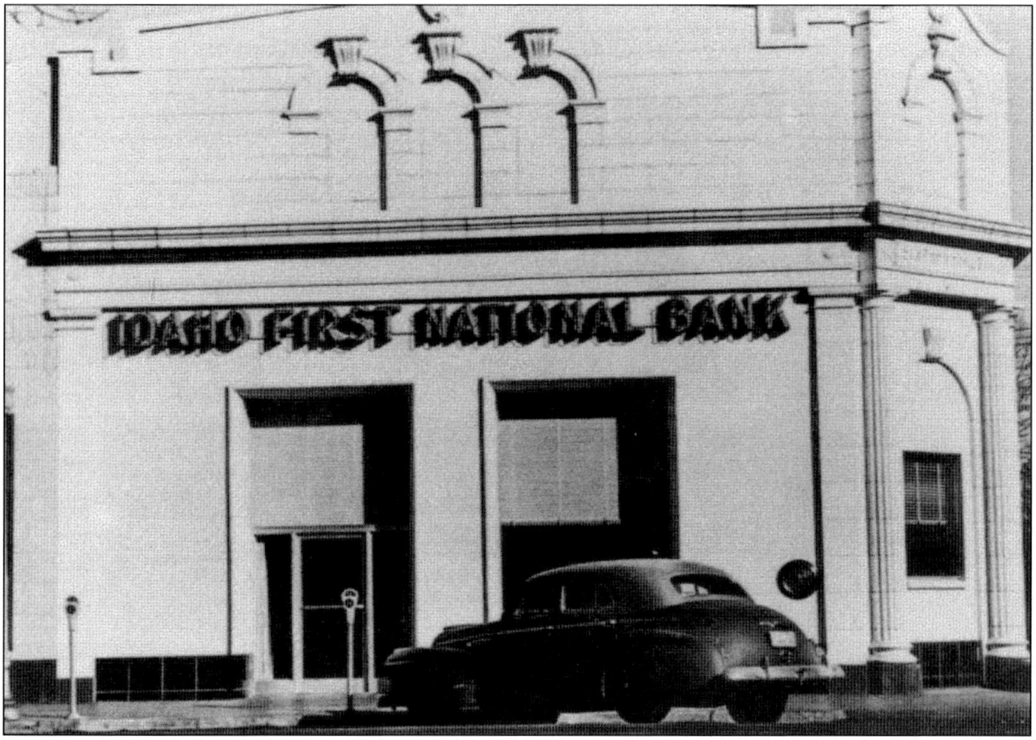

The Idaho First National Bank on First Street between Eleventh and Twelfth Avenues was one of the two leading banks in 1941. The other was the First Security Bank on the corner of Eleventh Avenue and First Street, only half a block away. The company went through a number of mergers and has since disappeared.

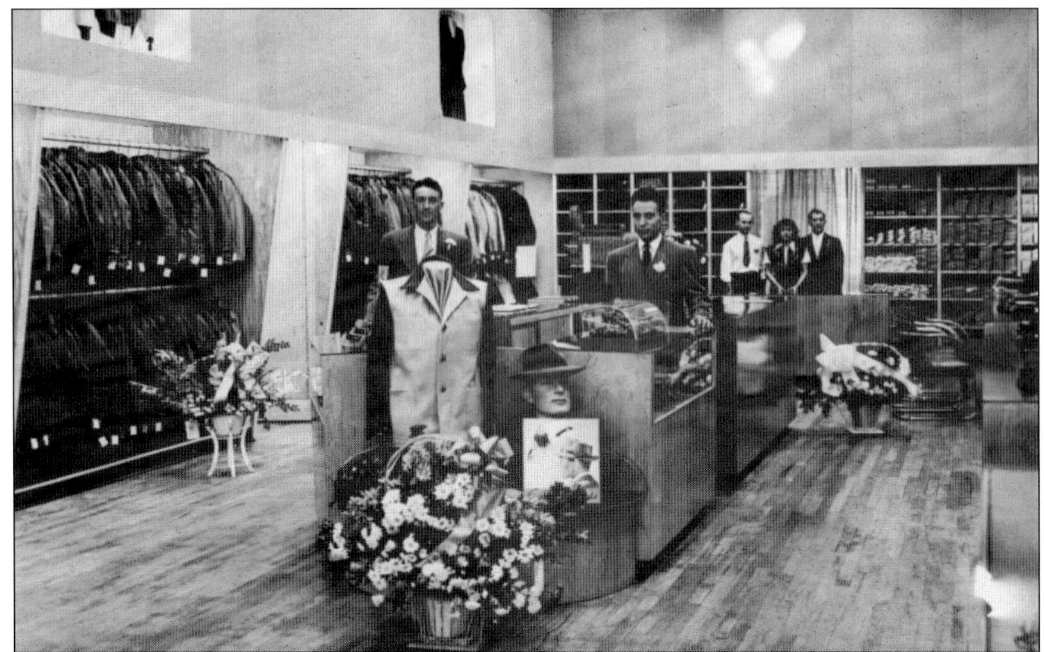

Nafziger-Banks clothing store had its grand opening in 1946 on First Street. Pictured here in the foreground are the owners, Howard Nafziger (left) and Chuck Banks. The store was the place for buying the latest styles coupled with top quality. It is still in business at the same location and is now owned by Dave Lancaster.

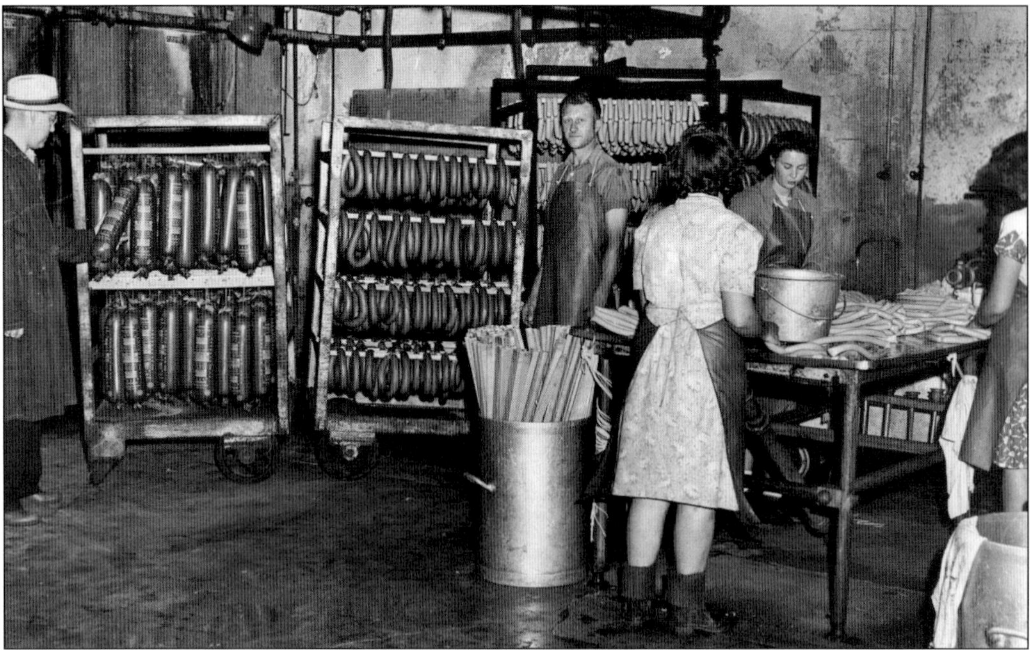

Here, sausage is being made in 1949 at Kings Packing Plant on Amity Avenue. The operation had expanded and been made more efficient over the years. George Kings was still making sausage 40 years after the photograph on page 28. Sausage was only one of the many Red Rose products put out by the plant.

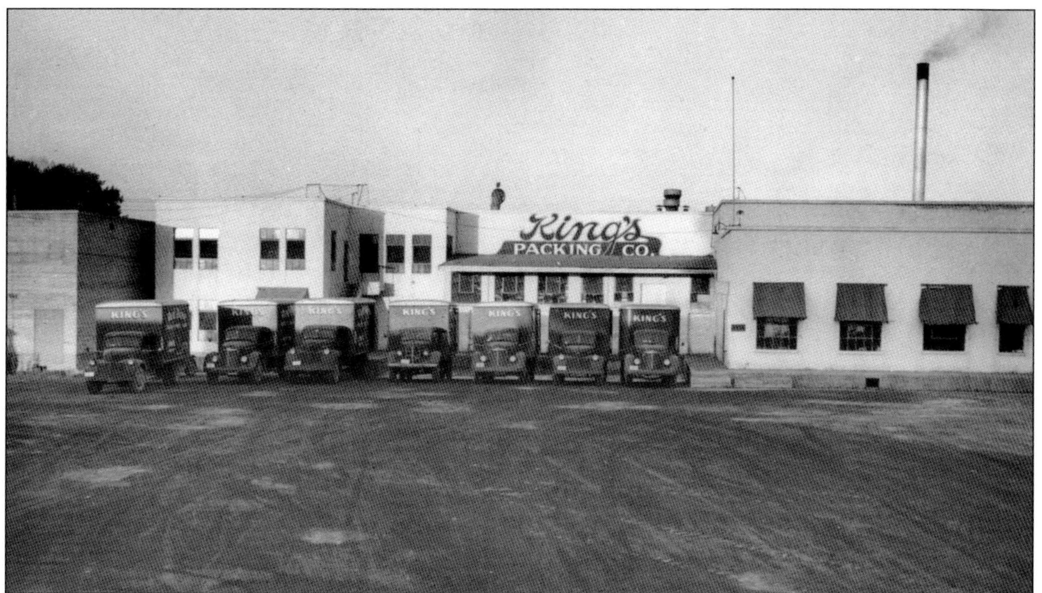

This exterior view of Kings Packing Company in 1949 shows the plant and a fleet of trucks. The Red Rose brand was sold in stores all over the Boise Valley and the state of Idaho. George King was one of the business pioneers in Nampa. A smaller packing plant, Ankeney's, was across the road from Kings.

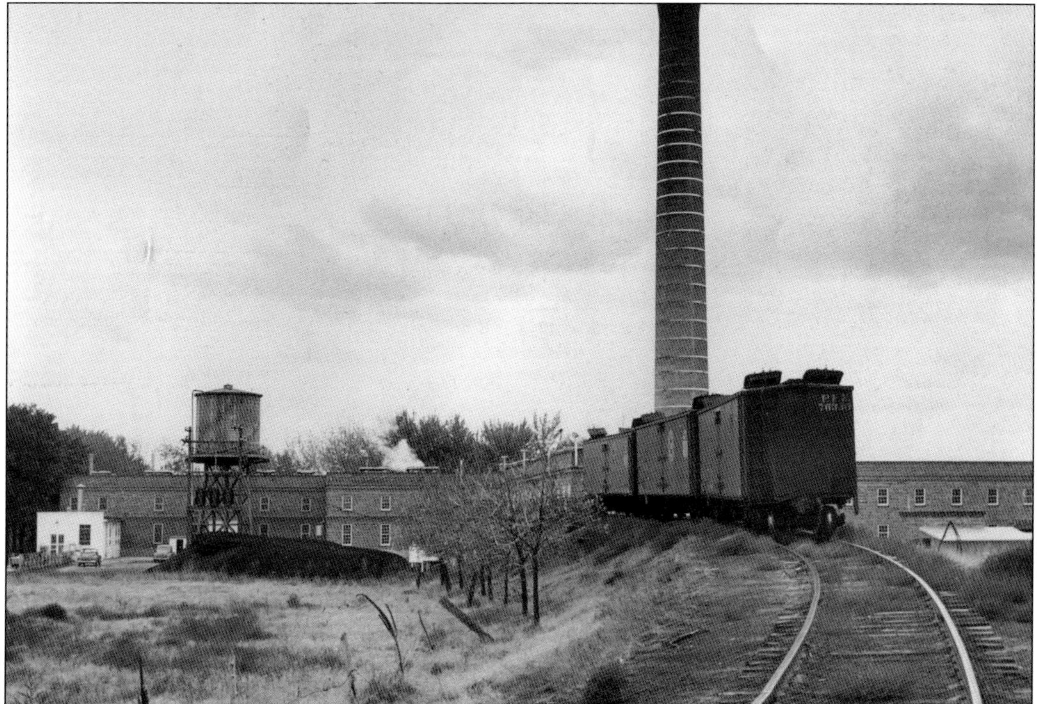

Carnation Milk Company is pictured in this 1949 image, which shows the rail transportation. The plant was near the site of the first sugar factory in Nampa. The company, which produced condensed milk then, is gone from the Nampa scene. There are now 51 condensed-milk producers in Idaho.

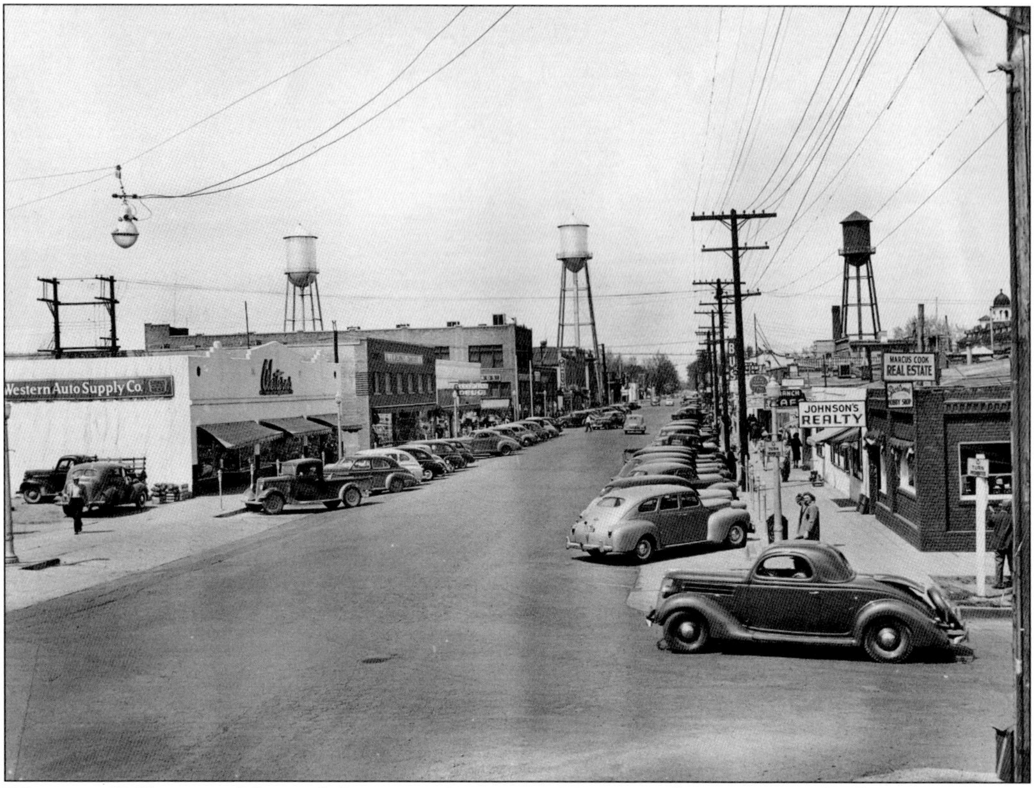

This is a 1945 view of Second Street in downtown Nampa. The stores on the left are Western Auto, Penny's, and Pennywise Drug. Just across Thirteenth Avenue is Montgomery Ward. On the right, the old sale yard at Fourteenth Avenue was replaced by Marcus Cook Real Estate. Even though the war was over, the new cars had not yet made it to Nampa's streets.

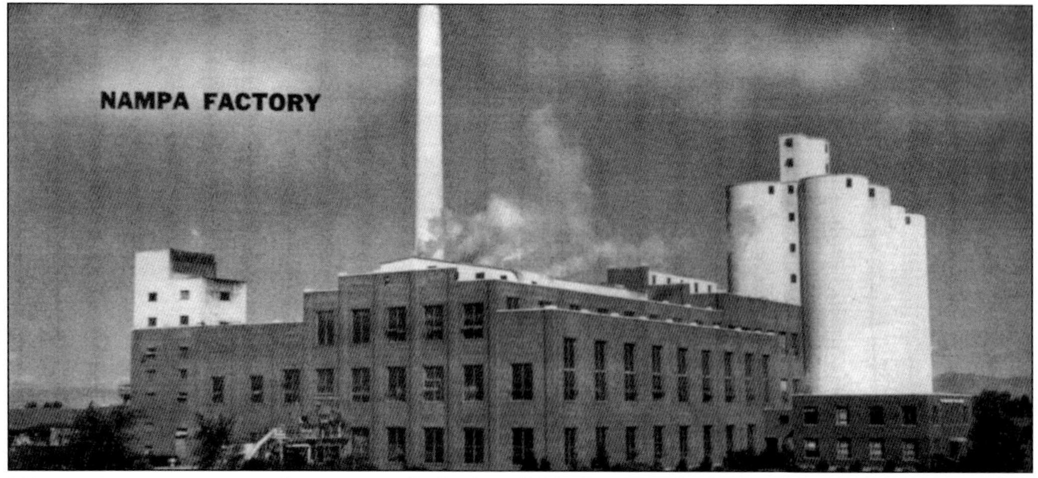

This is the current sugar factory as it looked in 1962. It opened on October 8, 1942, on Karcher Road and has been one of the top creators of jobs in the Nampa area. The sugar is marketed under the White Satin logo. Nampa's original factory opened in 1905, but a blight on sugar beets caused its closing, and it was moved to American Fork, Utah.

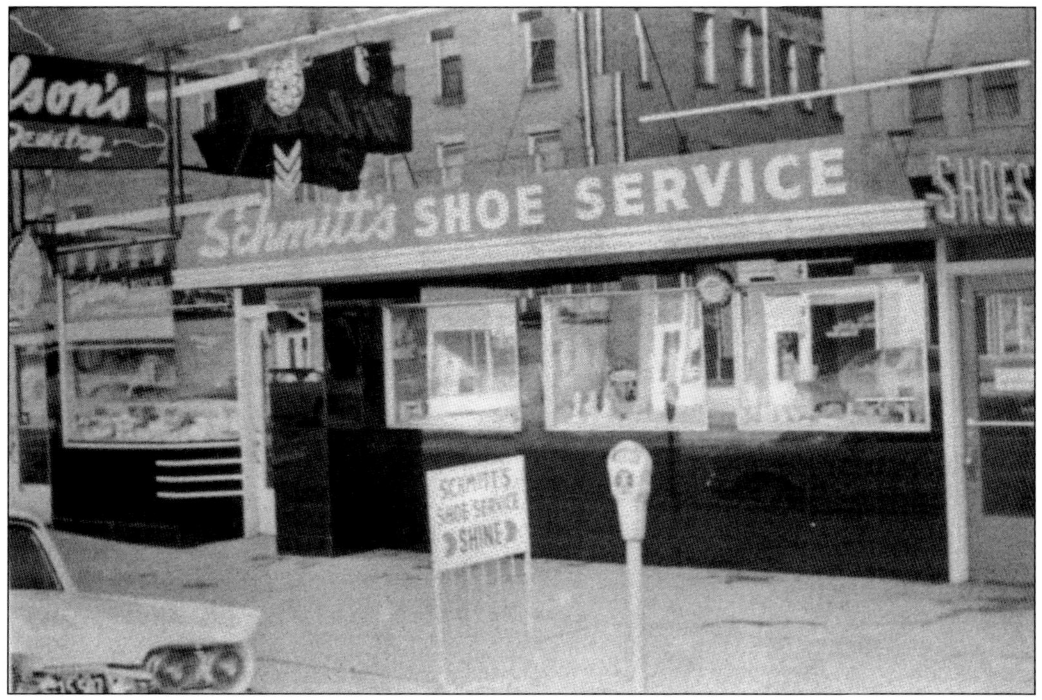

Seen here is a slice of Twelfth Avenue business in the 1960s. On the left is Wilson's Jewelry, owned and operated by Dean Wilson, which sold jewelry and did watch repair. On the right was Schmidt's Shoe Service, owned and operated by Howard Schmidt. The bicycle rack in front advertises Schmitt's Shoe Service and shoe shines.

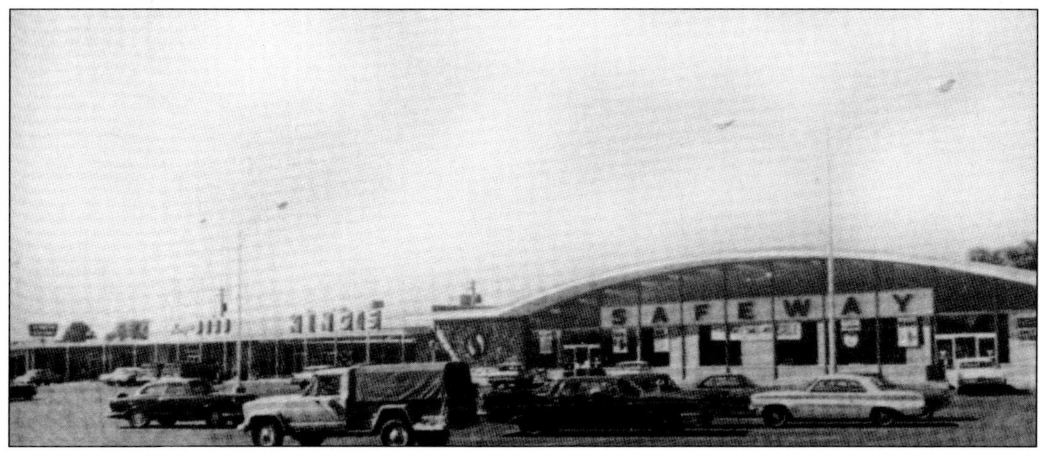

This Safeway store, pictured in 1966, was located on Ninth Avenue South. The original location for the company was across the alley from Albertson's on Third Street South. It was one of the big three at the time, along with Albertson's and Consumers. Only Albertson's remains in business in Nampa today, though Safeway is still the third-largest grocery chain in the United States.

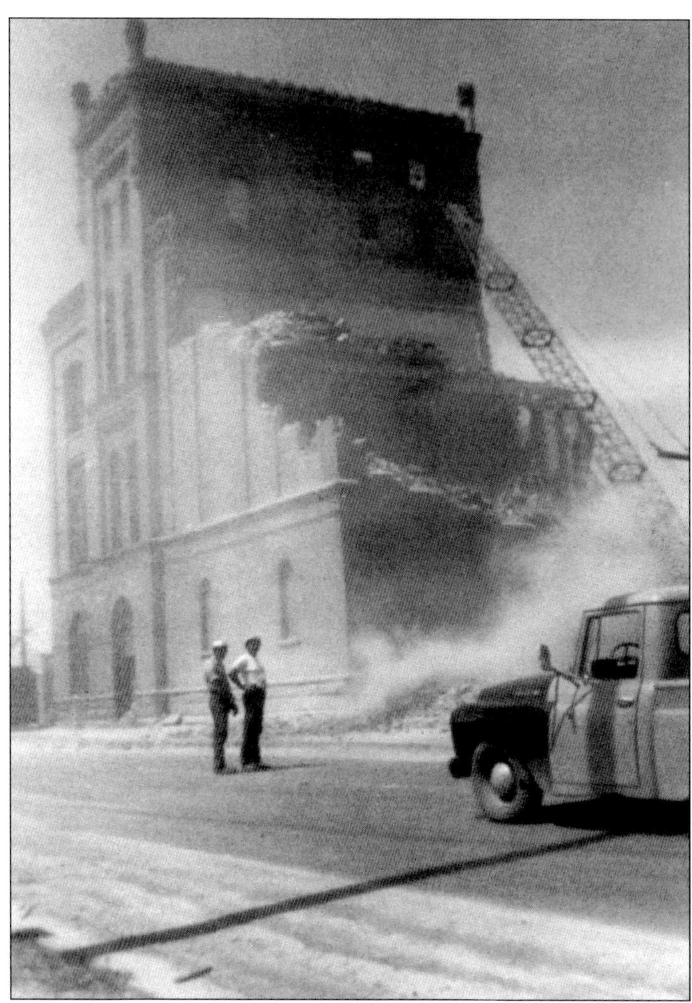

The Crescent Brewery was demolished in 1966. Its demise ended the life of one of Nampa's two most photographed and promoted buildings (the other being the Dewey Palace Hotel, also gone). The old bottling house and the Lockman house still remain at the original location on Ninth Avenue and First Street North.

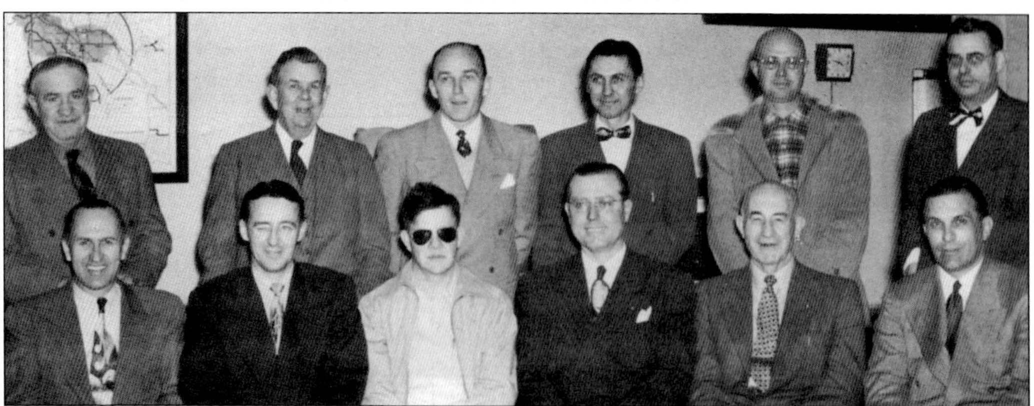

The Nampa Chamber of Commerce is pictured here at mid-century. These were the movers and shakers of business in Nampa. Each man represented a different business. The members are, from left to right, (first row) unidentified, Howard Nafziger, Bill Shaw, Doyle Cain, R. Mangun, and John Alsip; (second row) Walt Garrity, Windsor Lloyd, Homer Davies, Jim Kalbus, Frank Bevington, and Ike Corlett.

Three

Restaurants, Hotels, and Entertainment

Nampa has always been a town that supported its restaurants. From the Delmonico in the 1890s to the fast-food, cookie-cutter eateries of today, Nampans line up for the chow. There were better restaurants, like the Dewy Palace Grill and the Homestead; middle-of-the-road restaurants, like the Harmony and the Town Talk Café; and drive-ins, like the Toot and Tell, Kit Kat, and root beer stands. There were also downtown high school hangouts, such as the Parrot, Peter Pan, and Dixie's.

Entertainment included movies, sporting events, dances, various service club shows, and special events like the Eight Piano Symphony and the Snake River Stampede. Nampans like their diversions. People coming from out of town to attend these attractions had to stay somewhere, and hotels and motels fit the bill. The Dewey Palace stands alone as the most magnificent, a "palace" in the desert. Many others offered their hospitality to the weary traveler, including the Greystone, Commercial, and Lenox Hotels and places like the Nampa Chief.

This chapter gives a peek into this world where the laughter and tears flowed, diets were forgotten, and a warm bed was available to fall into.

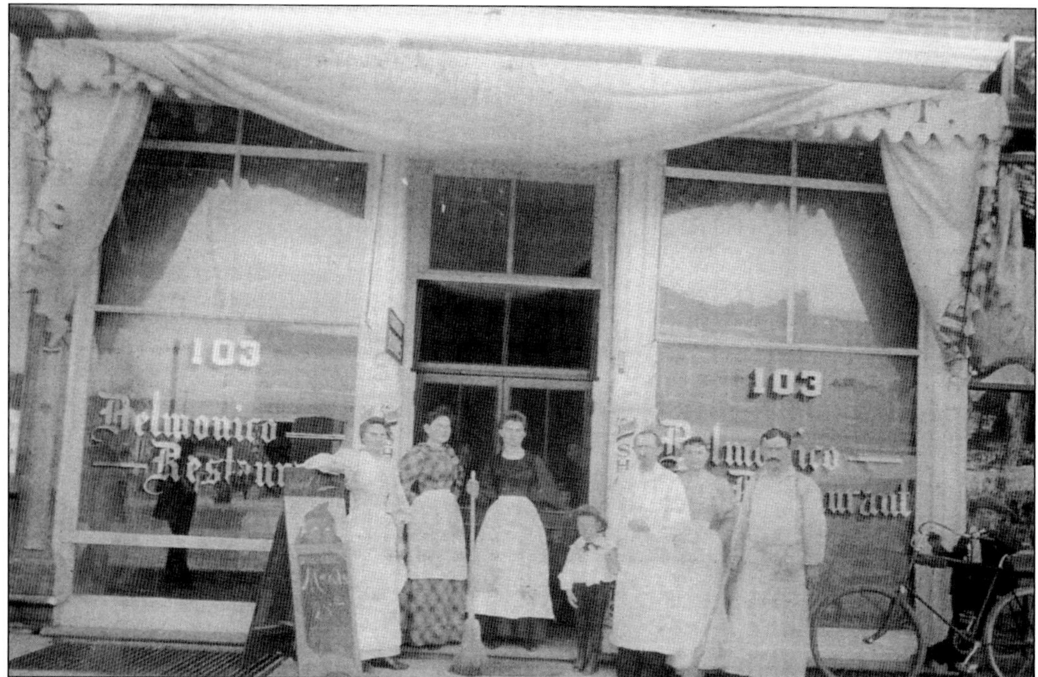

This is the Delmonico Restaurant, owned by a Mr. Hartman, in 1893. The people in the photograph are unidentified. This was one of the first sit-down restaurants in Nampa, and while knowledge of the exact location has slipped away in the ensuing years, this image remains. It was most likely named after the famous New York Delmonico's.

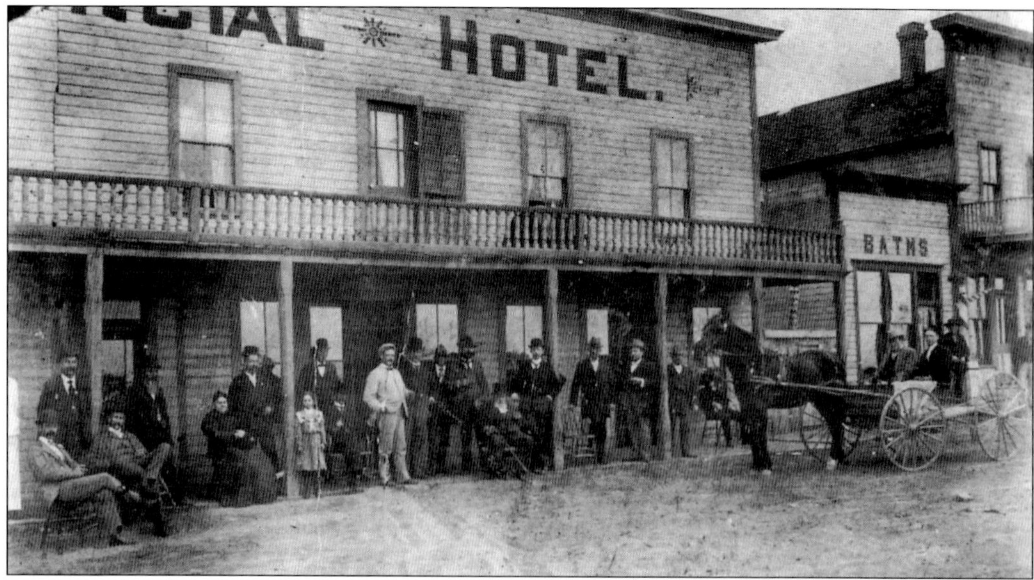

The Commercial Hotel on Front Street was the finest in Nampa until the completion of the Dewey Palace. It did not hold second place very long, however, as it burned in the great fire of 1909. This image dates to around 1898. Note the bathhouse next door. Many hotels of the time did not have bathrooms.

The Dewey Palace was the finest hotel between Denver and San Francisco, according to the 1904 travel book *Over the Range to the Golden Gate*. These front and back views give an idea of its size. The building in the back was the laundry. The hotel had everything a traveler wanted, including a restaurant, a bar, a barbershop, a bowling alley, and a special room for salesmen.

Pictured in 1903, the Strode Brothers Building was located on the corner of Front and Twelfth Avenue, kitty-corner from the new depot. The Cosmopolitan Saloon was at the ground-floor corner. The Imperial confectionery and newsstand was next door, and the business beside the Imperial was a real estate office.

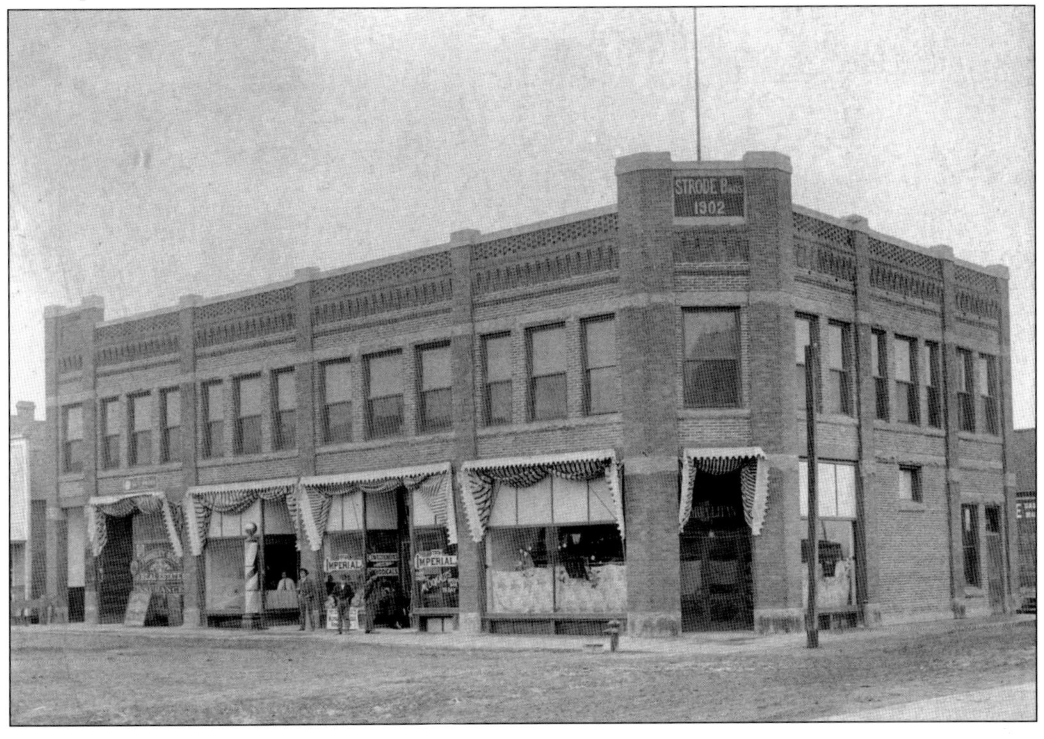

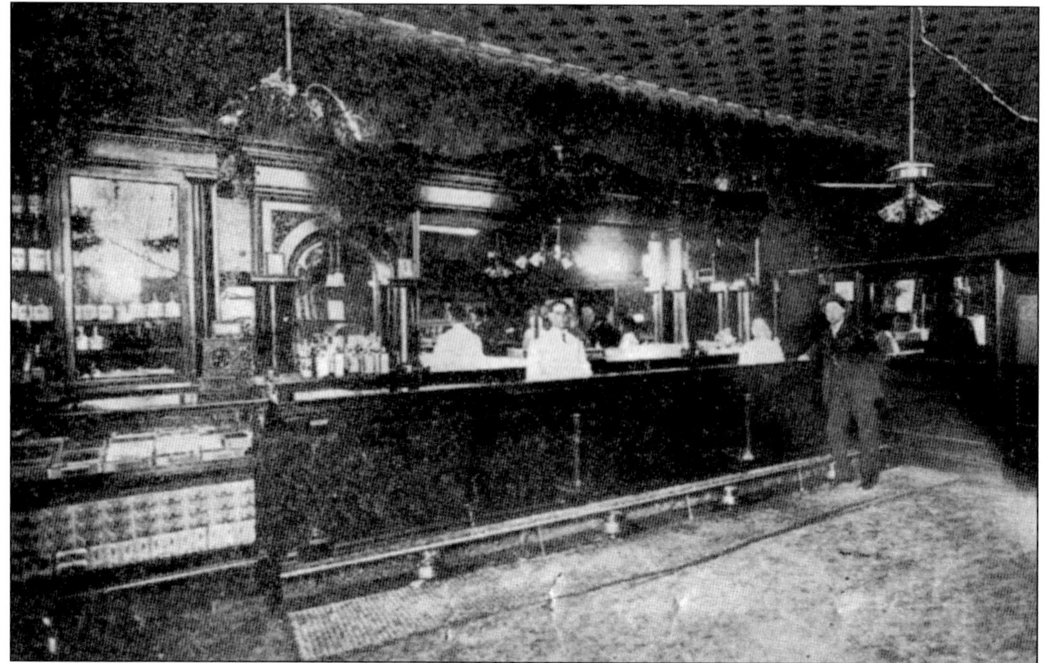

The interior of the Cosmopolitan Saloon is shown here. The tin ceiling, mahogany-backed bar, brass spittoons, and brass rail for feet were essential items any self-respecting bar owner would supply. The cigars in the case, the beer kegs, and the whiskey display did not hurt, either.

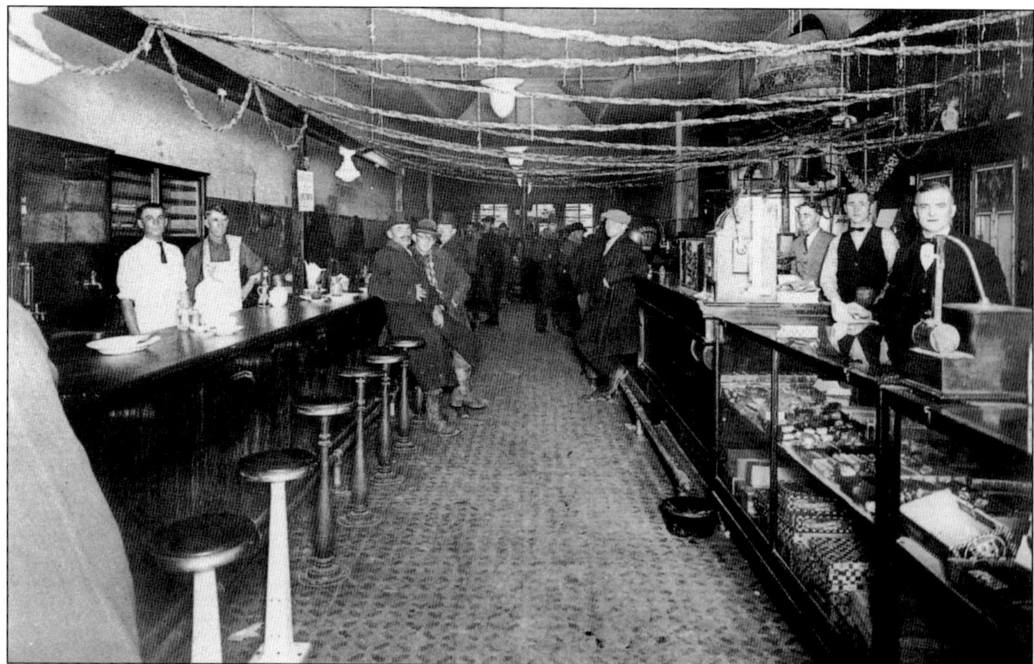

Pop's Cigar Store, owned by Pop Cox, is seen here around 1926. Cox was a bowling enthusiast, sponsoring both men's and women's teams for years. When Prohibition ended, he was one of the first to get a beer license. The store also added tables where patrons could play poker and other games with each other.

The Greystone Hotel is pictured here in 1926. Located on Twelfth Avenue South between First and Second Streets, it had one of the better restaurants in Nampa during the 1930s. Bessie Blackman was the owner in the 1920s and 1930s. It had a newsstand inside the hotel. The original name when it first opened was the Share House.

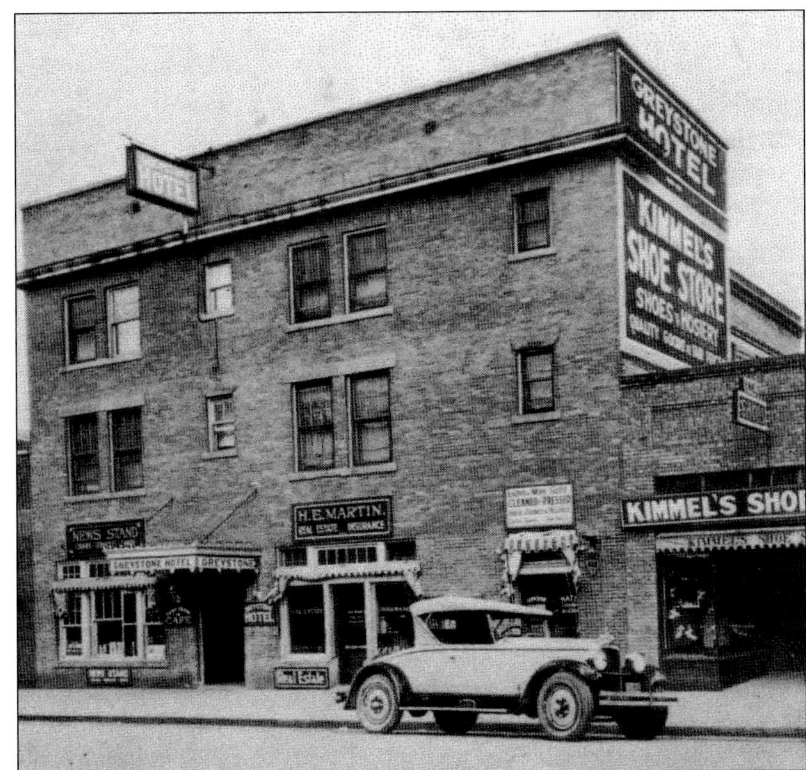

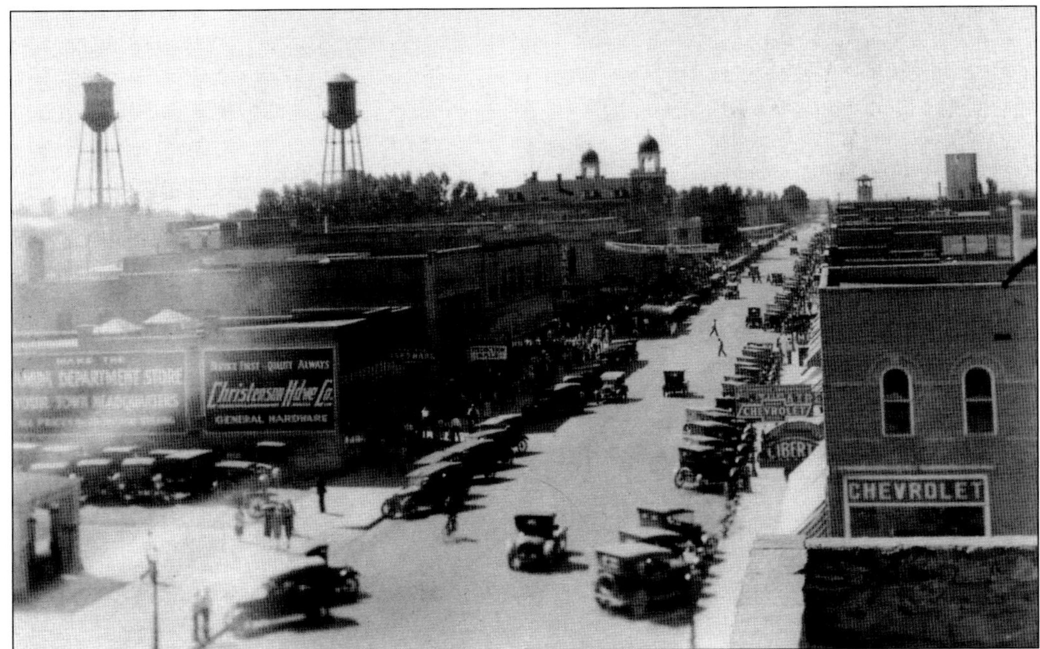

The Liberty Theater opened in 1919 and is shown here in 1927. Showalter Chevrolet was the corner building on the block; the theater was next door on Main (First) Street. This image must have been taken on a Saturday, as there are no parking places to be seen all the way to the fire station, and the sidewalk is quite crowded.

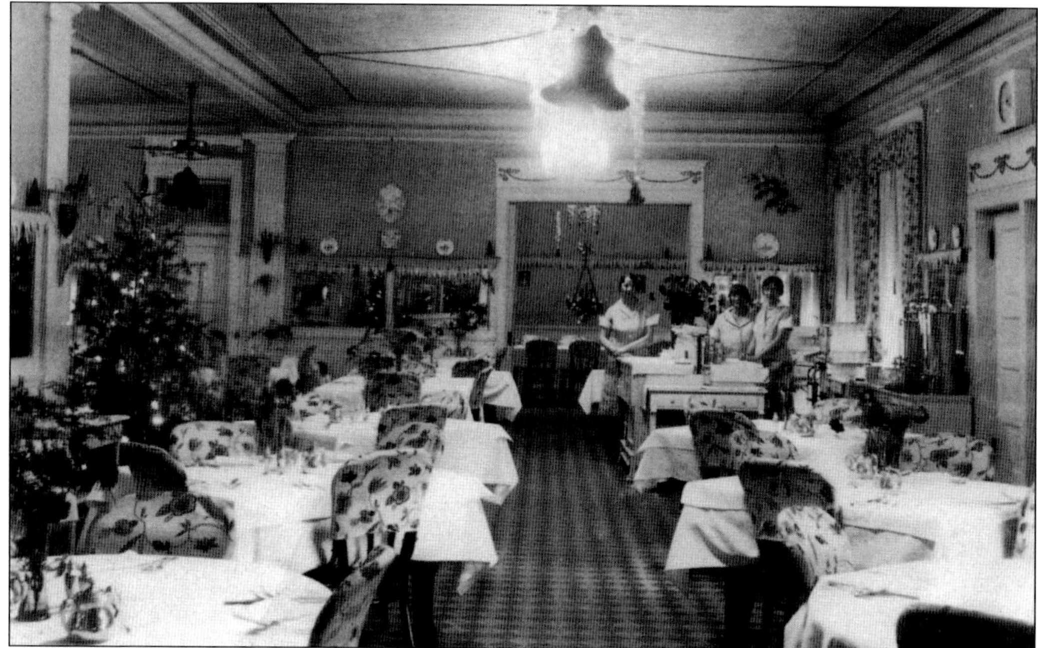

The Dewey Palace Grill was one of the best restaurants in Nampa. It was in the magnificent Dewey Palace Hotel. Here, the staff is waiting to seat guests. The restaurant featured intriguing ceiling decorations, and many service clubs held their luncheon meetings there in the adjacent private rooms.

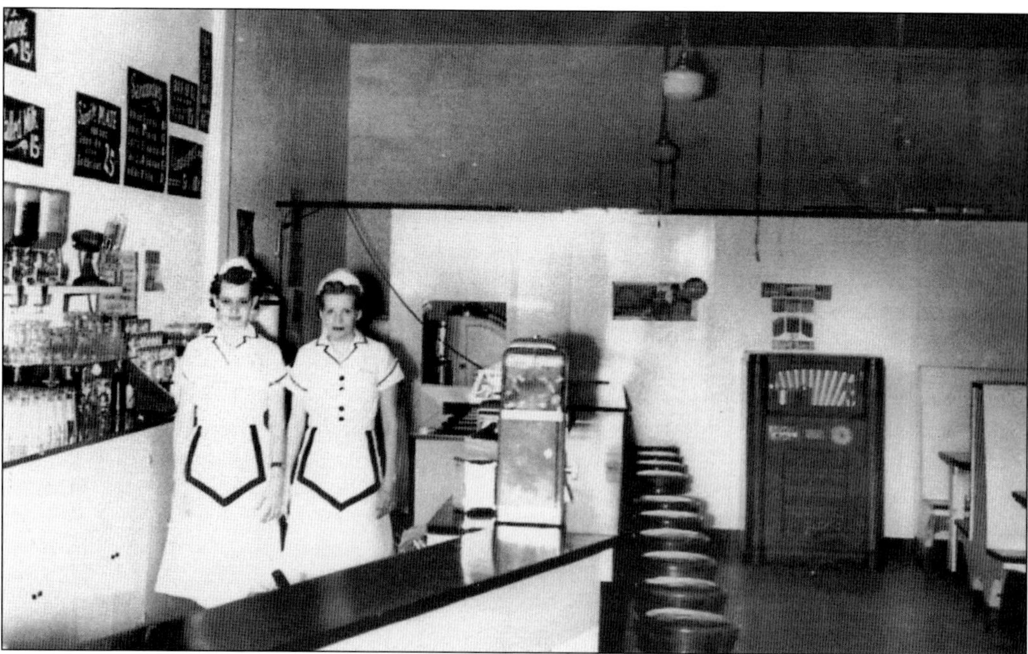

Charlene Ashcroft and Dixie Bohart pose proudly behind the counter of Dixie's Ice Cream Shop on Second Street in 1939. The shop was known for its burgers, milkshakes, and other soda fountain staples. Note the jukebox at right and the prices on the wall at left. This spot was popular with the high school set and adults alike.

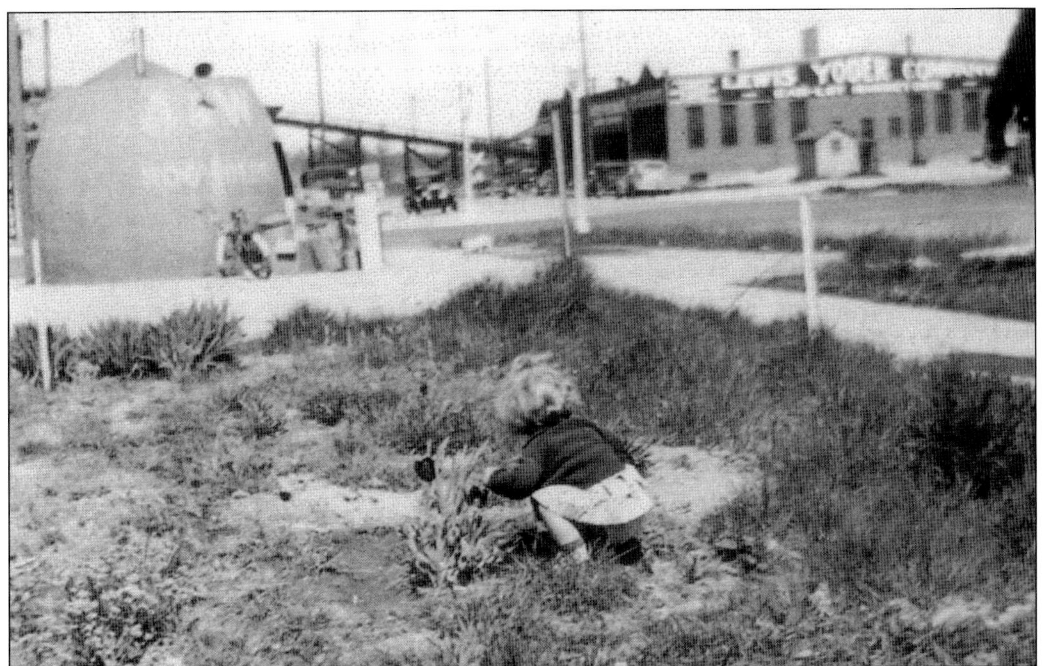

Little Sharon Lee is working in her garden on Fifteenth Avenue South by the A&W Root Beer Barrel. The stand also had a beer license, offering something for everyone. The Lewis Yoder Produce Company can be seen in the background. There was a second root beer stand with a beer license at the time, but its location is unknown.

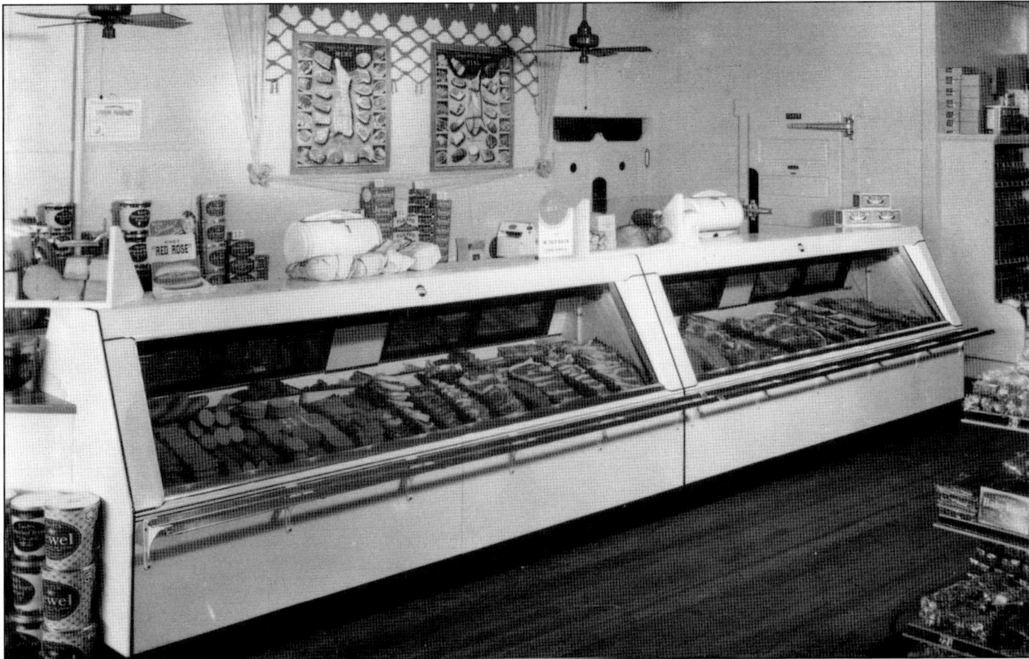

Kings Meat Market on Twelfth Avenue Road displays quality meat that was served in homes and restaurants of Nampa in 1940. The barrels at the end of the meat counter are items rarely seen today; they contained pure lard. The rack at the right displayed candy and other items.

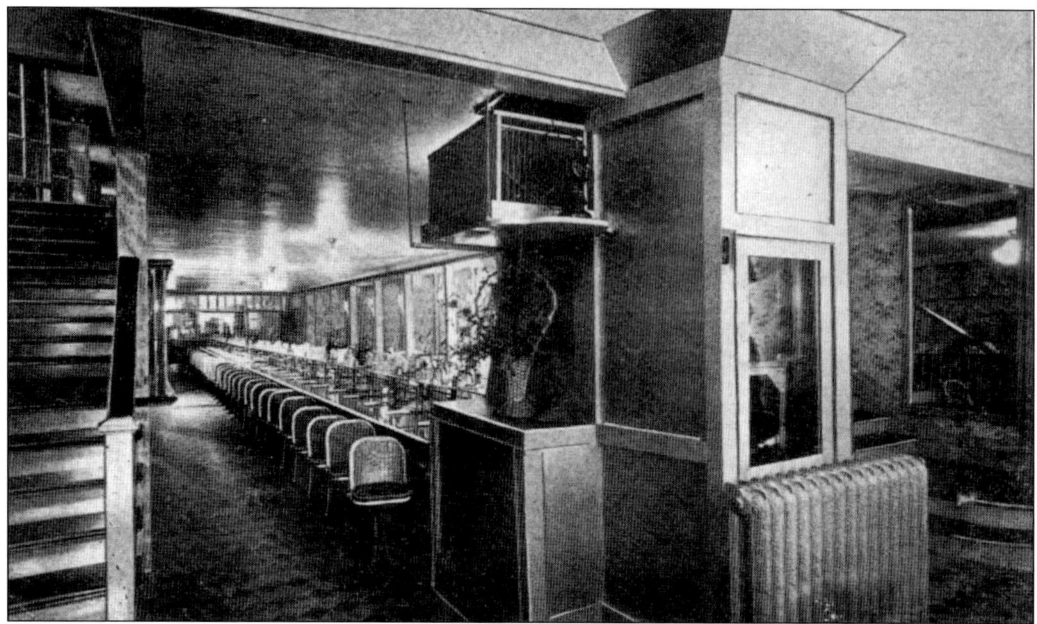

The Mecanafe was located in Boise, but crowds of Nampa people went there to eat. There were no waiters or waitresses; rather, the food passed by on a conveyer belt, and customers took what they wanted. The empty dishes told the establishment how much to charge. It was advertised as the restaurant of the future, but like a lot of advertisements, this assertion did not come true.

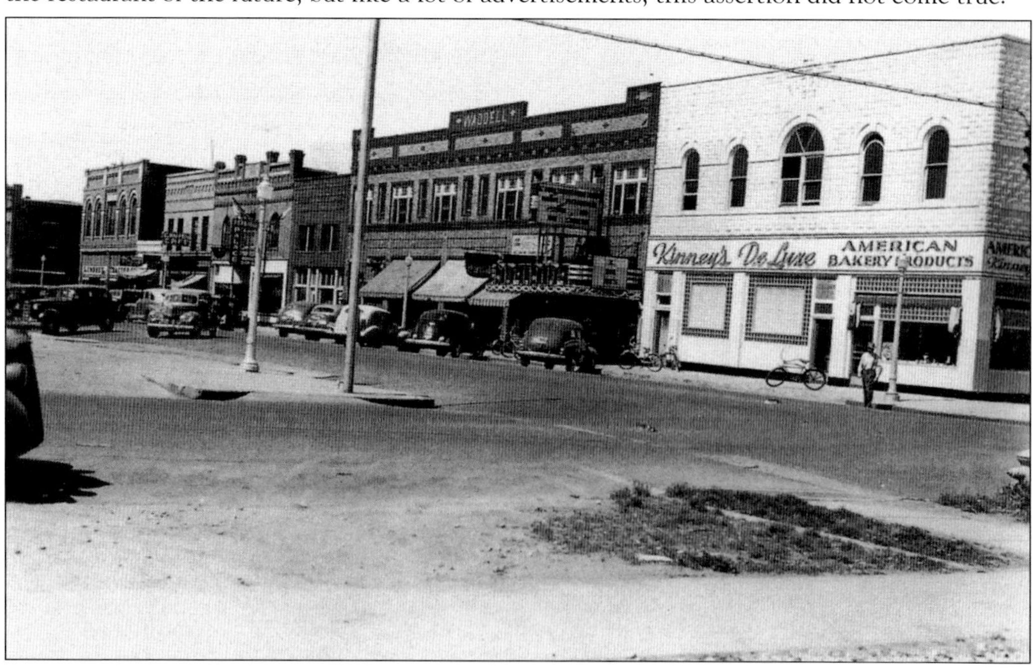

This is the corner of Fourteenth Avenue and First (Main) Street in 1944. Showalter's had been replaced by the American Bakery, and the Liberty Theater was now called the Adelaide. The Forbidden Palace and the Canyon Café (known in its last days as the Alibi Inn) were to the left. These buildings, along with the one to the right of the Forbidden Palace, were destroyed in an explosion in 1947.

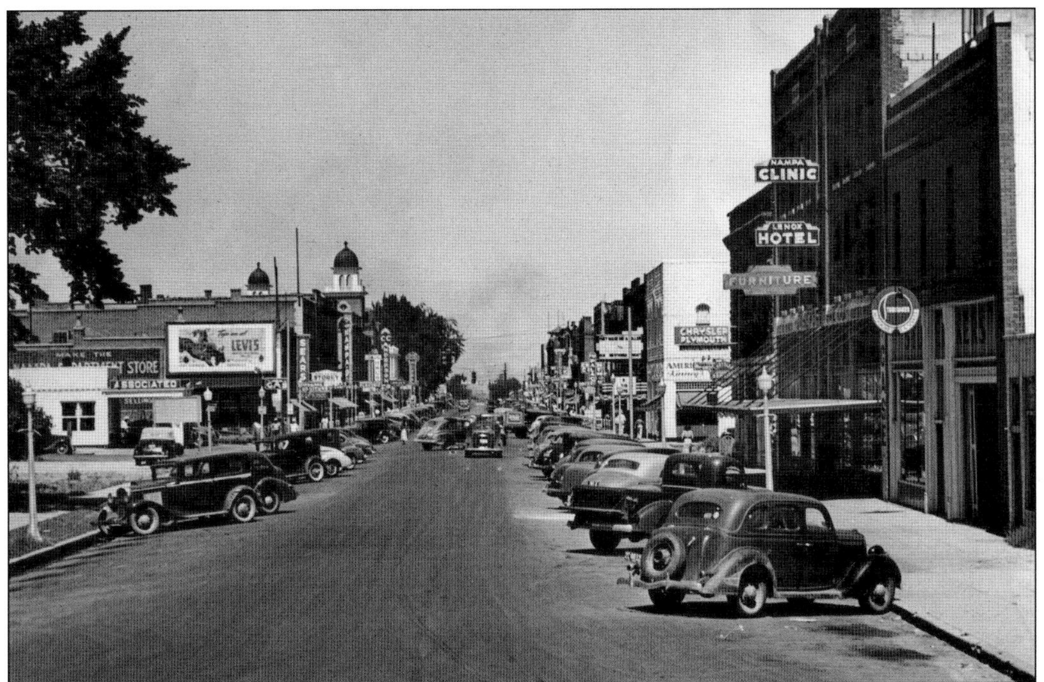

A half block up the street from the Adelaide was the Lenox Hotel, on the right. It rented rooms like any hotel but also contained the Nampa Clinic run by the Drs. Mangum. The Chrysler-Plymouth Dealer was on the corner, and the Forbidden Palace can be seen down the block.

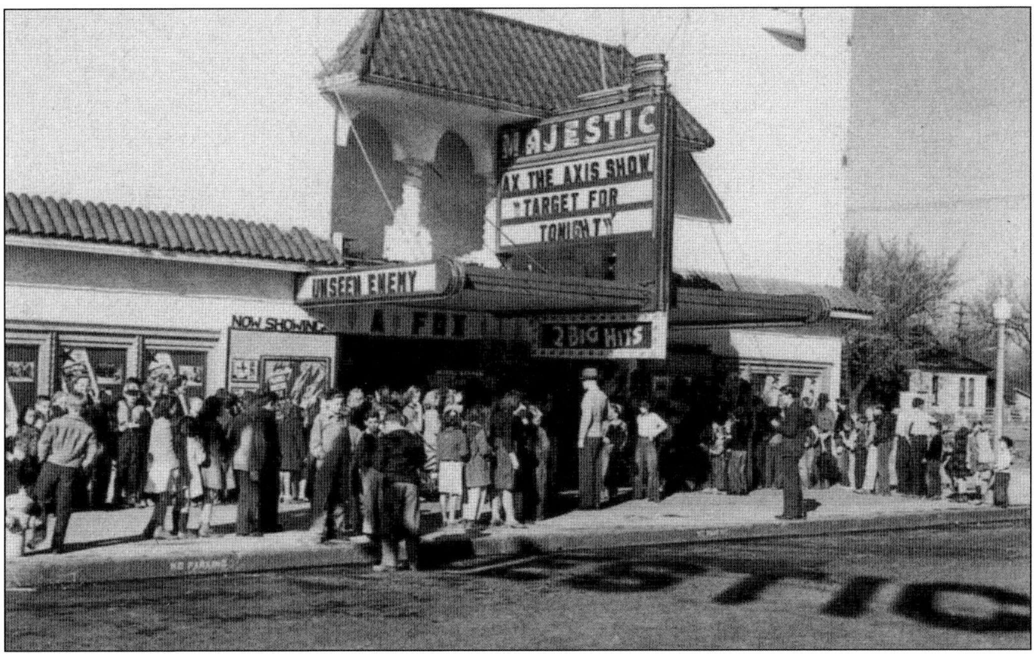

The doors of the Majestic Theater were about to open for the Saturday matinee in this 1944 image. Children flocked to these Saturday-afternoon showings of cartoons, serials, war movies, and Westerns there and at the Adelaide. The marquee displays "Ax the Axis Show," exemplifying the patriotic fever of the time.

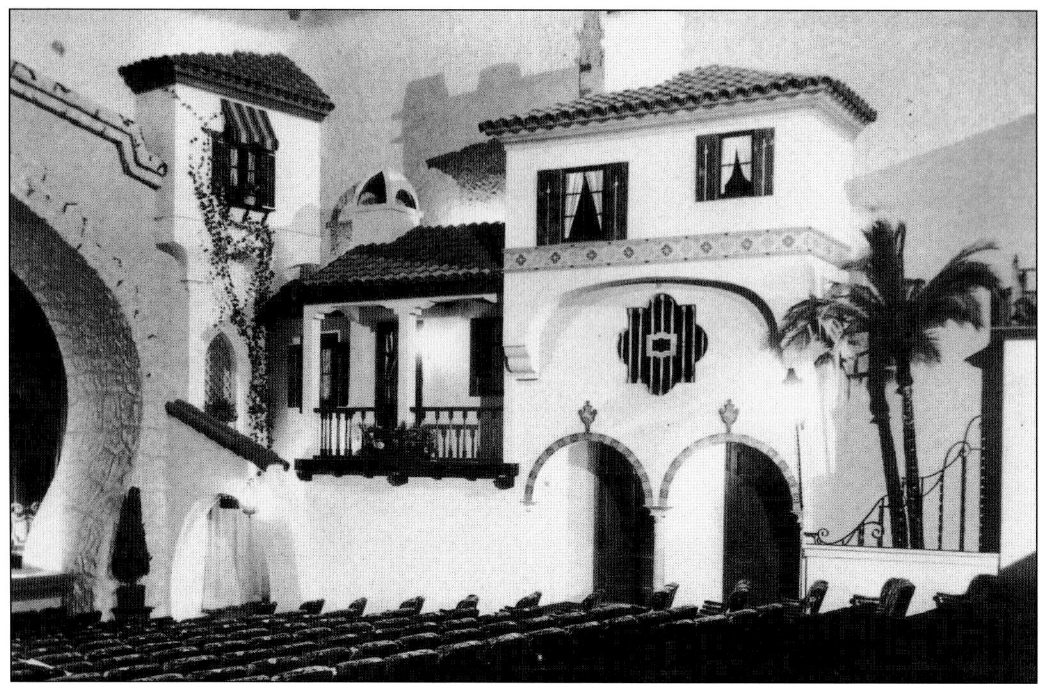

The interior of the Majestic is shown here. Both side walls were made to look like a Spanish town, with a bridge over the stage (visible at left) connecting them. There was a ramp leading to the balcony, where the ceiling had twinkling lights that gave an impression of stars. The lobby was sumptuous. The Majestic was a magic place, sorely missed when it burned down.

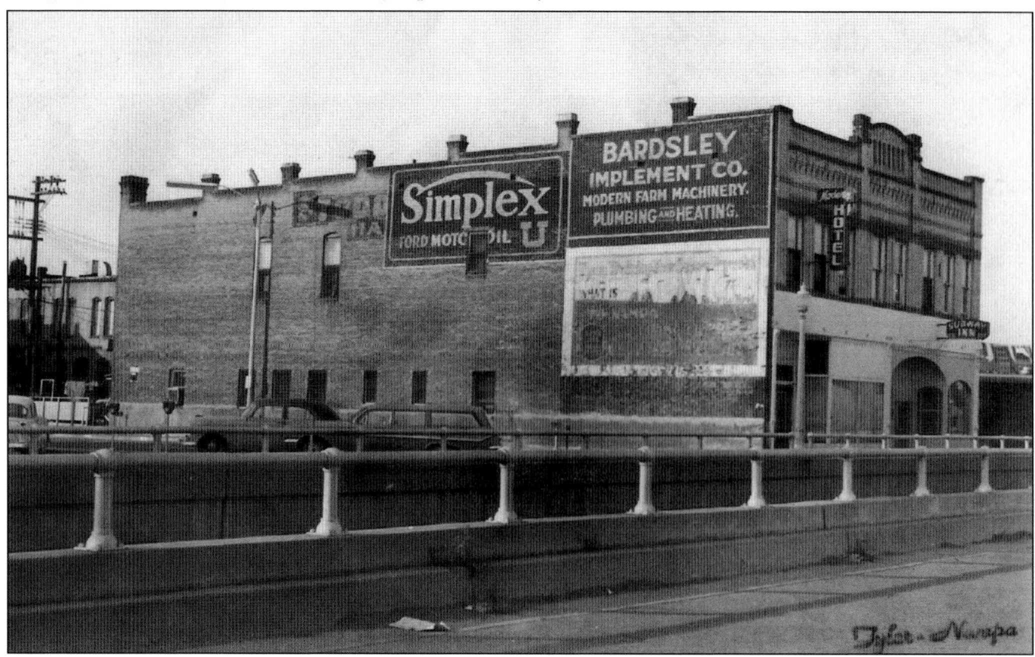

The Modern Hotel was located on Eleventh Avenue South beside the subway. It had a bar called the Subway Inn inside. The Modern was not competition to the Dewey Palace, which—despite beginning to look a little run down in 1946—was still the place to stay in Nampa.

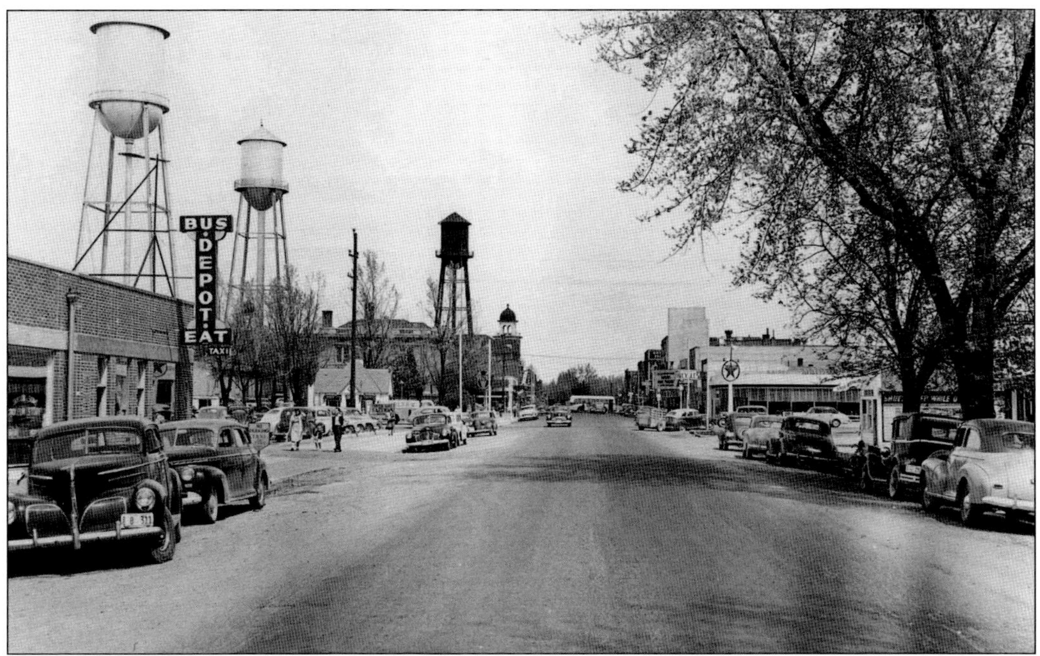

Construction of a new theater was met with excitement when announced in February 1946. It was the Pix Theater, and its slogan was "Pix picks the pictures." This photograph shows the theater on the right about a block down Twelfth Avenue South. The Greyhound bus depot is on the left, and Nampa's water towers are in the background.

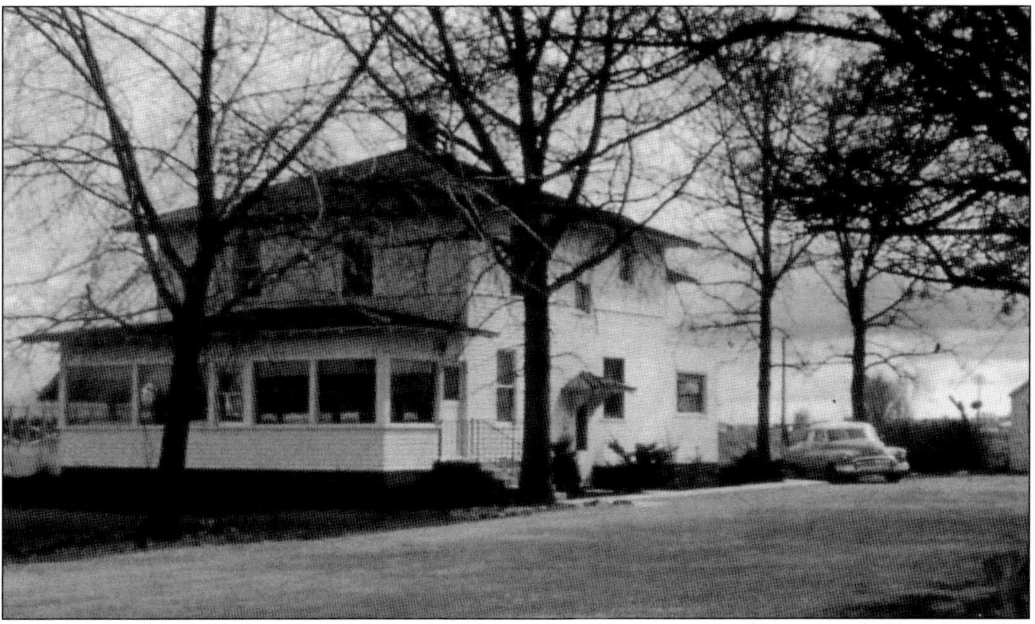

The Homestead was opened in 1952 by Doyle and Elizabeth Cain and Bob and Kathryn Williams on Lake Lowell Avenue. It was unique, offering only chicken and steak but serving it family style, with baked or mashed potatoes, vegetables, fresh-baked hot rolls, and their famous honey rolls. A selection of pies and ice cream came for dessert. It became the most popular restaurant in Nampa.

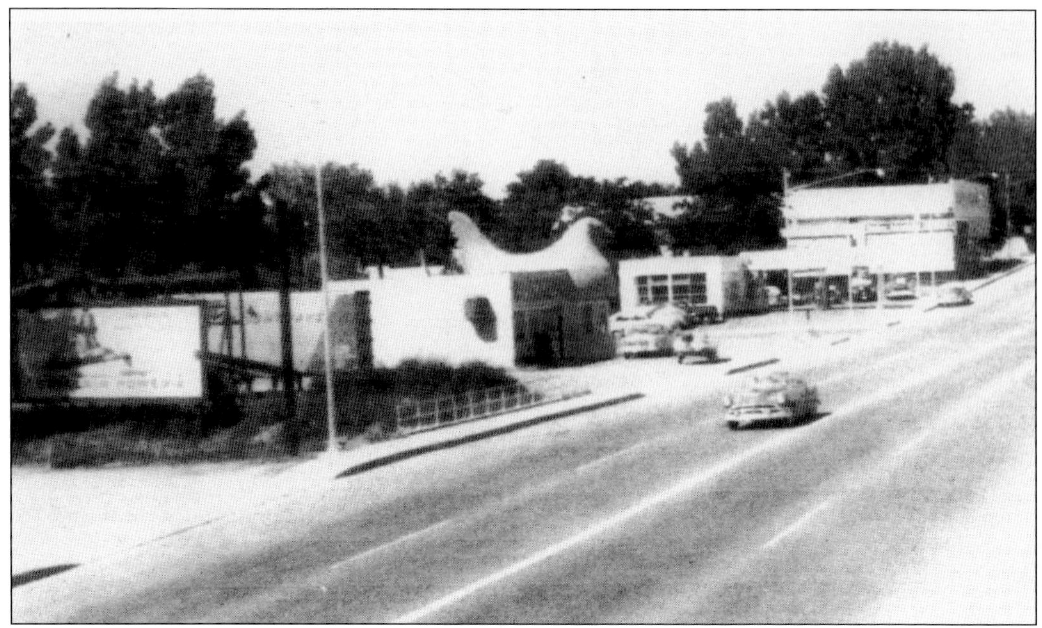

The Chicken Inn restaurant was the most unique-looking restaurant in Nampa. Located on Eleventh Avenue North, its specialty was, obviously, fried chicken. The building, in the shape of a chicken, gazes down on a 1953 Pontiac traveling down the four-lane street. It is another relic of the past that is now gone.

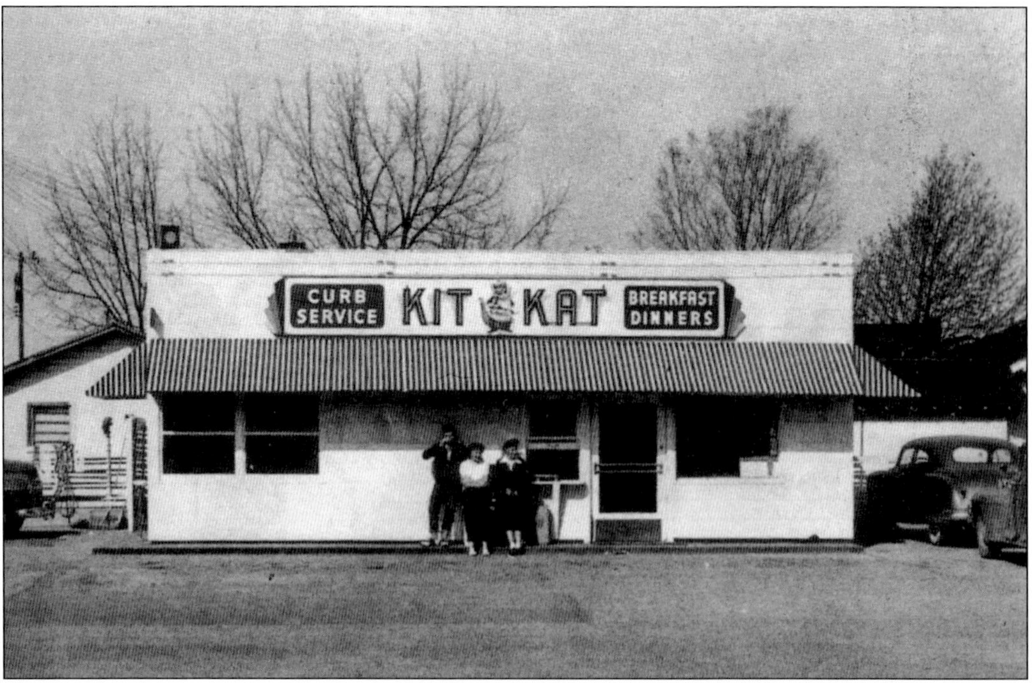

The Kit Kat drive-in was right across the street from the high school in the 1950s. The restaurant's hamburgers, hot dogs, and soft drinks brought in huge lunchtime crowds from the school. The high school was turned into West Junior High in 1956, but this development did not hurt those lunchtime crowds. The girls in the photograph are sporting their 1950s styles.

Four

Churches, Schools, and Public Buildings

Everyone in Nampa remembers the school they went to, the public buildings they conducted business in, and the churches they attended. Many are gone now, but those memories remain. Most early schools are gone, turned to dust by the relentless engine of progress. Church buildings fare better. They may have had facelifts and additions or been totally remodeled, but when the congregations moved to new buildings, other church communities seem to have taken up residence in the old sanctuaries. Even public buildings have gone the way of the dodo. Nampa's city hall was razed, and a new one built on the spot where many residents went to high school.

Many of the old buildings live only in photographs today. Chief among them are the Dewey Palace Hotel, Chicken Inn, and Crescent Brewery. These were torn down. The Greystone Hotel, Case Furniture building, old Commercial Hotel, Drake Drug, Forbidden Palace, and others were destroyed by fire or explosion. Drake Drug was rebuilt after the fire, but the Forbidden Palace became a sales lot for boats in the 1960s.

Theaters have not fared well at all. The Empress, Orpheum, Unique, and Crystal all faded from the local scene over the years. The Majestic burned, the Adelaide was converted to something else, and the Pix closed, was neglected, and fell into ruin, although the shell is still there.

This chapter goes back to rediscover those memories and maybe make new revelations of the past.

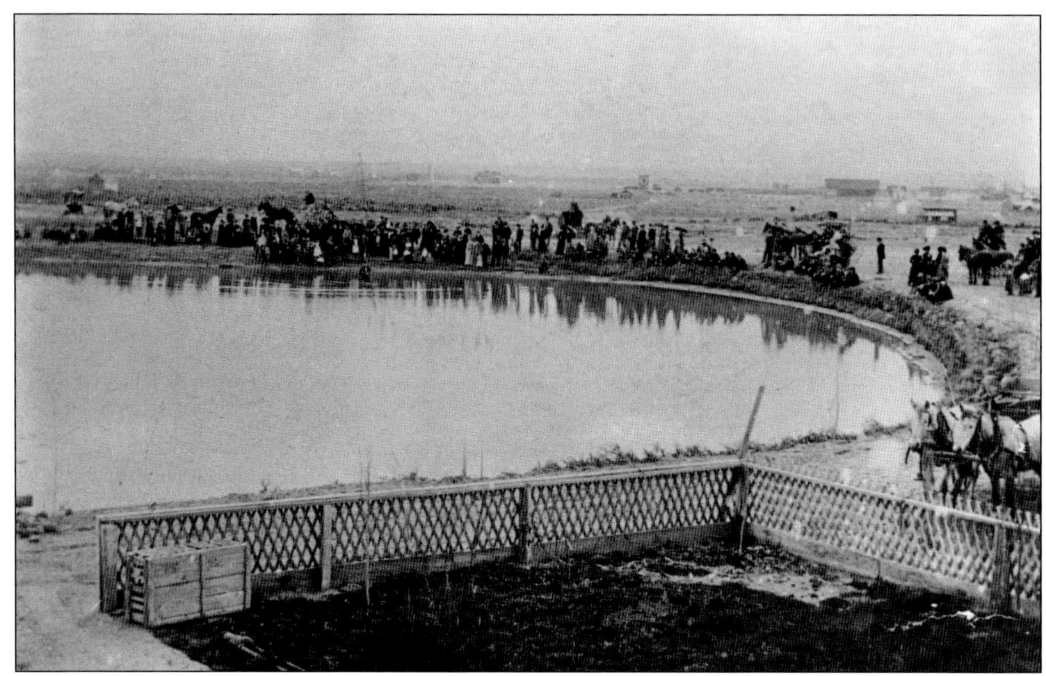

This scene depicts a baptism in Lake Ethel in 1891. Such ceremonies moved inside as churches were built around the city. It is included here to show that religion was and is an important part of life. Over a decade later, the lake would become part of the E.H. Dewey estate, with a beautiful home and trees lining the drive.

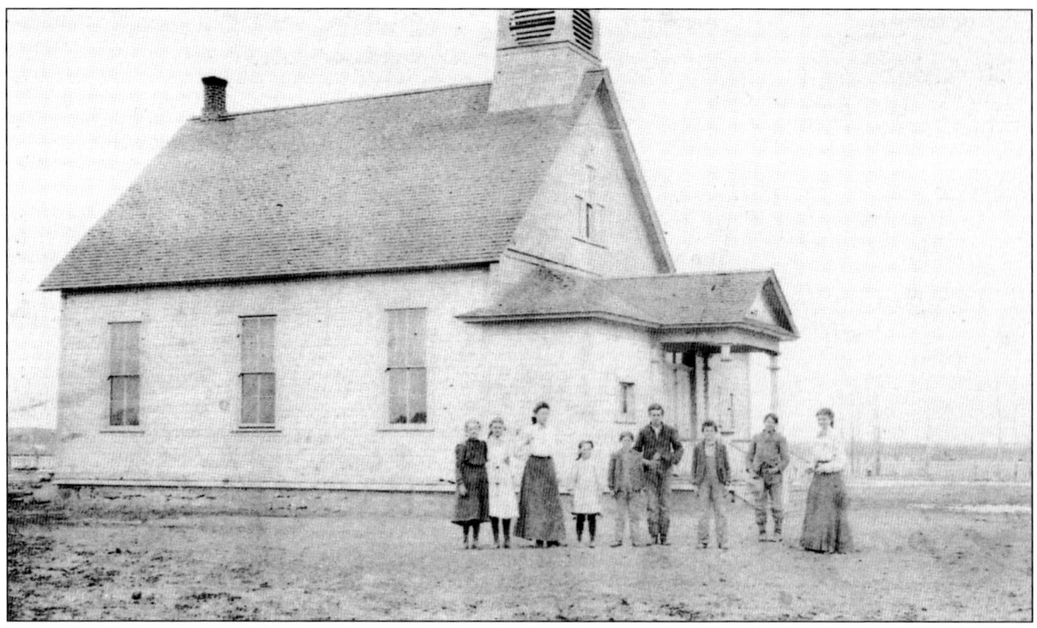

In 1904, this school occupied land covered by the waters of Lake Lowell when the dam was built in 1907. Even though it was not very large, the building was moved south of Nampa to the Scism District, where it fit the needs of the area. It was still attended by rural schoolchildren as they learned their ABCs.

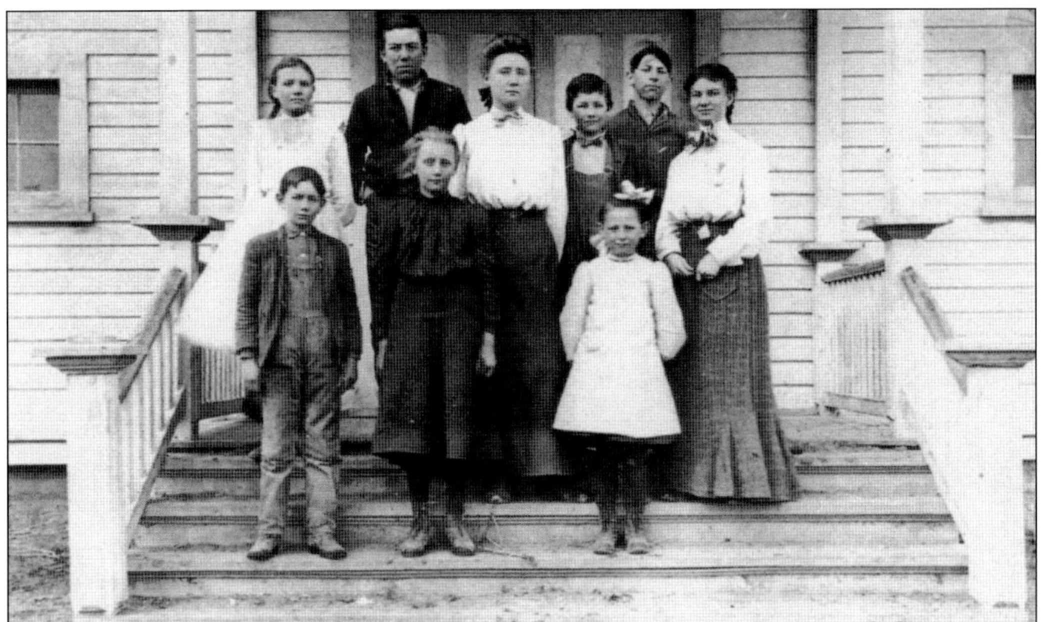

These are the students who attended the school on the previous page. The name of the school at the time has been lost in the past. The students included Abby Gott, T.N. Harris, Ruth Harris, two Esgates, and three O'Haras.

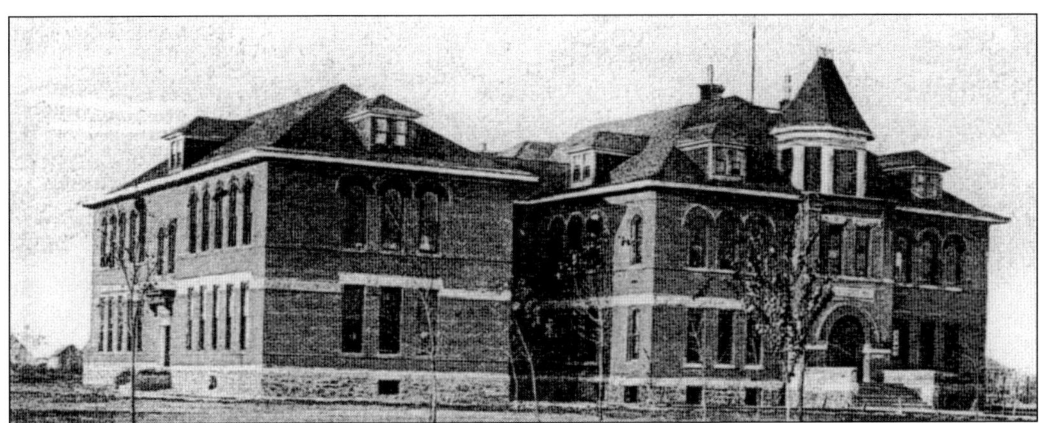

Kenwood School, pictured here around 1905, was the first real public school. It served as the junior high and senior high school until 1919, after which it was used as a grade school. Junior high students attended certain classes there in the 1950s, such as band and orchestra. It was located on Twelfth Avenue South between Fifth and Sixth Streets.

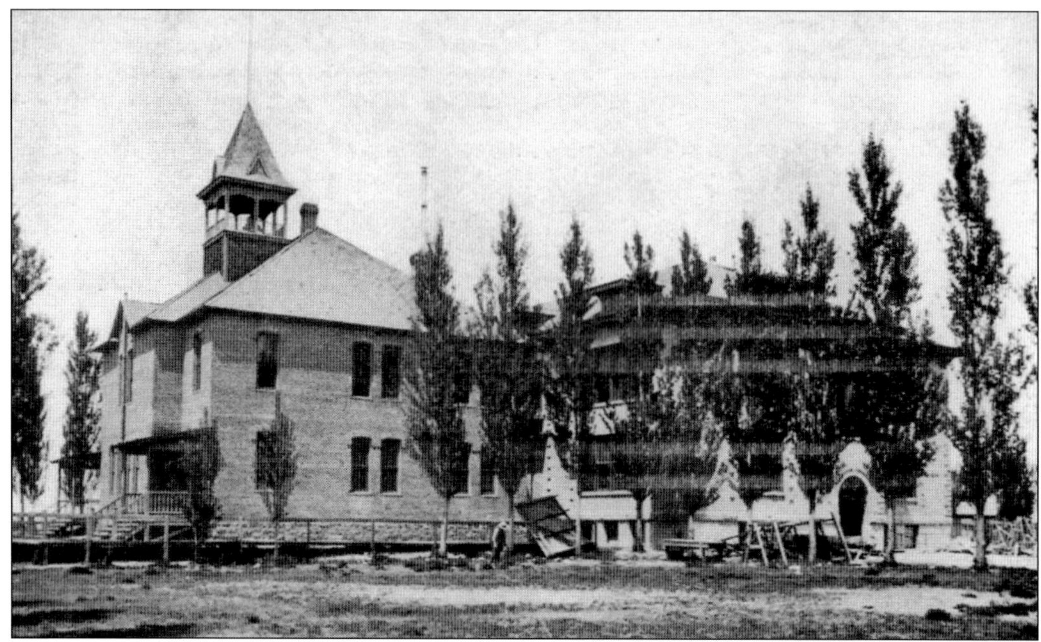

The two Lakeview schools are shown here. The one on the left was the first, and the one on the right was the second (it is still being used today by a charter school). The reason both were there was that the school board did not trust the contractor to have the new school done by September 1907. The board was right; it was not done until November, and the old school was used until the new one was completed.

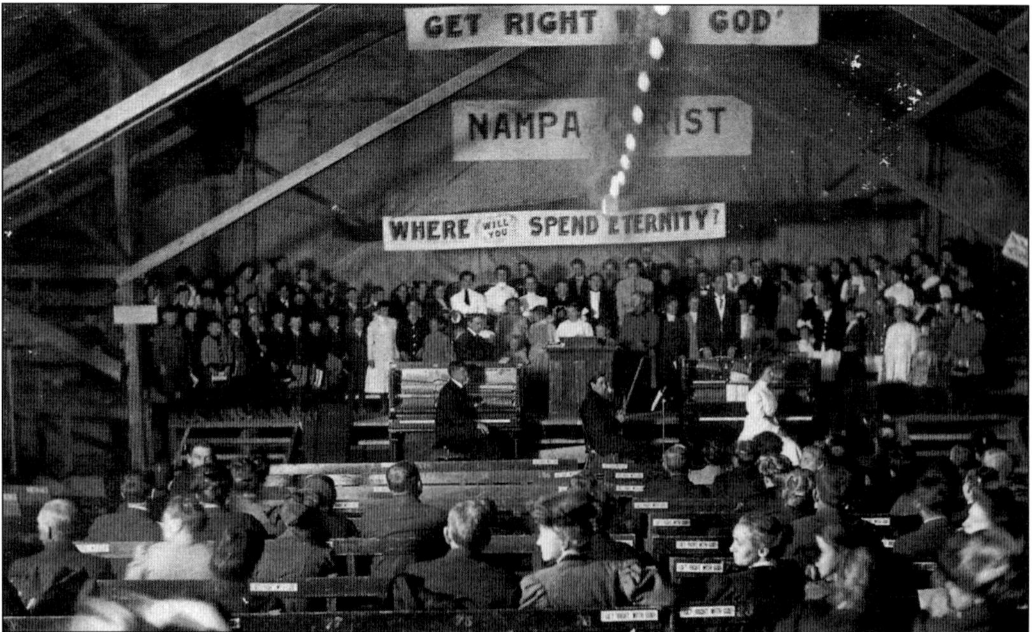

This Hicks evangelist meeting is underway in 1909. The location is unknown but looks like a temporary structure. Many churches brought evangelists to town to draw new people into their congregations. The banners give the impression of advertising for members. These traveling ministers found a temporary home in almost every church in Nampa through the years.

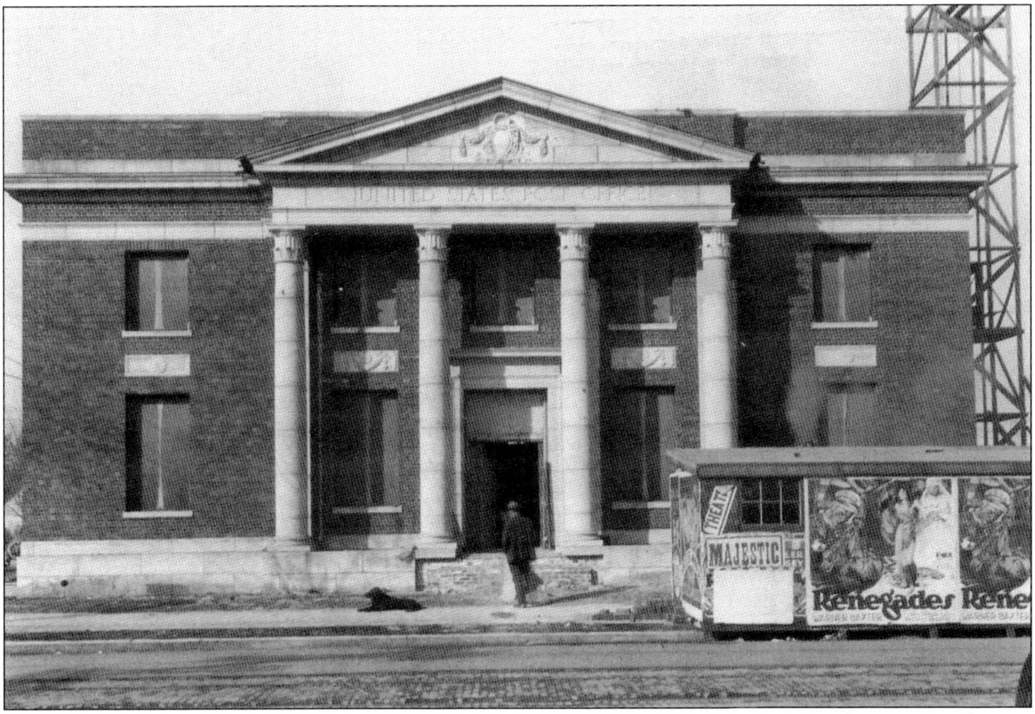

Nampa's federal post office is nearing completion in this 1931 shot. It is still in use today on Eleventh Avenue and Second Street South—an oddity, as the town has grown about 10 times in population since its opening. Note the Majestic Theater movie advertisements on the temporary construction building on the sidewalk.

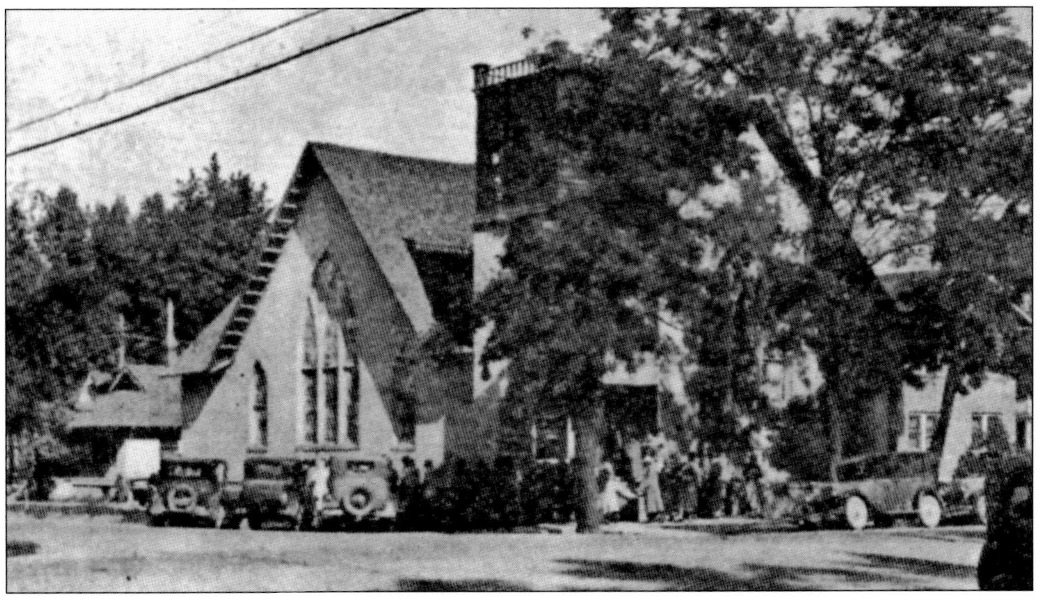

This was the Church of Christ (First Christian Church) in 1933. The minister was Lester Jones, who came to Nampa in 1927. He saw the completion of a new church at Seventh Street and Twelfth Avenue South that was dedicated May 8, 1949. The old church still remains and has been home to a number of congregations.

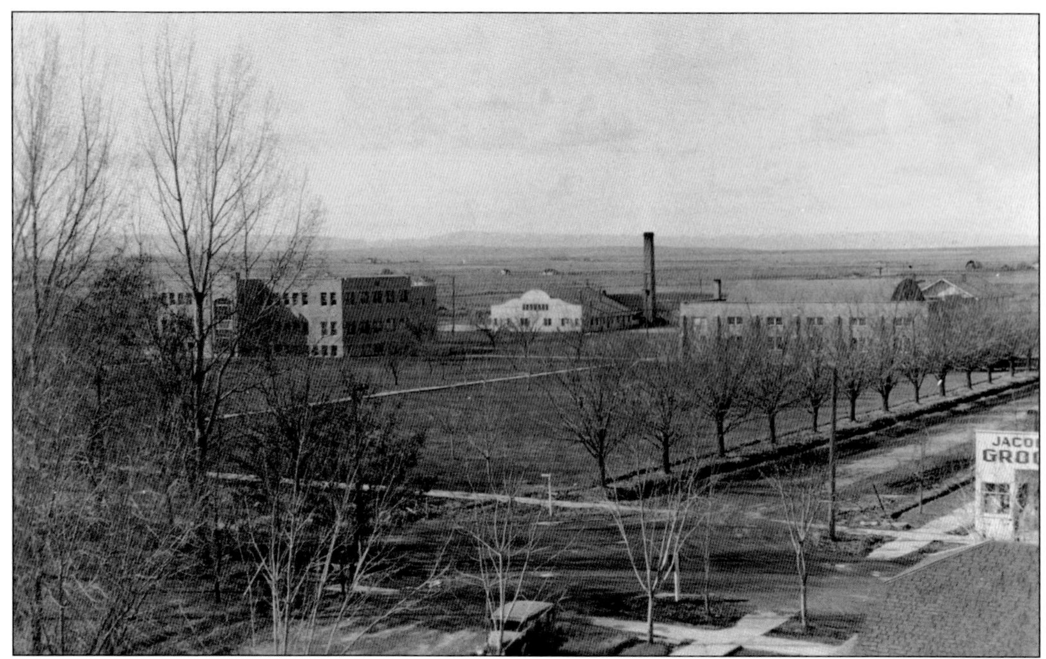

This photograph was taken of the Northwest Nazarene College campus in 1933. The school was definitely on the outskirts then, and its growth since that time is staggering. It added the old Kurtz Park and other land to the campus and is now Northwest Nazarene University. Jacobs Grocery in the right corner was later Campus Corner Grocery.

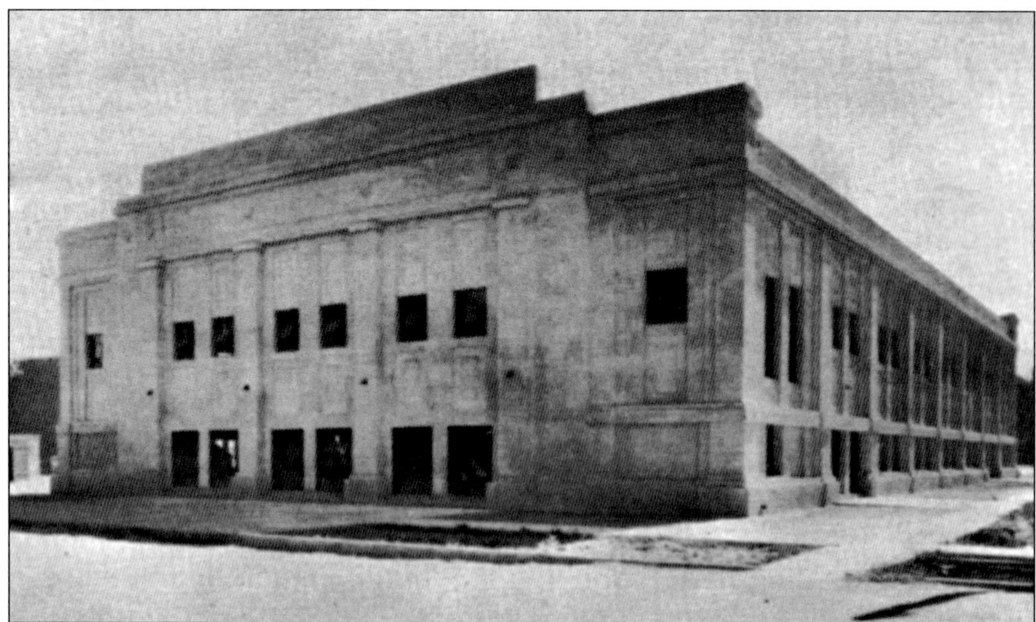

Central Assembly Building (also known as Central Auditorium) was completed in 1937 by the Works Progress Administration of Roosevelt's New Deal. It was added to the junior high school that was finished in 1929. The auditorium still stands today, and many memories of basketball games past surround the structure. Both Nampa High School and Northwest Nazarene College used the edifice for years.

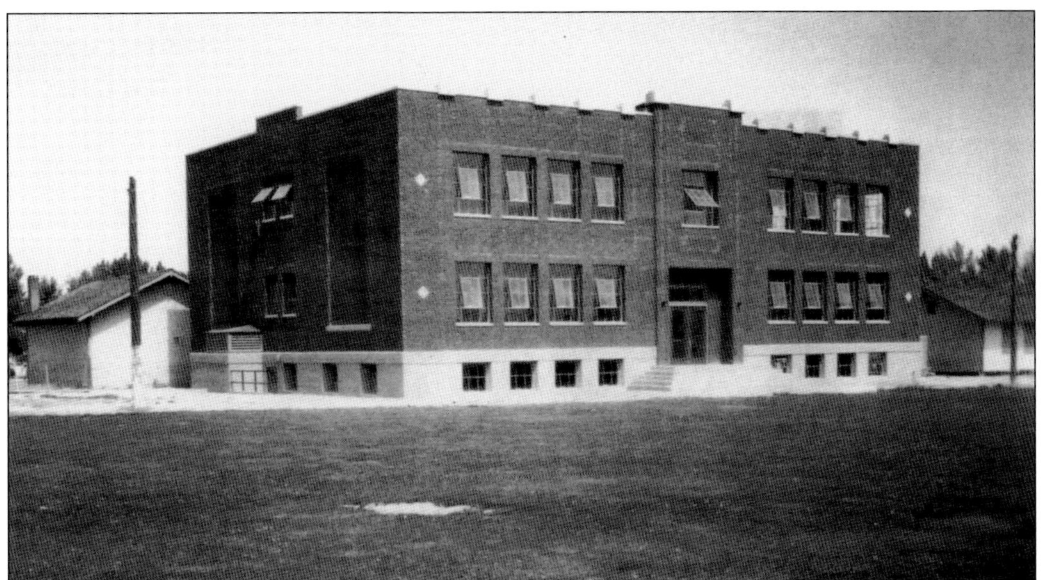

The year 1937 was a big one for school construction. In addition to Central Auditorium, Eastside Grade School (pictured here), and Roosevelt Grade School were completed. The two grade schools had been using cottages or small, wooden buildings to house their students. The Eastside campus is a park today.

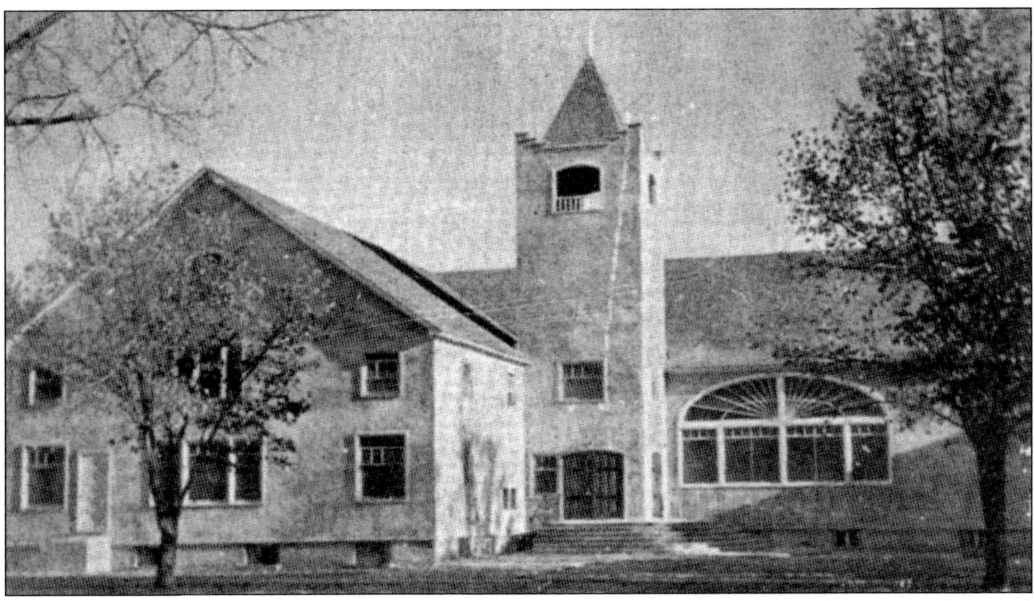

The First Church of the Nazarene, pictured in 1940, has undergone massive remodeling and additions over the years. It has grown from a corner church to cover almost two square blocks, including the parking lot. Fifteenth Avenue South no longer goes through the campus. The church is well attended and continues to grow and improve the surrounding neighborhood.

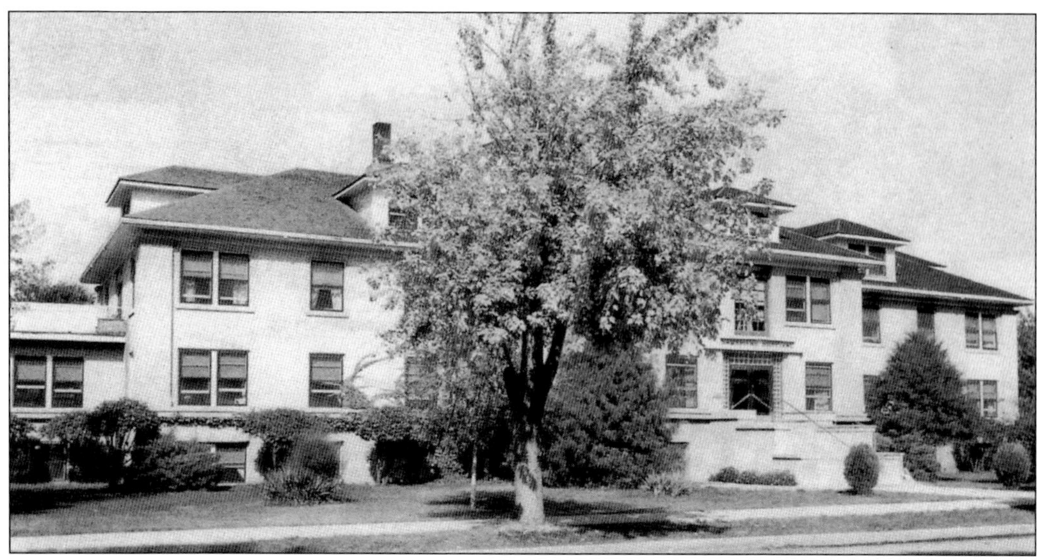

The Samaritan Hospital was built by the Nazarene churches in the early 1930s. Dr. Tom Mangum was a driving force in its completion. A nursing school was a part of the complex. The building is still there today, but it is no longer a hospital. It is now part of the Northwest Nazarene University campus.

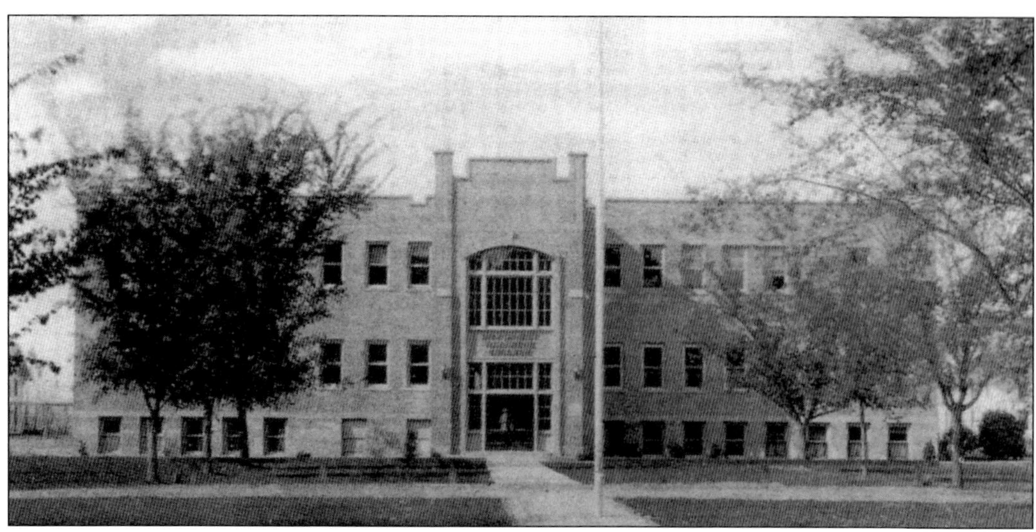

The Administration Building on the Northwest Nazarene University campus, seen here around 1940, has welcomed many a new student to the school. The college opened its doors in Nampa in 1913 and has been a major part of the city, growing steadily over the years since. The building is still in use today.

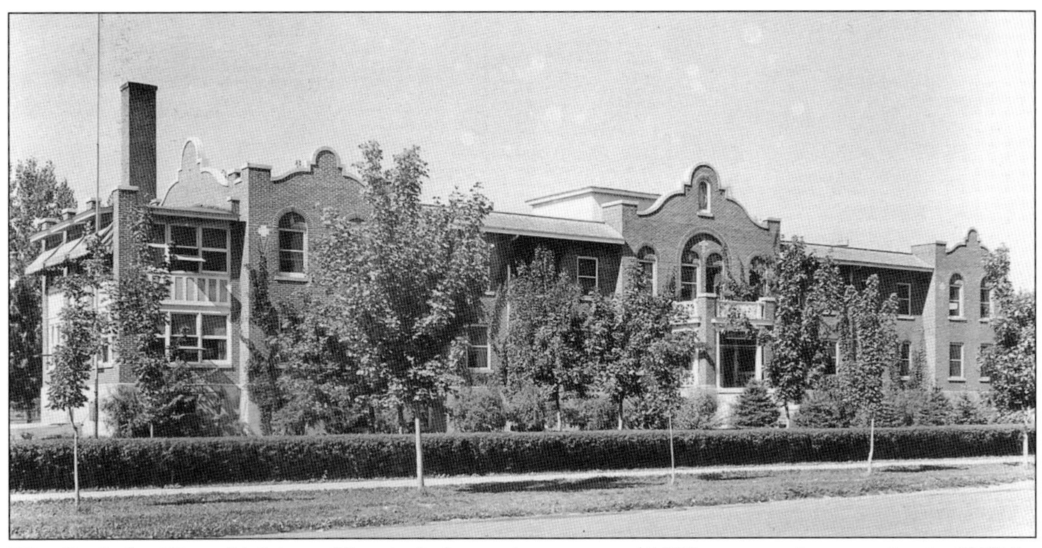

The Catholic Church's Mercy Hospital, shown here around 1950, was put into service in 1919. It, like the Samaritan Hospital, had a nursing school in conjunction with it. It served the community for many years but is now boarded up, only a ghostly reminder of the past.

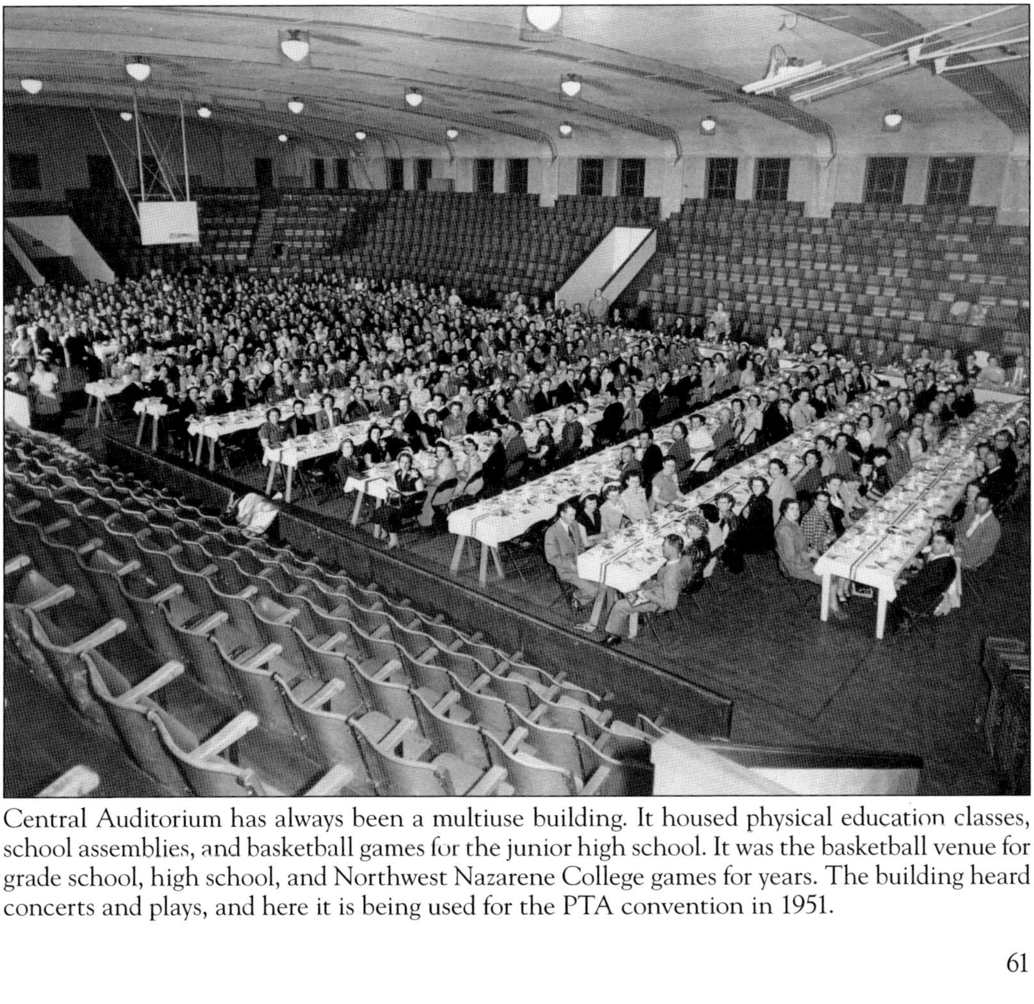

Central Auditorium has always been a multiuse building. It housed physical education classes, school assemblies, and basketball games for the junior high school. It was the basketball venue for grade school, high school, and Northwest Nazarene College games for years. The building heard concerts and plays, and here it is being used for the PTA convention in 1951.

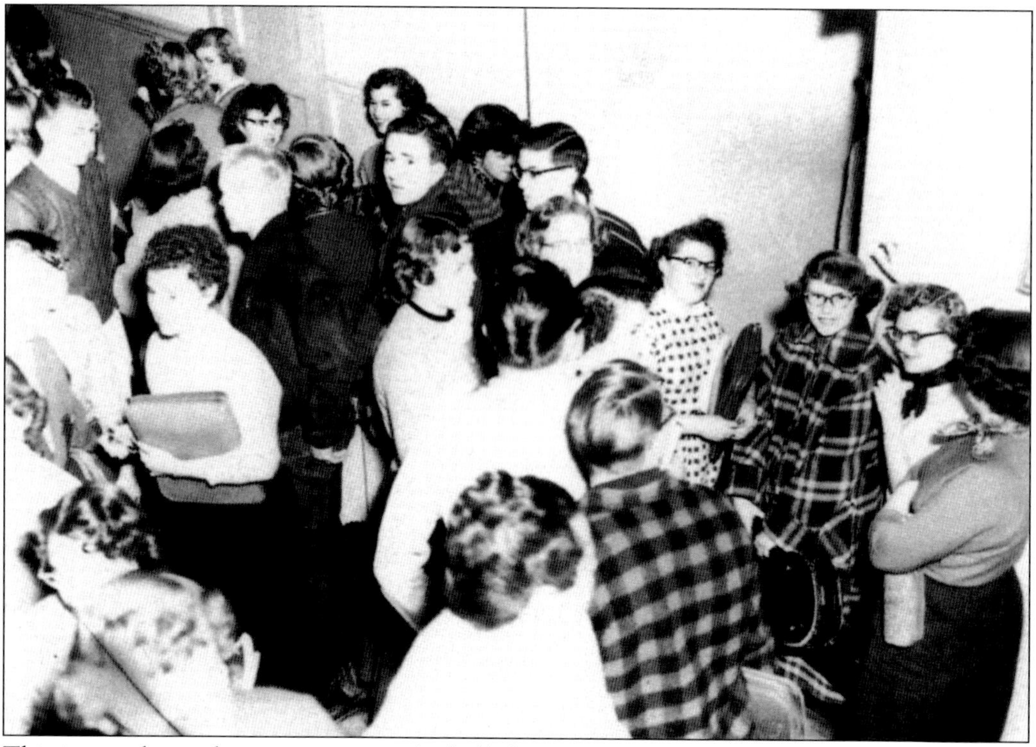

This image shows the congestion in the halls between classes at the old high school in 1954. This was one of the reasons for the new school on Lake Lowell Avenue that opened in the fall of 1955. Among those in the photograph are Bob Pepply, Pat Herr, Kathy Roth, Scott Murray, Bob Deihm, Ron Coyle, Ms. Birks, and Illa Mae Higgins.

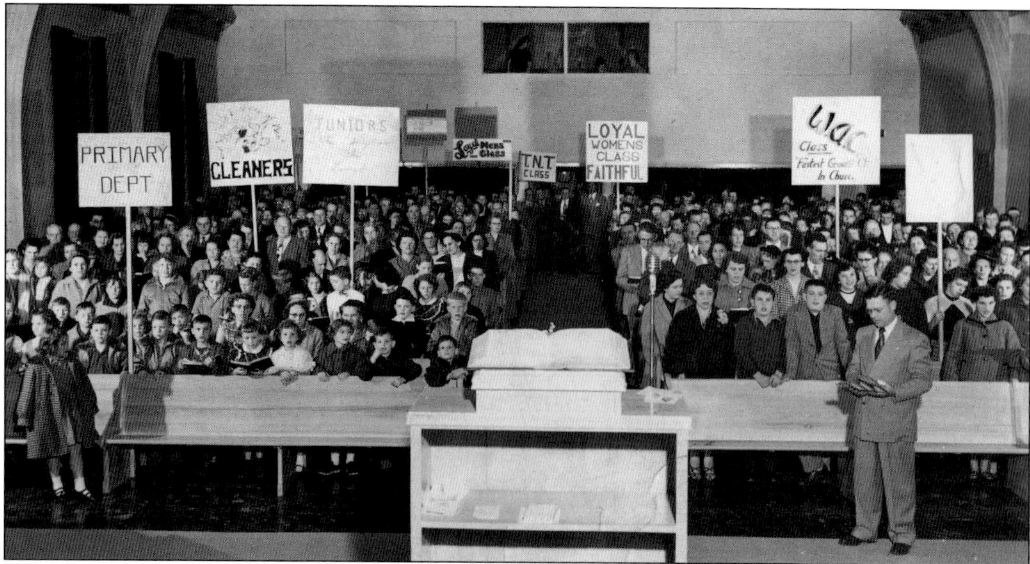

Located then and now on the corner of Twelfth Avenue and Seventh Street South, the sanctuary of the Church of Christ (First Christian Church) building that was completed in 1949 is seen here. The Golden Glow Tower next to the church was a project of the congregation. The windows in the back wall mark the "cry room" for families with young children.

Five

Downtown and Neighborhoods

The face of Nampa changed many times over the years. The commercial center took on new looks when various buildings were added, given facelifts, or razed. Architectural styles changed both in the business district and in the residential neighborhoods. Homes ranged from palatial to just functional, as in any city. Memories are filled with big houses owned by the prominent citizens, but there were also other, smaller homes that people lived out their lives in, and their memories are just as important.

Streets went from dirt in dry weather to mud on rainy days. For example, in August 1920, Mayor H.H. Keim had been badgered about doing something to remedy the deplorable condition of Seventeenth Avenue South. He finally listened when, after a rainstorm, he was driving his delivery wagon down the street and became hopelessly mired in the mud. He had to call Young Transfer and Storage to pull him out. Soon after, a successful movement to pave the city's streets began. Today, there are multiple lanes on the streets and highways, and it is hard for modern youngsters to even imagine anything of the sort happening in this city.

This chapter looks at a cross section of the city as the years passed by.

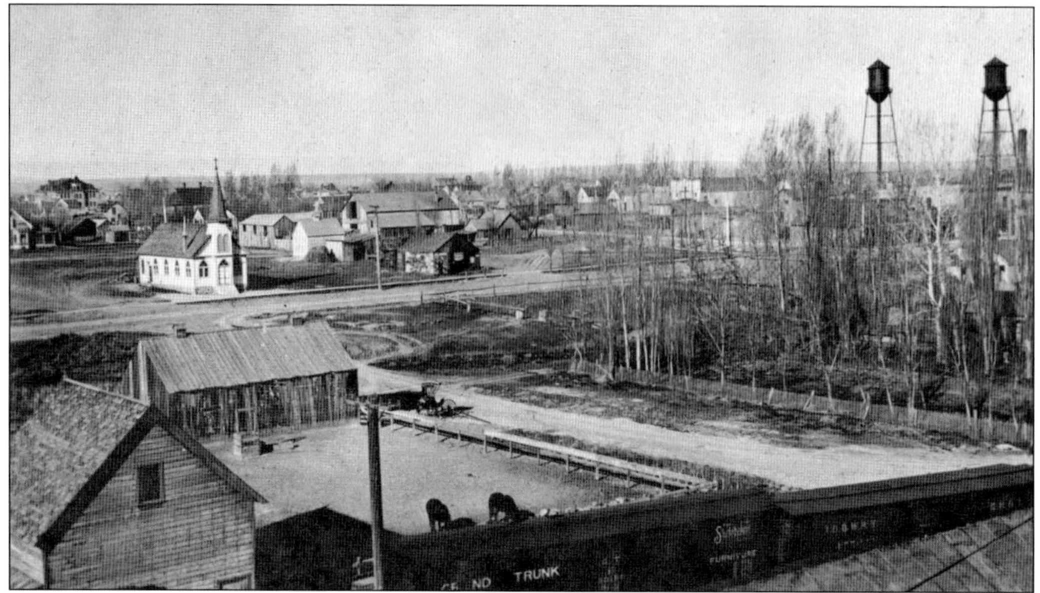

Looking across Front Street toward the business section in this 1902 image, one can see Kenwood School in the background and not much past it. Dr. J.C. Joyner said it was possible to hunt rabbits and pheasants a block past the school at that time. After Kenwood, the next house was the Hasbrouck mansion.

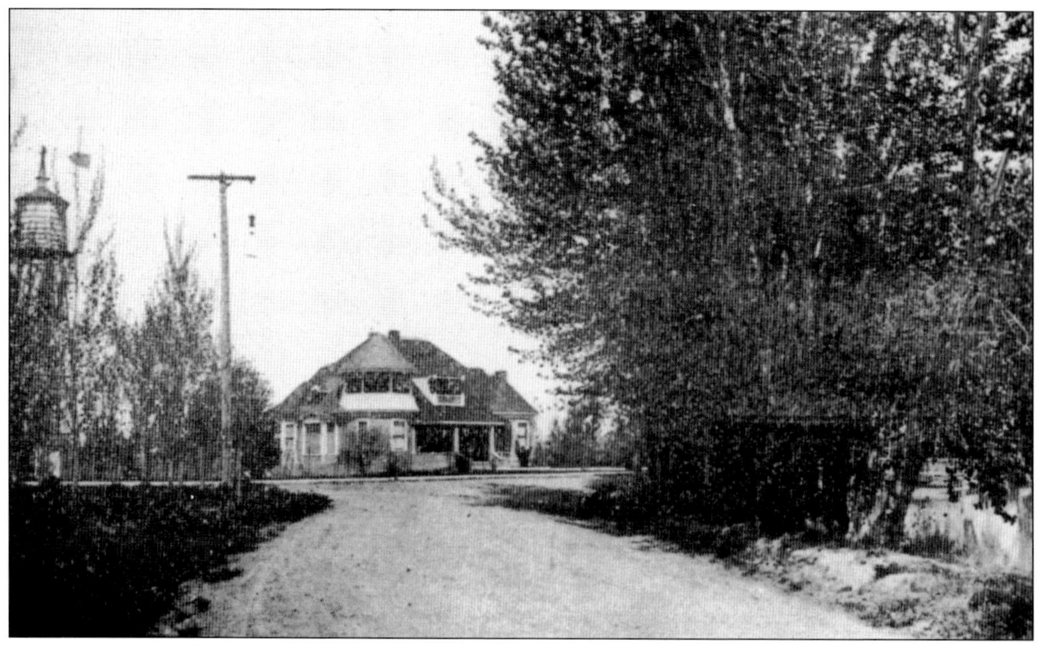

The E.H. Dewey home was located on Lake Ethel. In 1910, it was one of the showplace homes in Nampa. A postcard was sold that said it was a typical Nampa home—there was no truth in advertising then. It was called the Park House in later years and was used for community meetings before falling into disrepair. Today's Lakeview Park was the Dewey estate.

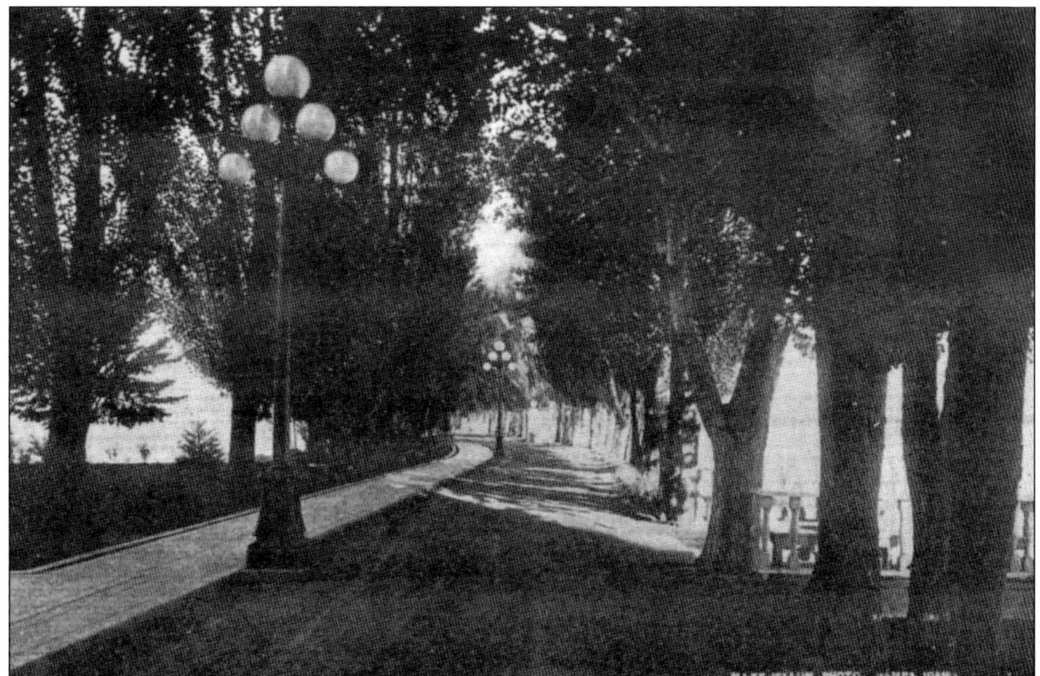

This is the driveway around Lake Ethel to the Dewey house. The lights were electric, as Dewey owned the power company. The estate had a water tower and its own water system. Dewey had started and continued to run the water company. He made a lot of money, and showed it in the pride he took in his estate.

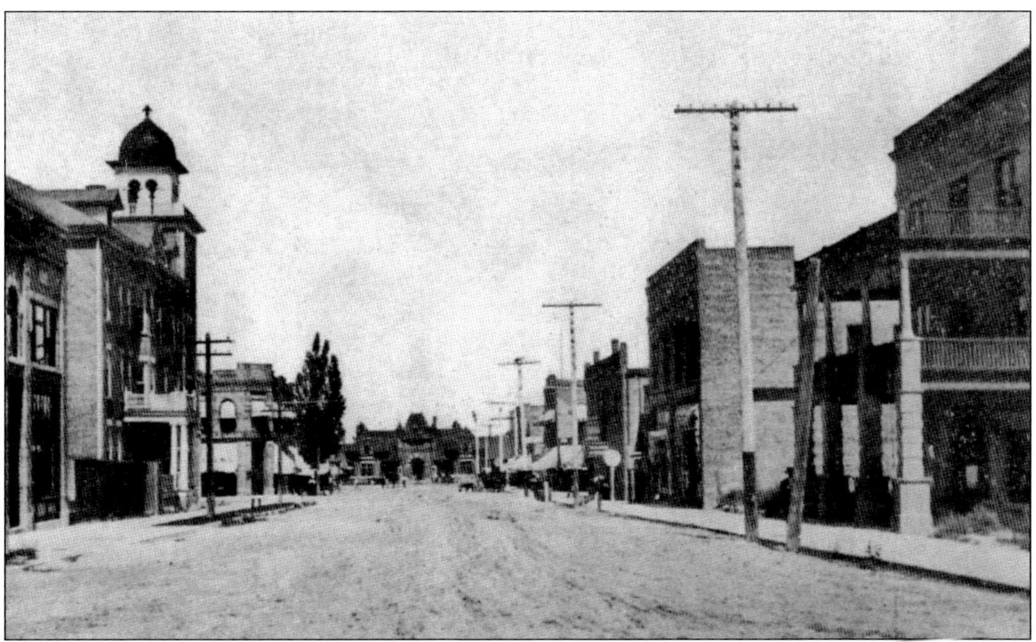

Looking down G Street (Twelfth Avenue) in 1907, the streets are dirt. The Greystone Hotel (Share House) on the right, the Dewey Palace and the Burns-Fox building on the left, and the Oregon Short Line depot at the end of the street dominate the scene. The sidewalks were wood.

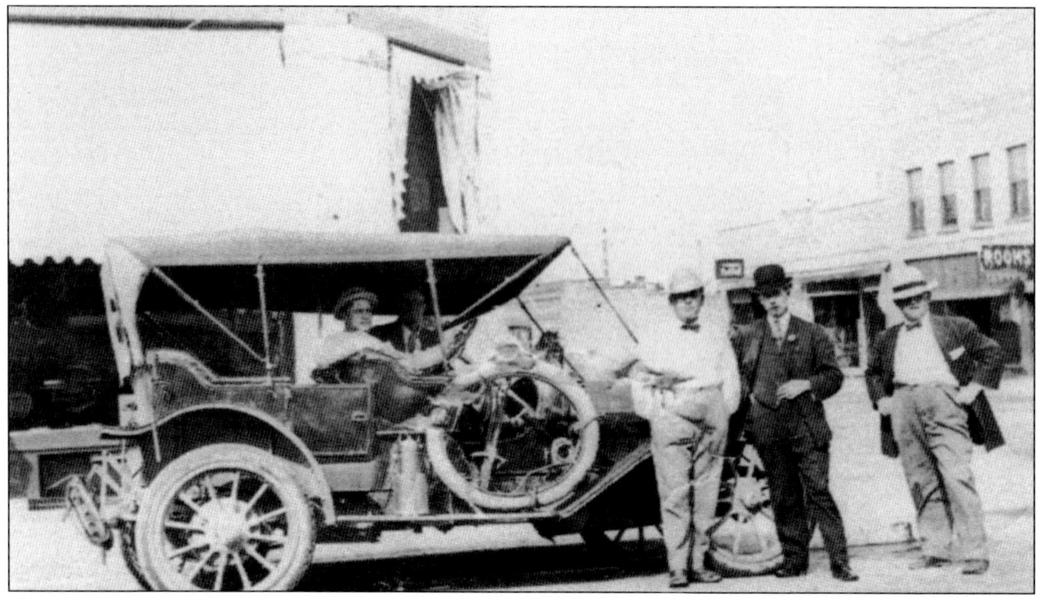

The Stoddard brothers pose with their friends in front of an automobile, not a common sight in 1907. E.H. Dewey bought the first car, a Cadillac, in 1905. The Stoddards owned the building housing the Cosmopolitan Saloon at Twelfth Avenue and Front Street and also Stoddard Hardware on First Street and Thirteenth Avenue South.

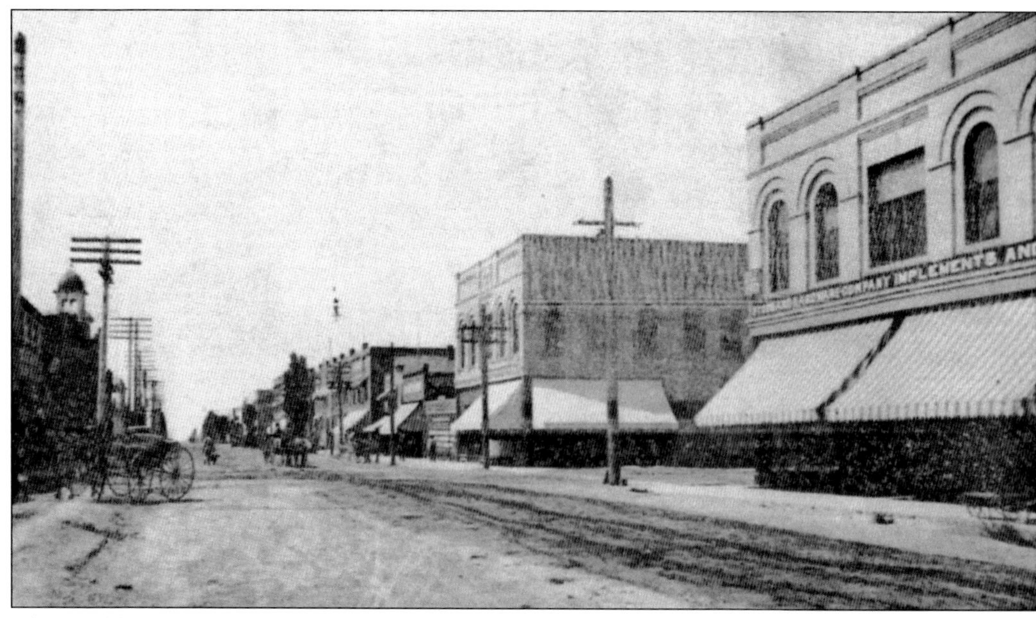

The Stoddard Hardware Company noted in the previous photograph is seen on the right around 1908. The edifice across Thirteenth Avenue is Fred Mock's Blue Eye building, named after the 1905 book he wrote. Take note of the horse-drawn transportation, with not an automobile in sight. Cars did not start to become common until after 1910.

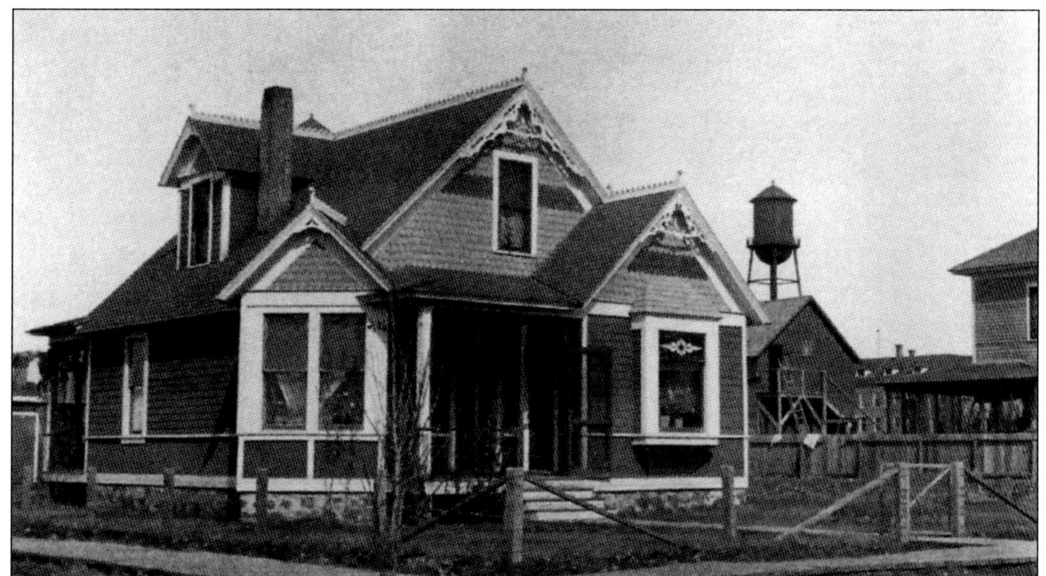

The O.G. Reinhardt house at 223 Thirteenth Avenue South is pictured here in 1910. This was a typical Nampa house for the time, and many of the area's homes were of this caliber. Almost all had outbuildings, as chickens, rabbits, and other small animals were raised on the property for the owner's consumption.

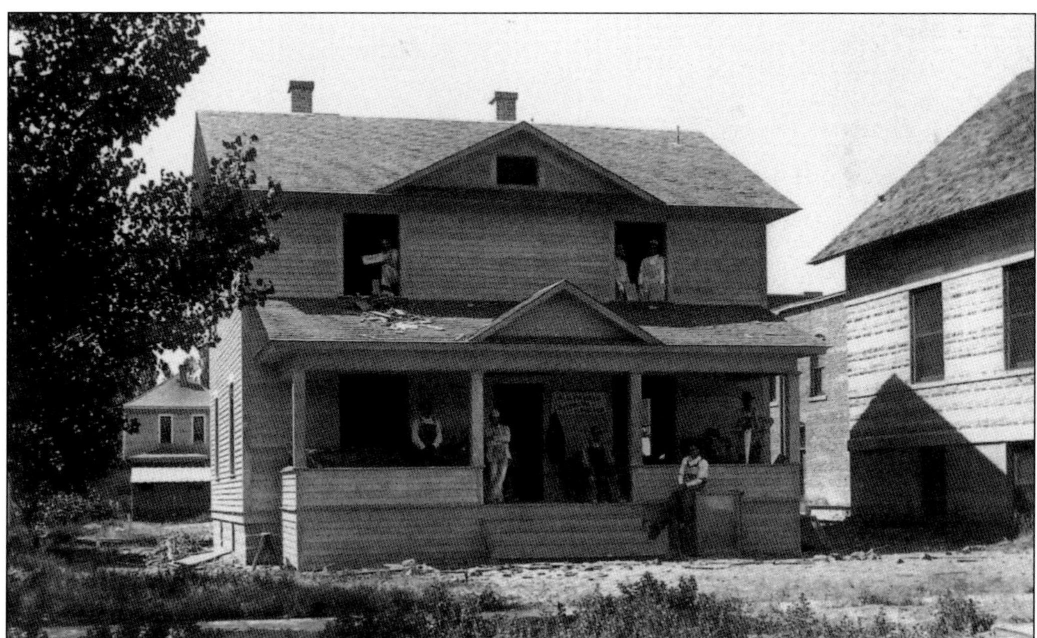

This house was under construction at 209 Fifteenth Avenue South when this photograph was taken in 1919. It was being built by the Frantz Construction Company. It was the Dodd family home from the 1940s to the 1960s. The building on the right was the Presbyterian church, now a bookstore.

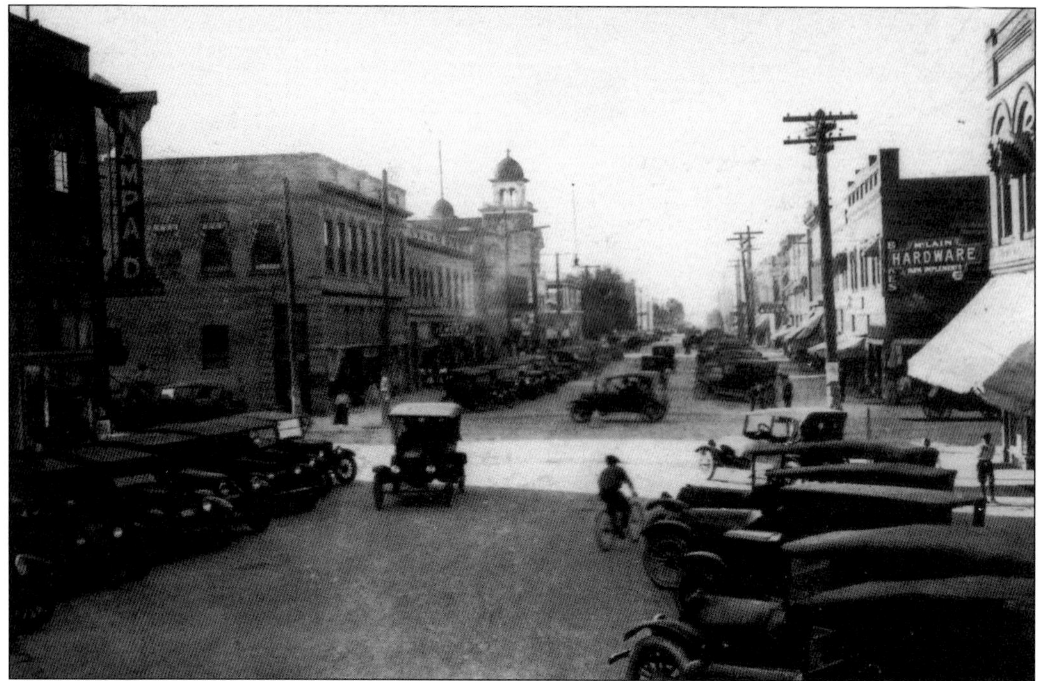

Here is Main Street on an active Saturday in 1925. The town was busier, and the streets were paved. In contrast to earlier times, parking and traffic were beginning to be a problem. There were still no traffic lights, however. Stoddard Hardware had given way to McClain Hardware, and the Nampa Department Store was now Falk's Nampa D.

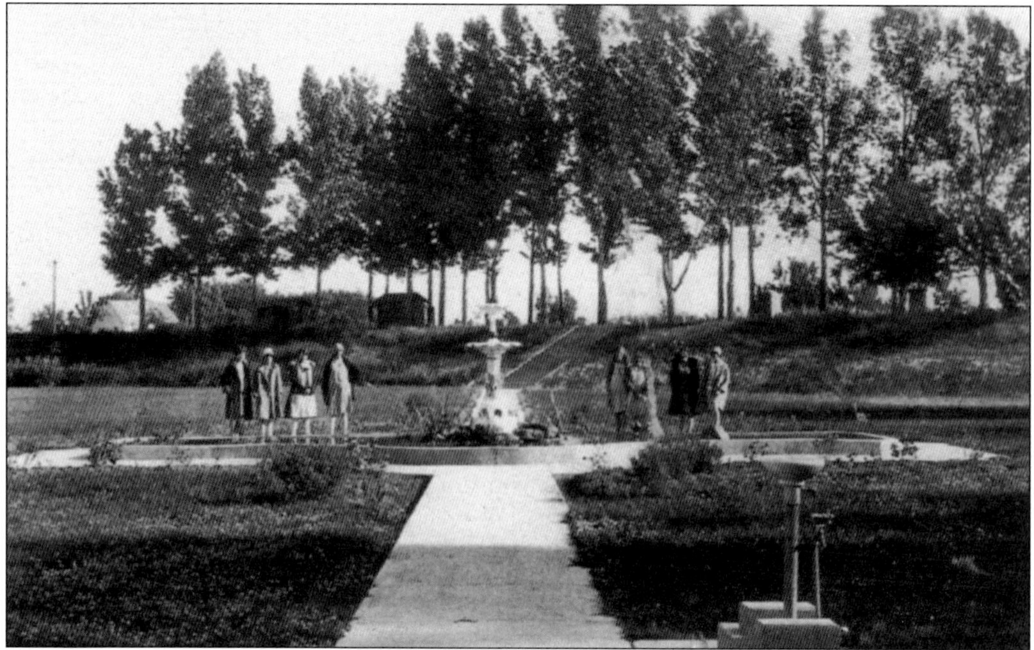

It was 1927, and Lake Ethel was gone, having been drained by E.H. Dewey because of a lawsuit. Here, some girls pose by the fountain where the waters of the lake once lapped against the incline behind them. The area where they stand came to be known as "the bowl."

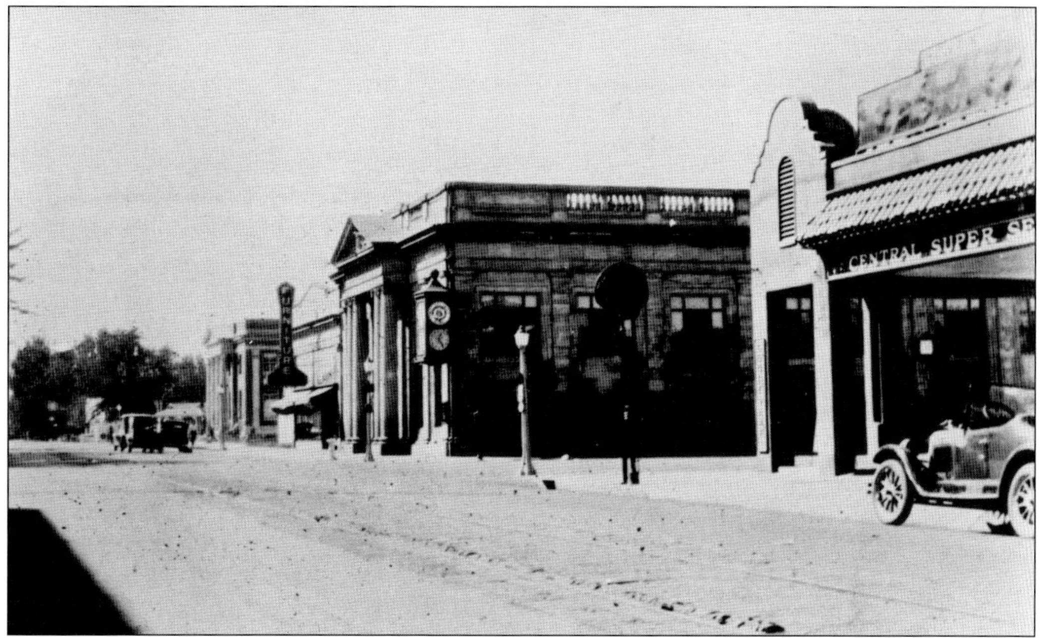

Service stations were starting to spring up all over town in the 1920s. Central Super Service is on the right, and the First Security Bank is across First Street. This was before the subway was completed on Eleventh Avenue. There was a railroad crossing on Eleventh Avenue, though, making it a good place for a service station.

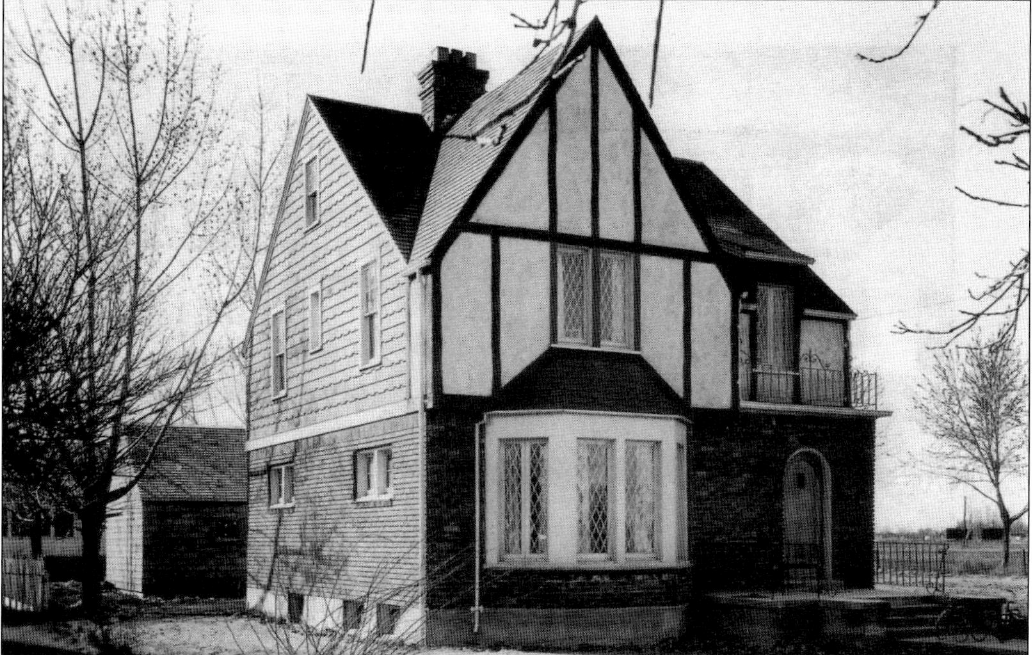

By 1938, the architectural style of homes was changing. Arch Taylor's new home, pictured here on Yale Avenue, was a good example. Taylor owned a service station nearby called Yale Park Service. Yale Avenue contained numerous fine homes at the time, and this house, although added onto and remodeled, is still there today.

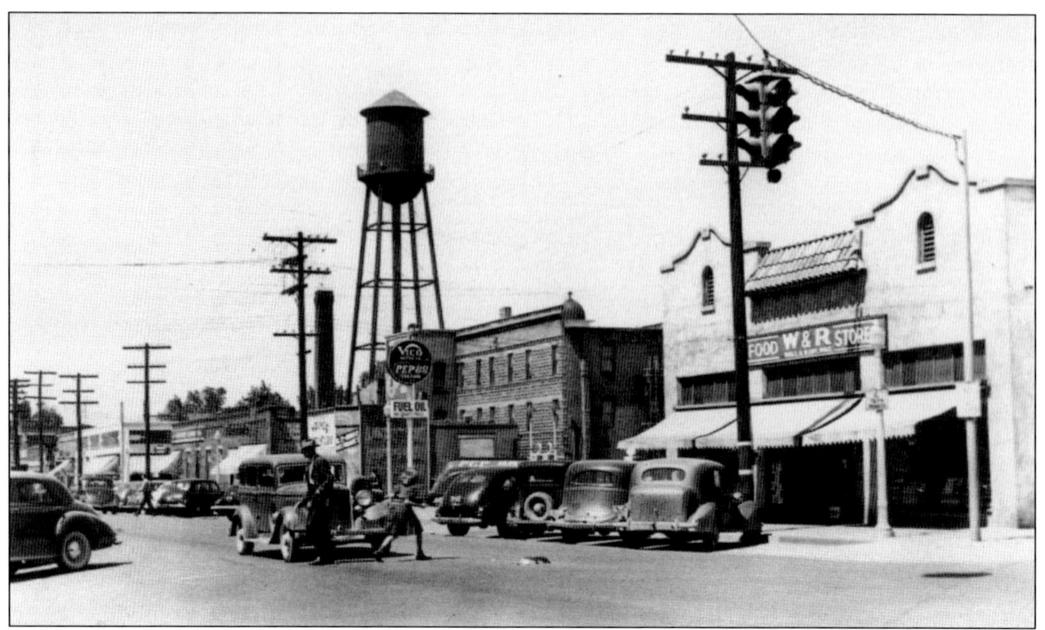

This is the corner of Thirteenth Avenue South and Second Street as it looked in 1940. The addition of traffic lights is noticeable. The W&R Store was Wall & Rawlings. The service station advertises Vico Pep 88 gasoline, a brand that has long since been gobbled up by larger petroleum companies. Montgomery Ward was to the left, out of sight on the corner.

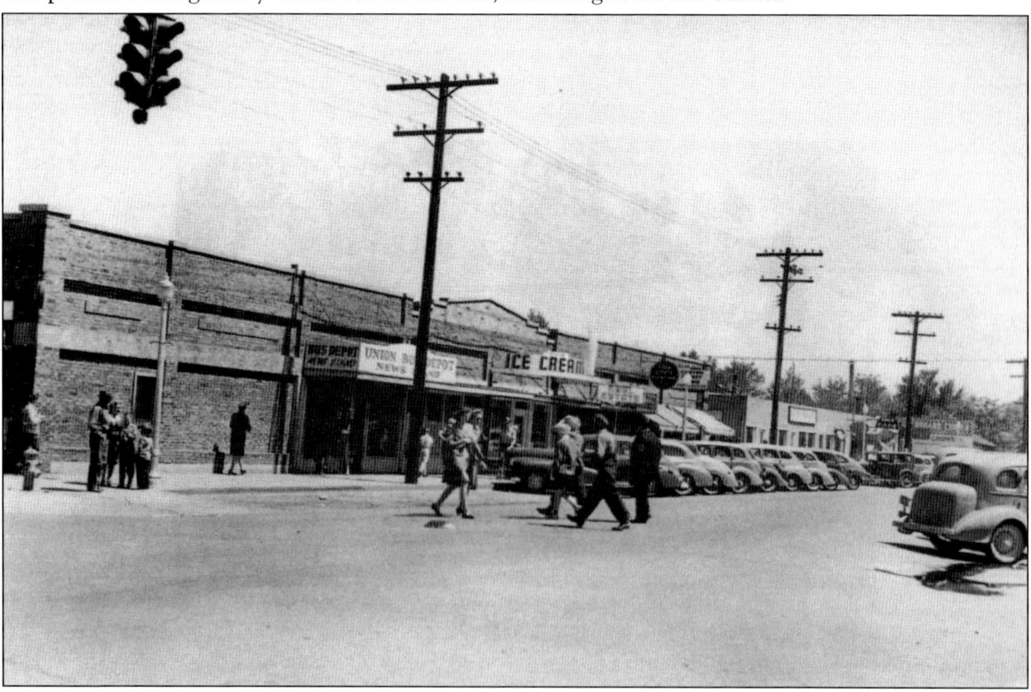

This image looks the other direction down Second Street at Thirteenth Avenue the same year. The Union Bus Station, on the left, serviced local stages and Trailways. Dixie's ice cream shop is just beyond the Second Street entrance to the depot. There was also one on Thirteenth Avenue. There were still many cars and pedestrians. The town was growing.

This 1941 photograph was taken in front of C.C. Anderson's Golden Rule Department Store on Main Street. A crowd was always there on Saturdays and sale days, as well as during the Christmas season. The store across the alley was also C.C. Anderson's—it was the appliance department, where Bendix and Frigidaire were the major brands.

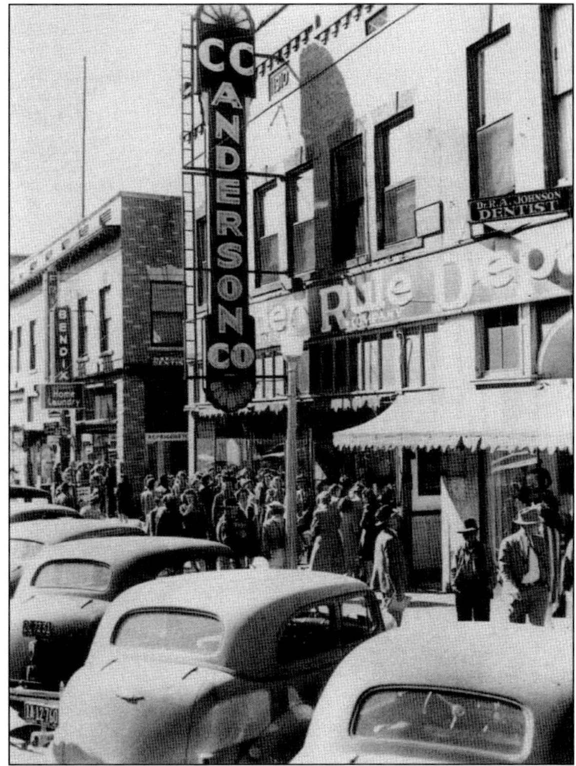

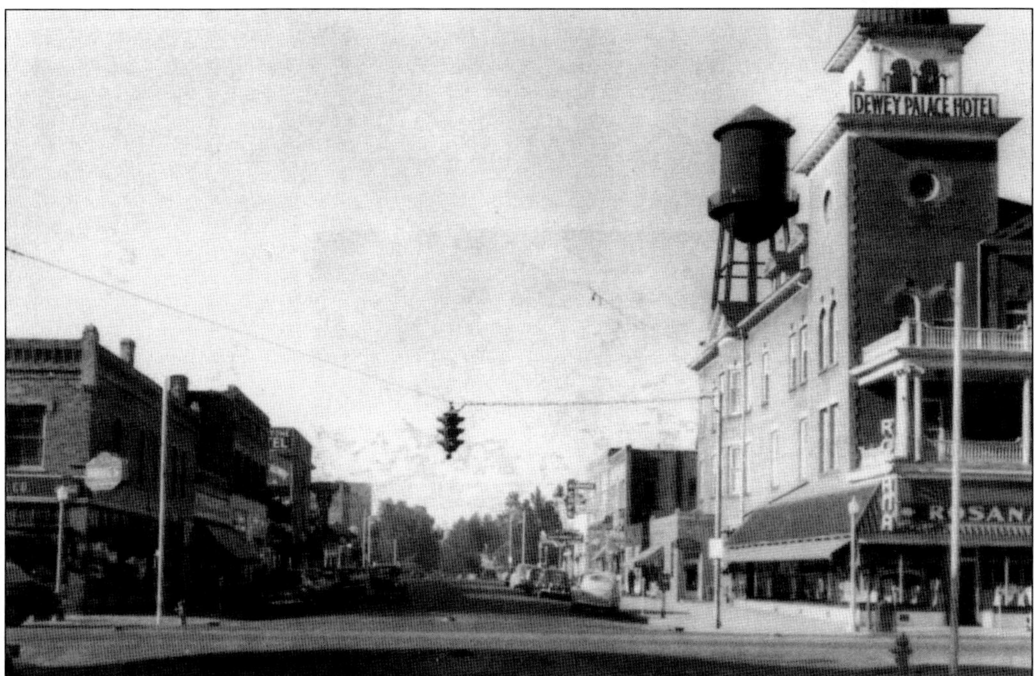

This 1940s view looks down Twelfth Avenue South at First Street. The hanging stoplights previously mentioned have gone the way of the horse and buggy. Vic Stolle Drug was on the left, and the Dewey Palace, which contained Rosanna's Shop, was on the right. Both are now gone.

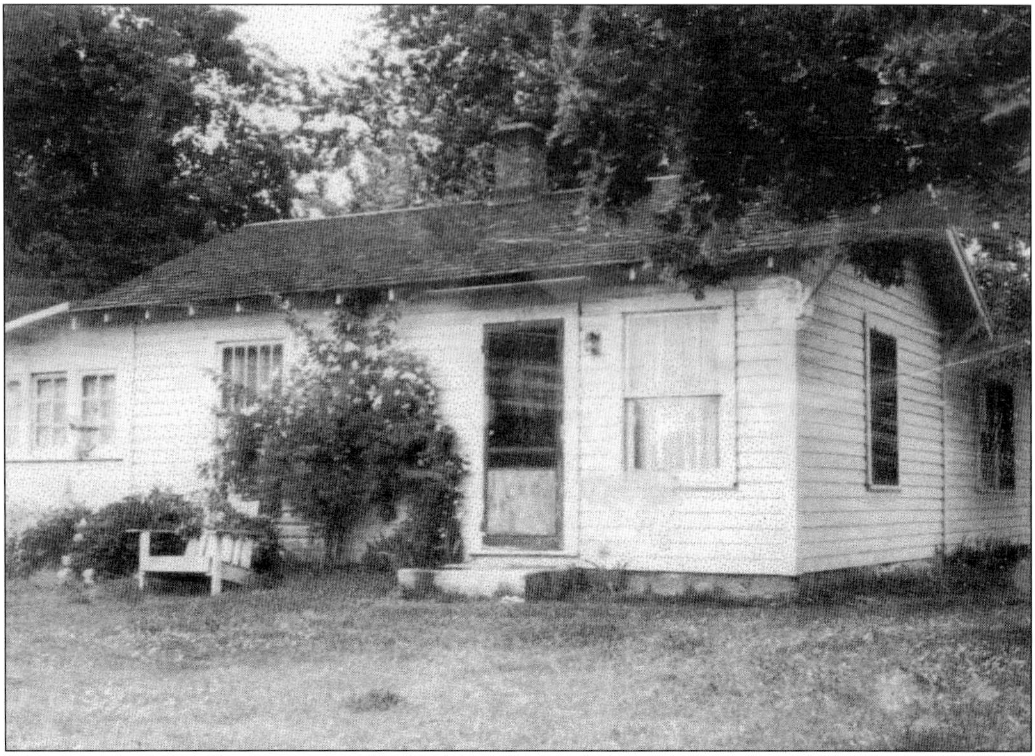

This house was built in the 1930s and is at 134 Elmore Street. It is a two-bedroom, one-bath home used for many years as a rental. It was on the opposite end of the housing spectrum from the Arch Taylor and E.H. Dewey homes. The latter two houses were within a block and a half.

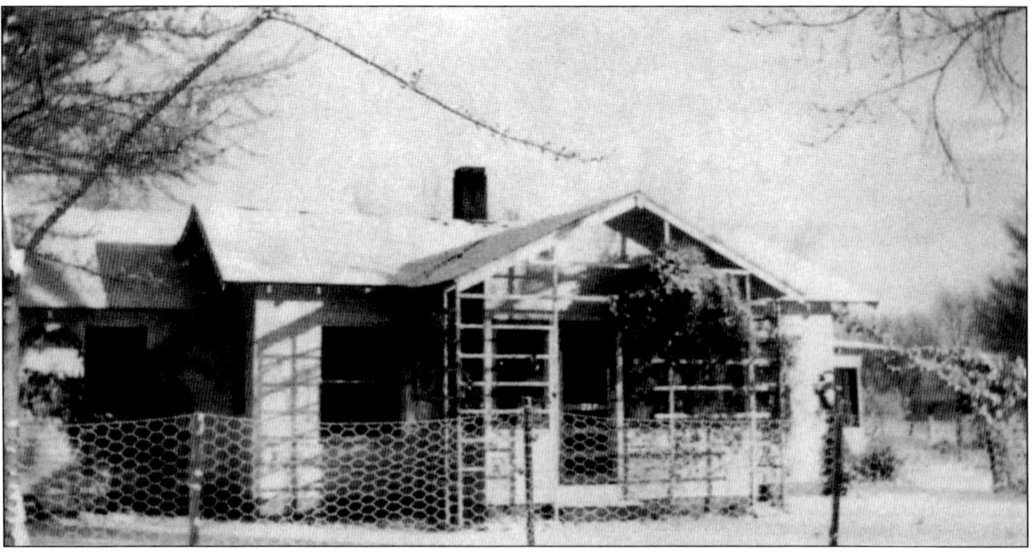

This house was at the Corner of Elmore Street and Canyon Avenue. In 1947, it belonged to Mrs. Carson, who had an extensive flower and vegetable garden on the property. It is known that she had a son, Bob, and a daughter, Frances. The house is still there, although it has been remodeled extensively.

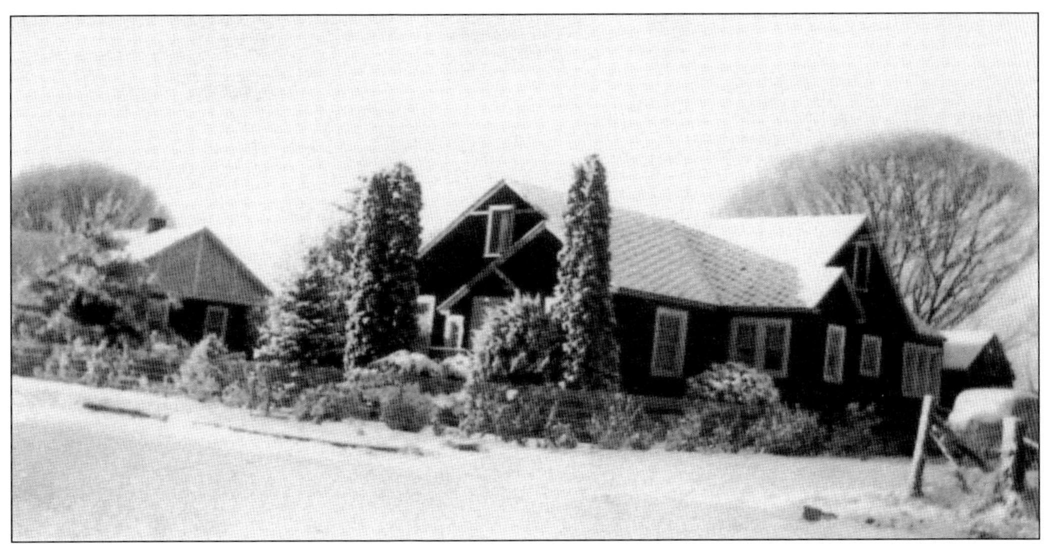

Kitty-corner from Mrs. Carson's home was the Cain house, facing Canyon Avenue. Doyle and Elizabeth Cain bought the house in 1943. It and the house next door were built by Tom Hahn. These three structures represent the contrast between Nampa homes. The Cain house was a five-bedroom, one-bath home in 1943. The Cains' granddaughter Shannon Jones owns the house at present.

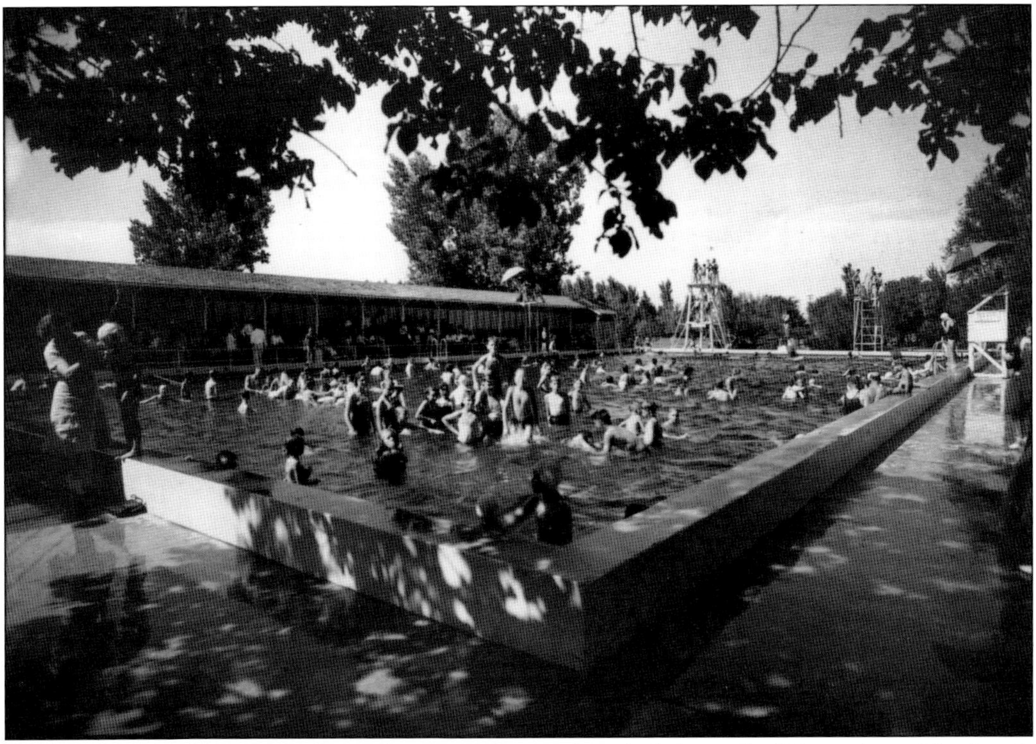

The municipal swimming pool at Lakeview Park was where kids from all of Nampa's neighborhoods spent many happy summer hours. The tall structure on the left was a diving tower with two levels. The one on the right was one of two diving boards. The towers with umbrellas were the lifeguards' seats.

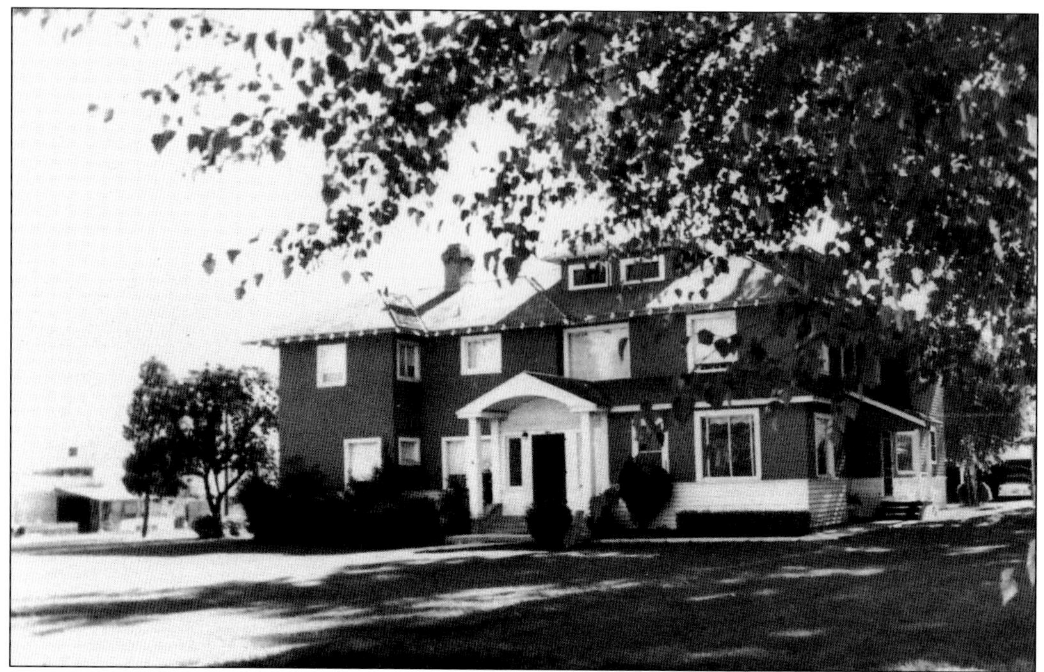

The C.R. Hickey home was one of the outstanding homes of the wealthy in Nampa. This photograph was taken in 1957. Hickey was a banker, insurance man, and investor. His mother had been one of the first to homestead in Nampa. The house is still there and still magnificent.

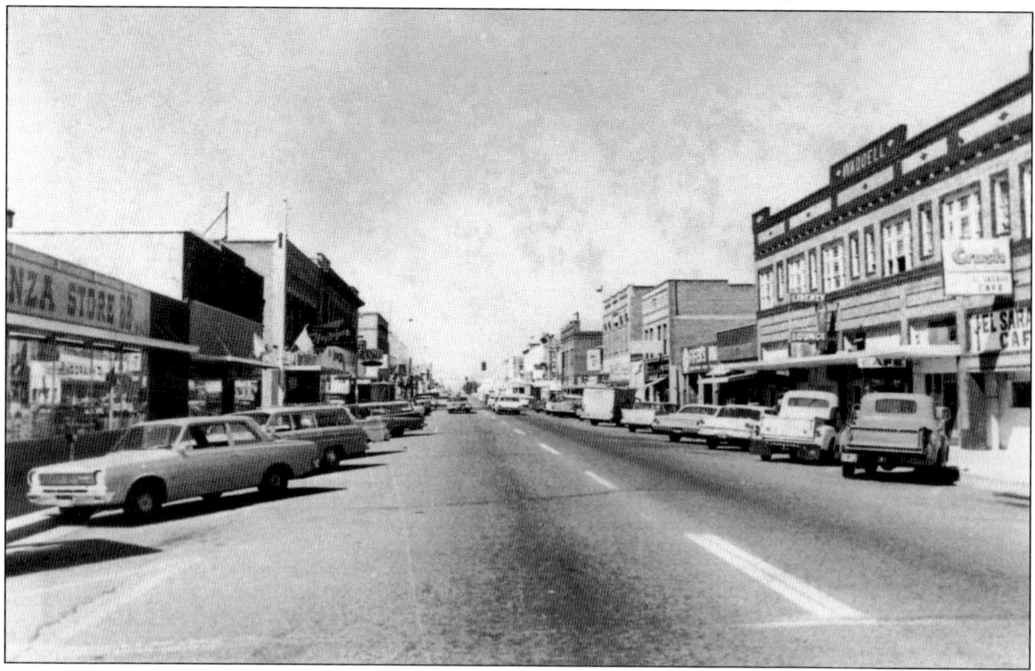

By 1960, the Adelaide Theater was gone. The entrance now contained the El Serape Café. The Waddell Building once housed the Liberty Tavern, Liberty Sweet Shop, and the Liberty Theater, and was later home to the Adelaide. The only Liberty left was the Liberty Lounge. The Bonanza store was located at left on the corner of Fourteenth Avenue and First Street South.

Six

Radio

This chapter is about the media, though it is labeled "Radio" as there are more photographs of radio personalities. Newspaper reporters are basically a faceless bunch, though newspapers were in existence in Nampa since almost the beginning. Radio did not make an impact until the 1920s, and the first station that caused excitement in Nampa was in Boise. KFAU was the Boise High School station. It was on the air only a few hours a day and ran the tried-and-true format of music and local talent. Some of the performers heard over the valley's crystal sets and radios were Nampa people. It is hard to imagine today the impact radio had in the 1920s and 1930s. It was free, it was in one's home, and the equipment could be built by anyone. Excitement was at a fever pitch when it was announced that Nampa was getting its own station in 1930.

The station had the call letters KFXD and went on the air in Nampa on May 4, 1930. The location was on the corner of Twelfth Avenue and Eleventh Street South. Frank Hurt built a small stucco building that housed the offices, studio, and transmitter. Two aluminum towers brought from Jerome were erected.

In 1935, Hurt hired a young salesman, Doyle Cain. He was to become the face and voice of the station over the next 27 years. Doyle started the station's play-by-play sports broadcasts, which included Nampa High School teams, Northwest Nazarene basketball, College of Idaho football, and periodic games played by small schools around the valley.

In 1962, Cain and Howard Nafziger bought a local religious station, KWLW, and changed the call letters to KAIN. They still cornered the sports broadcast market and were known as the "Sports Voice of Treasure Valley." The station dominated the sports scene with play-by-play and sports programs throughout the day.

Many local radio personalities are featured in this chapter, and their stories will hopefully bring back memories.

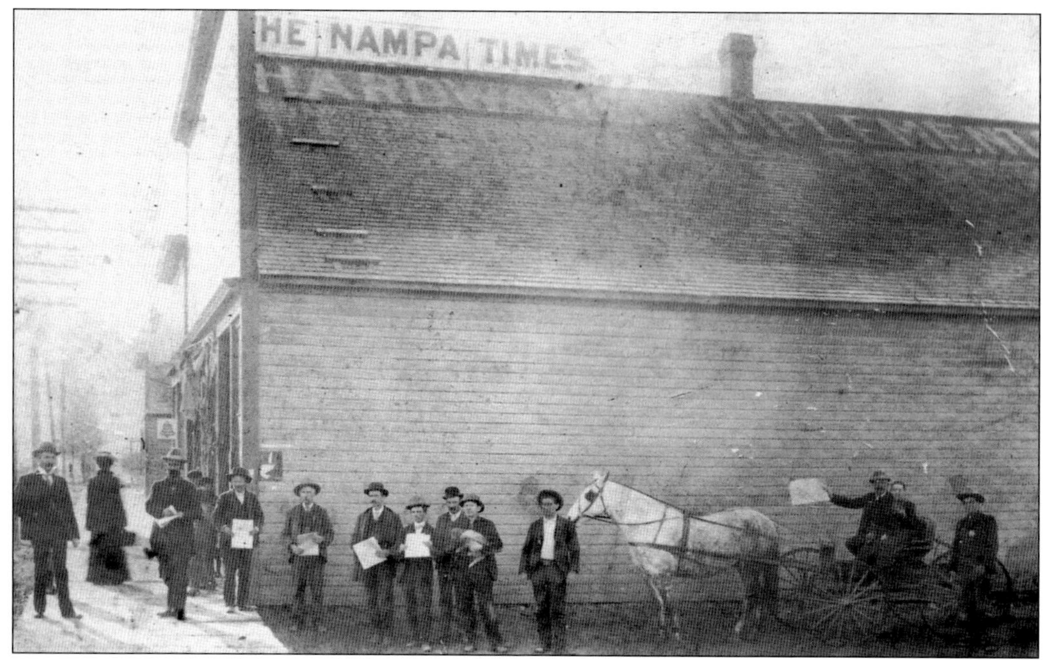

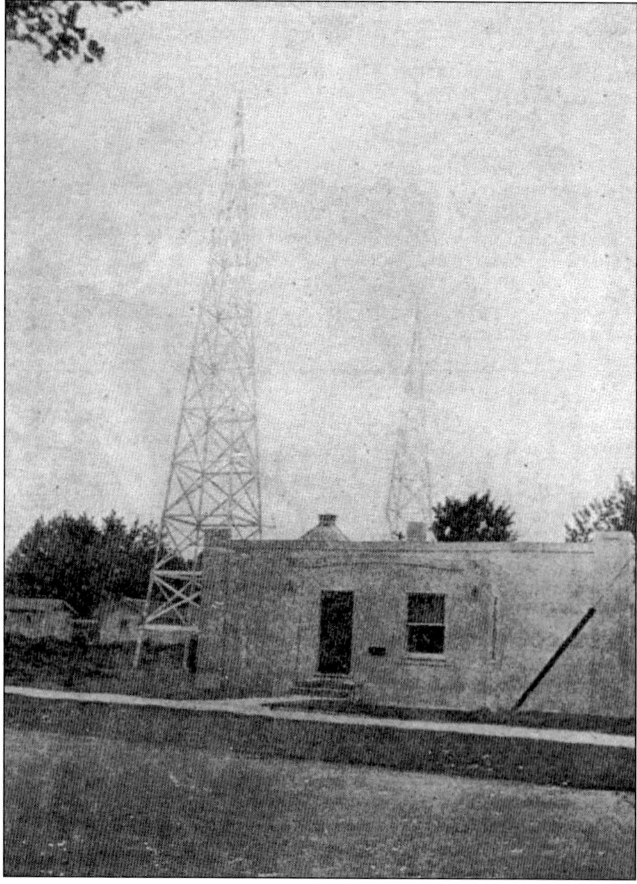

The *Nampa Times* stopped publication soon after this 1902 photograph was taken. The slack was picked up almost immediately by the *Idaho Leader.* The *Leader* stayed in business until the late 1930s, undergoing name changes to *Nampa Leader* and then *Nampa Leader Herald.* In the late 1930s, it was merged with the *Idaho Free Press.*

The original KFXD building was constructed by Frank Hurt in 1930. Stucco with two towers, it served the station's needs until 1934, when it was expanded and remodeled. The aluminum towers were damaged in a violent windstorm and replaced with a single 230-foot steel tower in 1935.

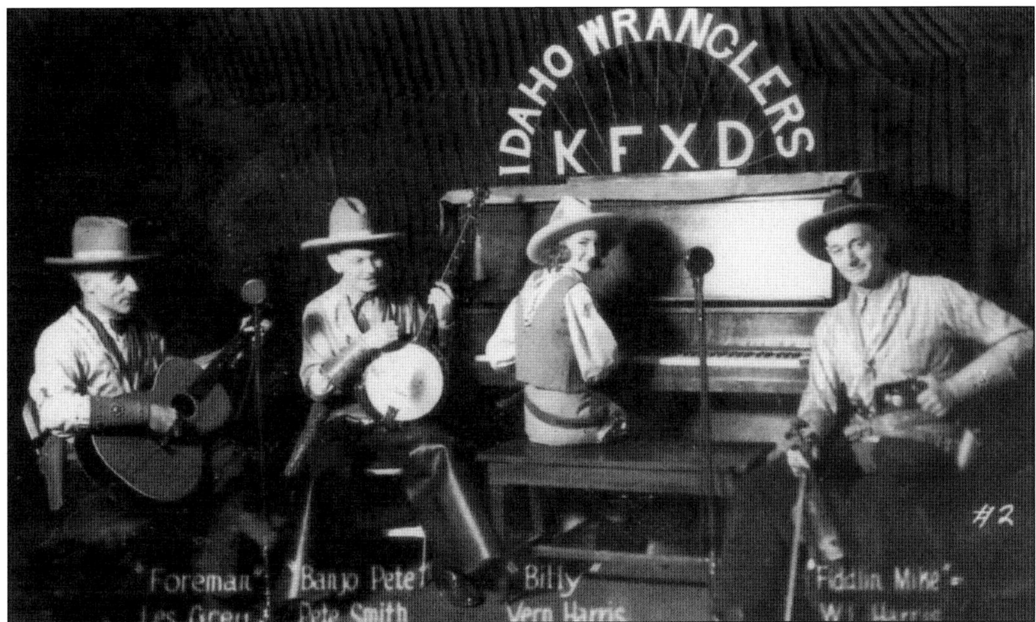

The Idaho Wranglers were a popular dance band in the 1920s and 1930s. They played at KFXD's grand opening in May 1930. They were so well received that they became a staple of the station's programming, sending their music out over the airwaves from the studio in the building. This photograph appeared in a booklet put out by the station in 1937.

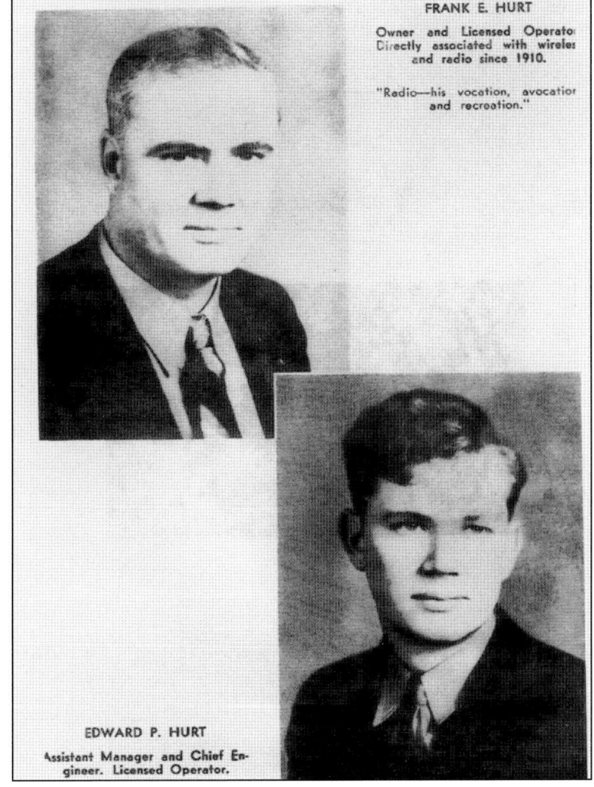
FRANK E. HURT

Owner and Licensed Operato
Directly associated with wireles
and radio since 1910.

"Radio—his vocation, avocatior
and recreation."

EDWARD P. HURT

Assistant Manager and Chief Engineer. Licensed Operator.

Frank and Ed Hurt were the owners of KFXD. This picture is from a rare booklet put out by the station in 1937. The publication showed that the station had expanded, with studios in Boise and Caldwell and private telephone lines connecting the three. They also had private phone lines to the sheriffs' offices in Canyon and Ada Counties.

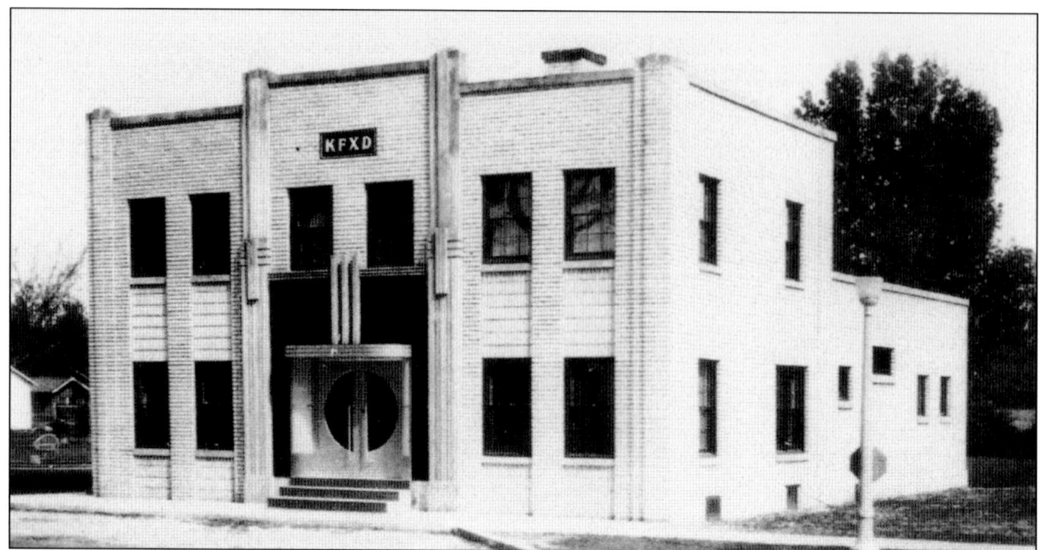

In 1937, this 50-by-70-foot, two-story, modern Art Deco–style building was completed. It had a soundproof studio, control room, offices, and a beautiful entry. The receptionist had an office to the right of the front doors. Frank Hurt and his wife lived in a luxury apartment upstairs.

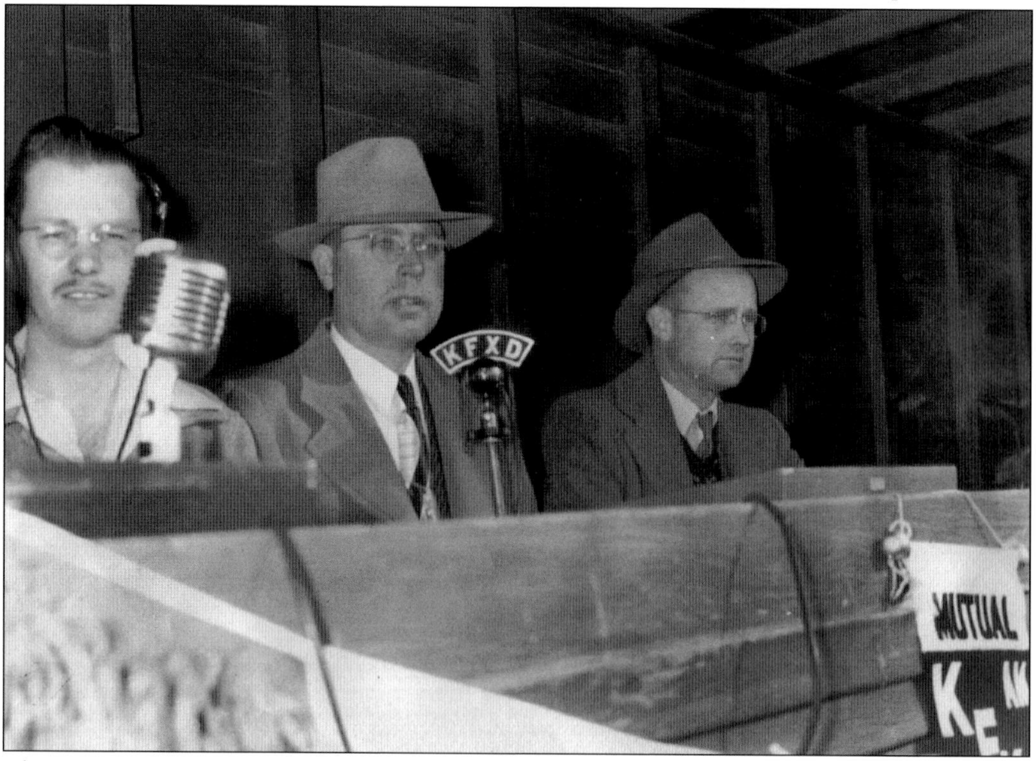

The KFXD sports crew is pictured at Hayman Field in Caldwell on the College of Idaho campus in 1947. From left to right are Jim Davidson, Doyle Cain, and Les Grass. Doyle did the play-by-play of the College of Idaho contest, while Jim read commercials during time-outs and filled in at halftime with observations of the happenings. Les was a spotter who pointed to the player making a tackle, among other things.

Floyd Bryant was the emcee of the popular "Early Bird" program heard from 6:00 a.m. through drive time. He also read the news and weather reports during his show. The photograph is from a 1949 booklet put out by the station. Bryant had been in radio for 10 years at the time.

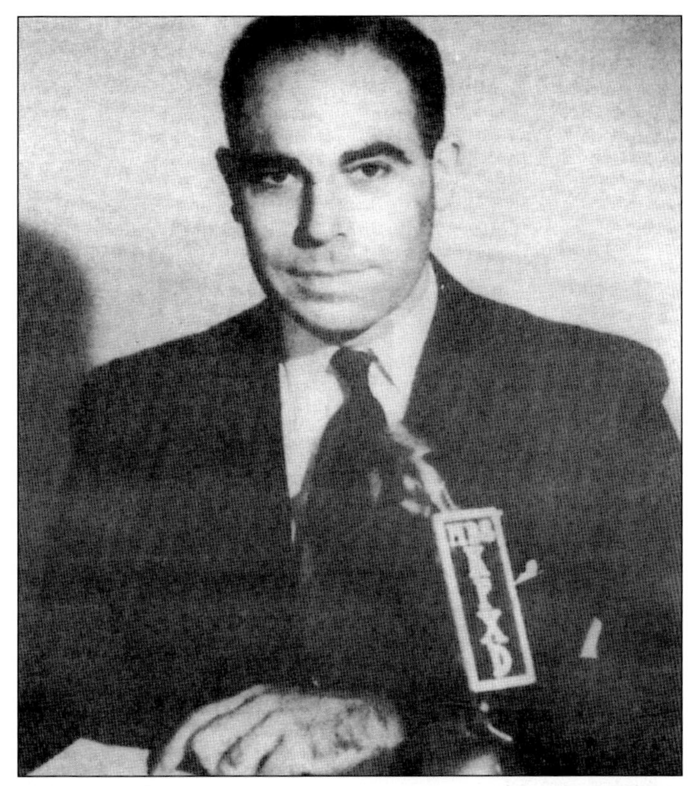

This studio photograph was taken in 1947 and shows, from left to right, Shirl Black, Doyle Cain, Jim Davidson, and Ralph Paulson. Pictures of this type were used for publicity purposes and were displayed in sponsors' windows. Many photographs were taken of the station's personnel for the 1949 booklet, including the receptionists, bookkeeper, and other off-air support.

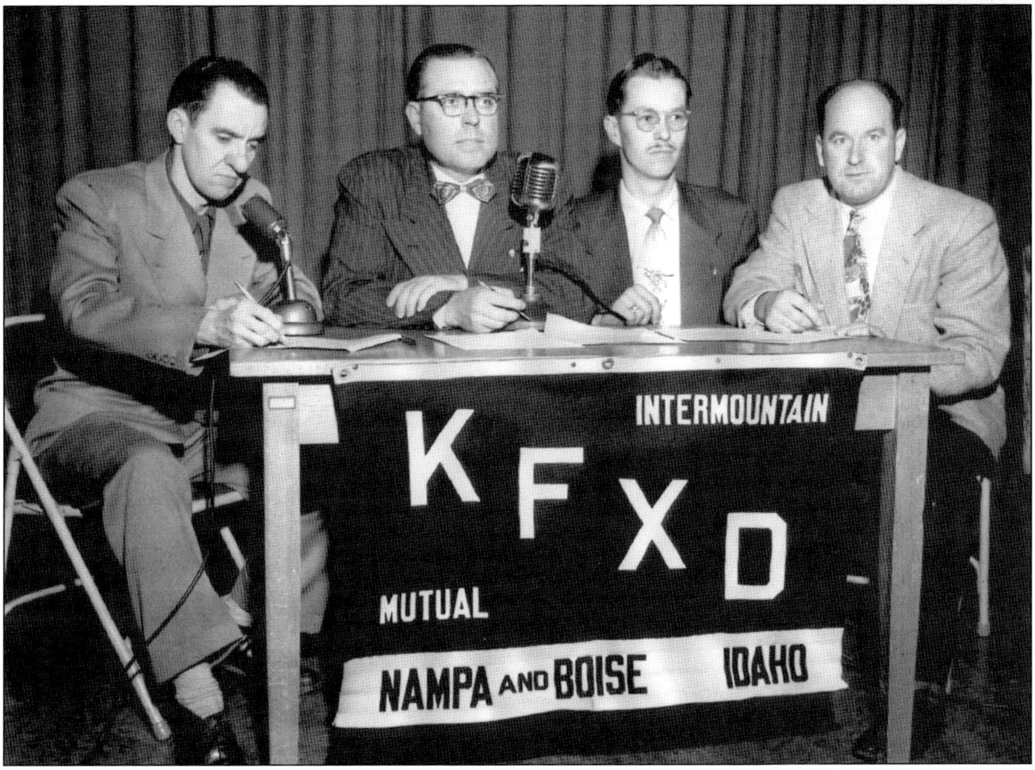

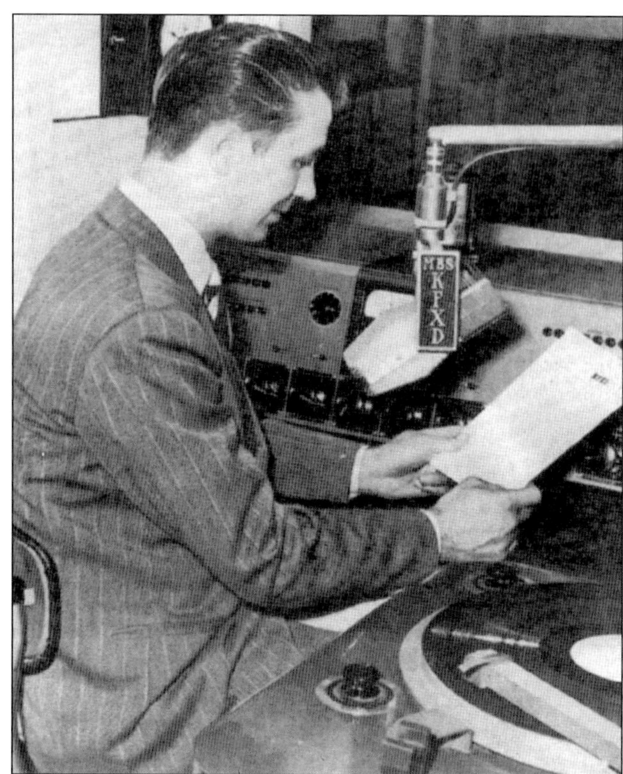

Ken Bort was one of the stars of the station. He was an entertainer, playing the piano at many functions even though he could not read a note of music. He was the announcer for the sponsors on game broadcasts and the genial foreman of the very popular "Snake River Stampede" program. He later went to work for KGEM.

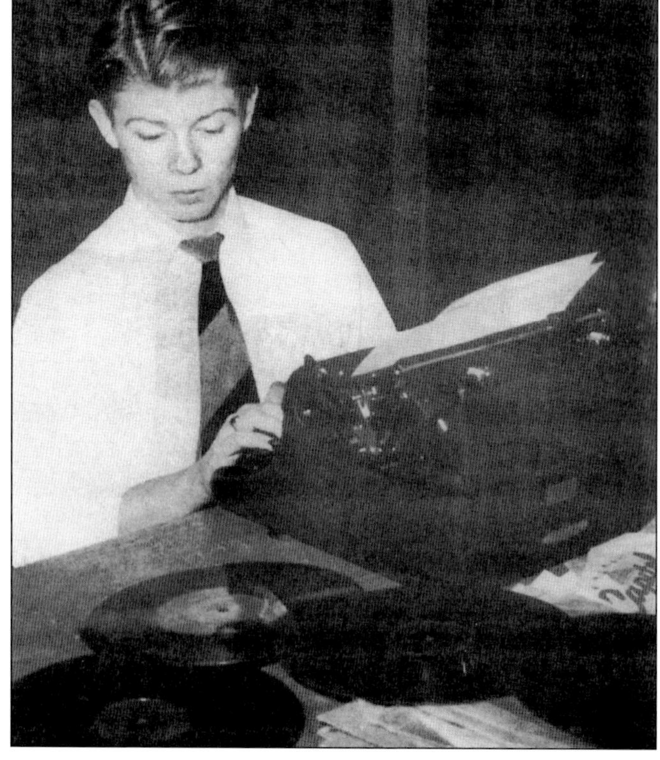

Herb Everritt was an advertising copywriter and on-air announcer. He was also the master of ceremonies and the late-night disk jockey on the "580 Record Revue" (580 was the station's location on the dial). The program was aimed at the young crowd and featured Top 10 records.

In 1949, Doyle Cain was on the air six days a week. He not only did sports broadcasts and daily sports programs, but was also the sales manager, with an enviable record of sales achievement. His popularity with the listeners and his rapid-fire delivery are still talked about by old-timers today.

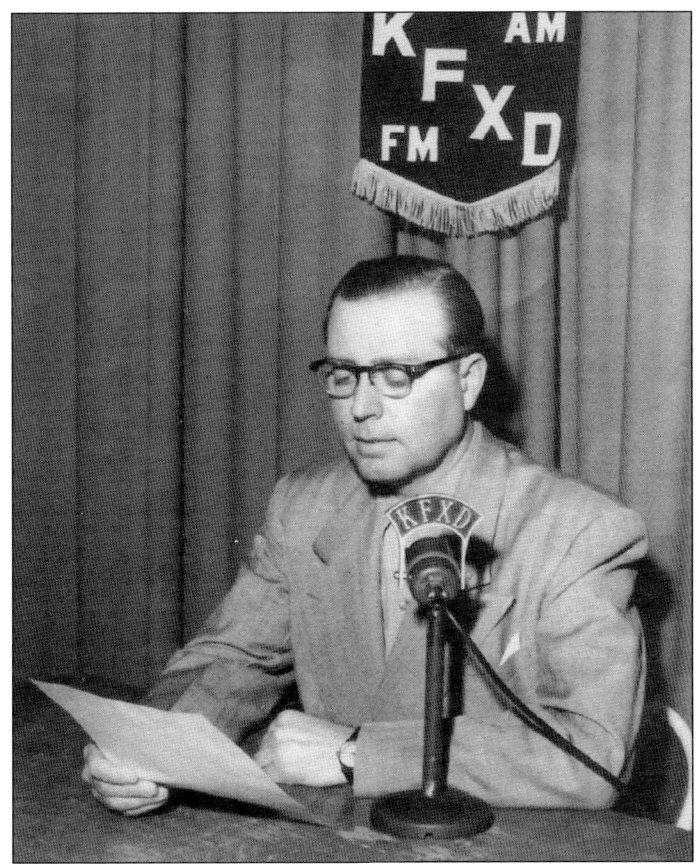

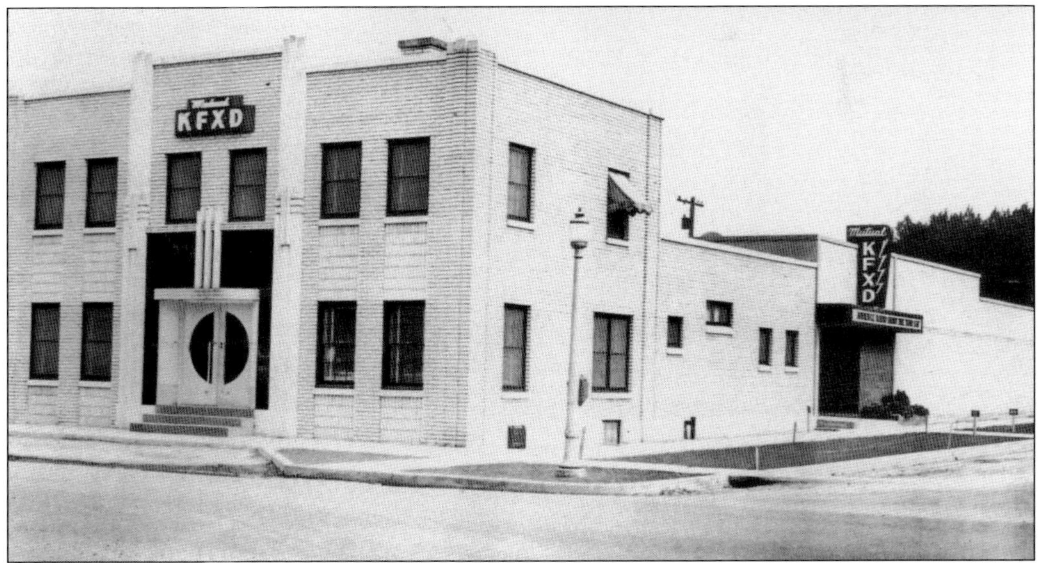

The station was expanded in the 1950s, with an auditorium added on the back of the original structure. It was used for live broadcasts, movies, and local entertainment, and was let out to local clubs, churches, and organizations. It was a full-sized movie theater, with a stage and lighting for live performances.

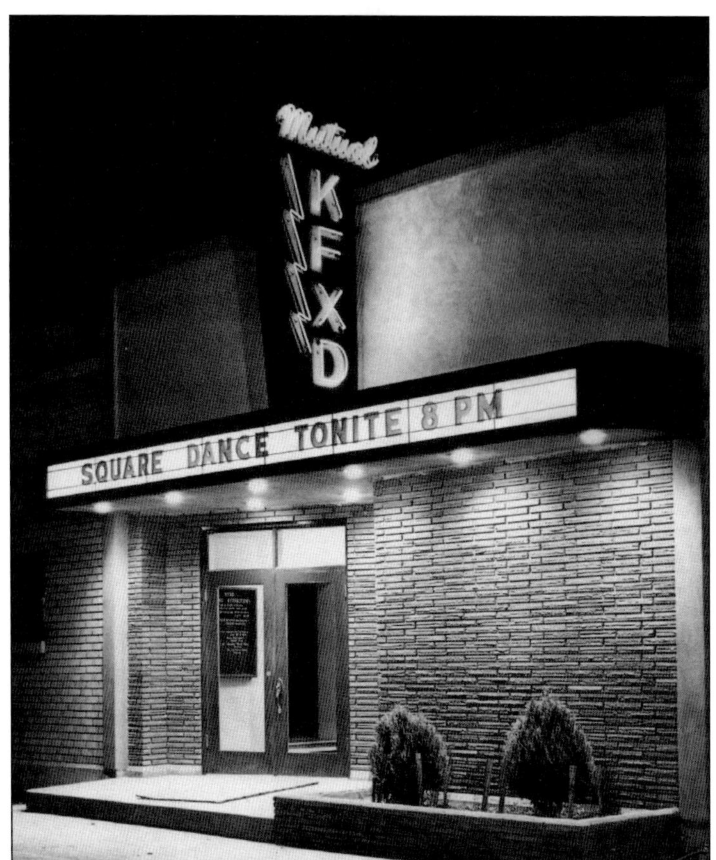

This image shows the inviting front entrance of the KFXD theater at night. The door seen through the glass entrance led into the station's offices. The building is still in existence today, but not as a theater. It was remodeled into offices. It was the dream of Frank Hurt to have a theater in conjunction with the radio station.

This 1954 interior view of the theater shows Earl McKeever, Nampa High School band director, leading his group as it is being broadcast over KFXD. The xylophone player in front is Barbara Tiegs. The upholstered seats all had arms and were very comfortable.

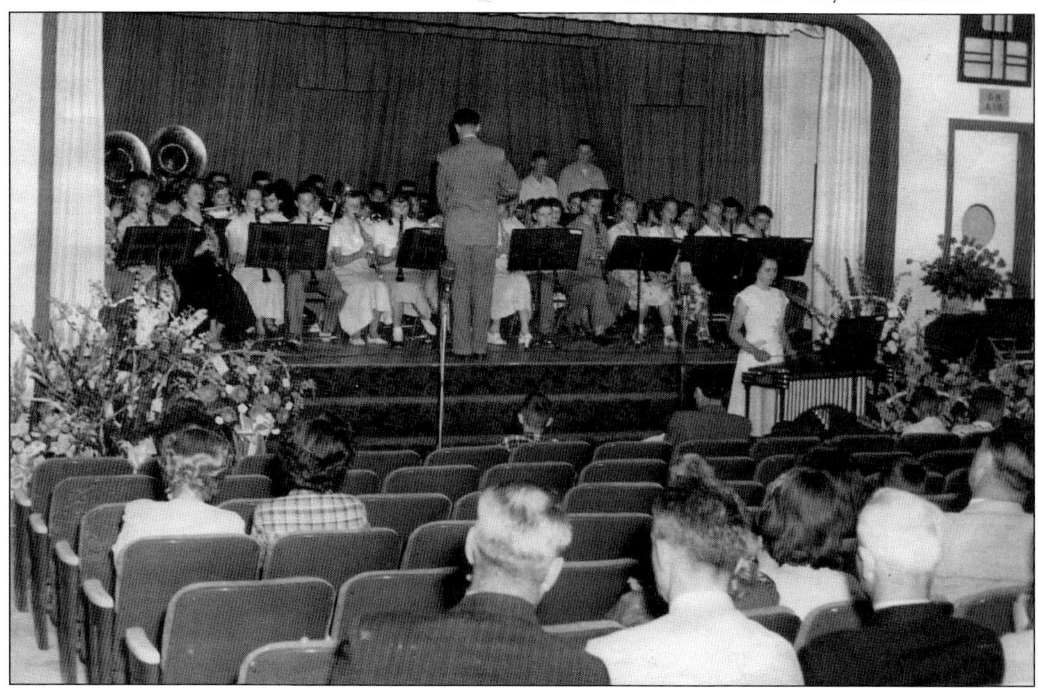

In 1950, a new transmitter building was opened on Amity Road near the Kuna-Meridian Highway. The location in Nampa was getting crowded as new and better equipment was purchased. The station had been approved for 5,000 watts of power and needed three towers to direct its signal away from stations in Fresno, California, and Calgary, Canada, that were on the same frequency.

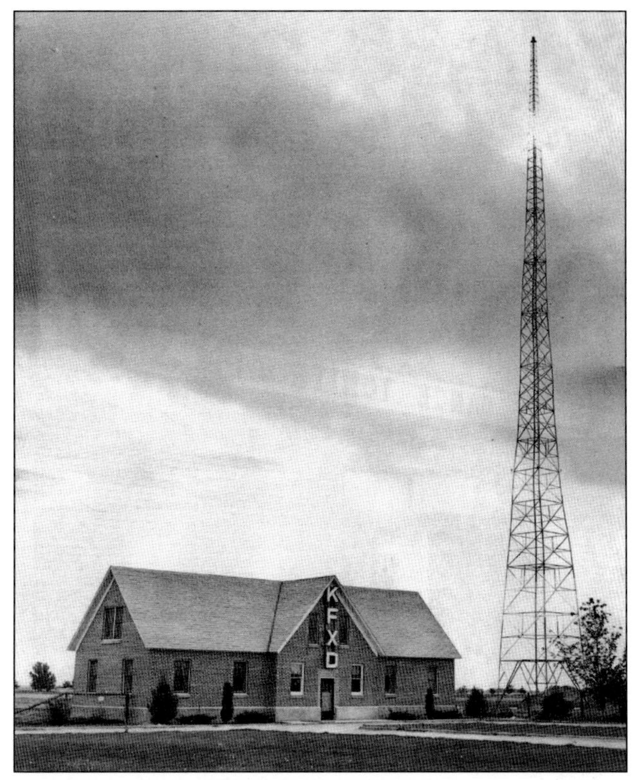

This is the KFXD sports crew on a baseball broadcast from Rodeo Park in Nampa. From left to right are Shirl Black, Doyle Cain, Rusty Johnson, and Ken Bort. Nampa High School, American Legion, and Nampa Clippers games were broadcast to radios all over the valley from the field. The booth had been built especially for this purpose.

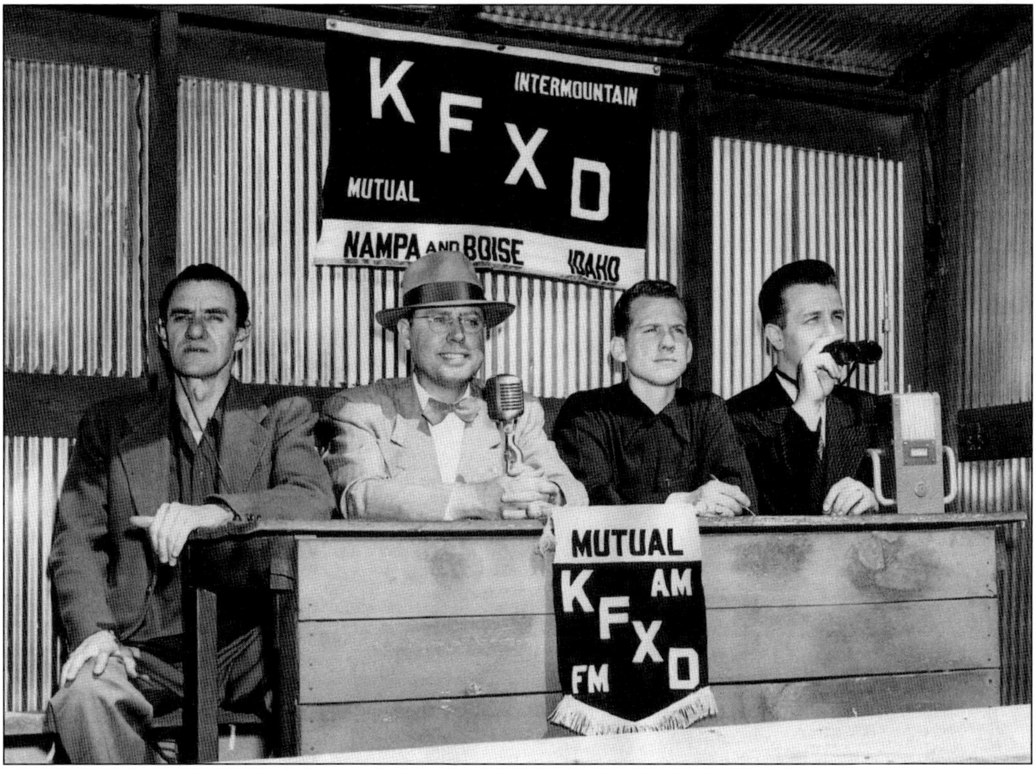

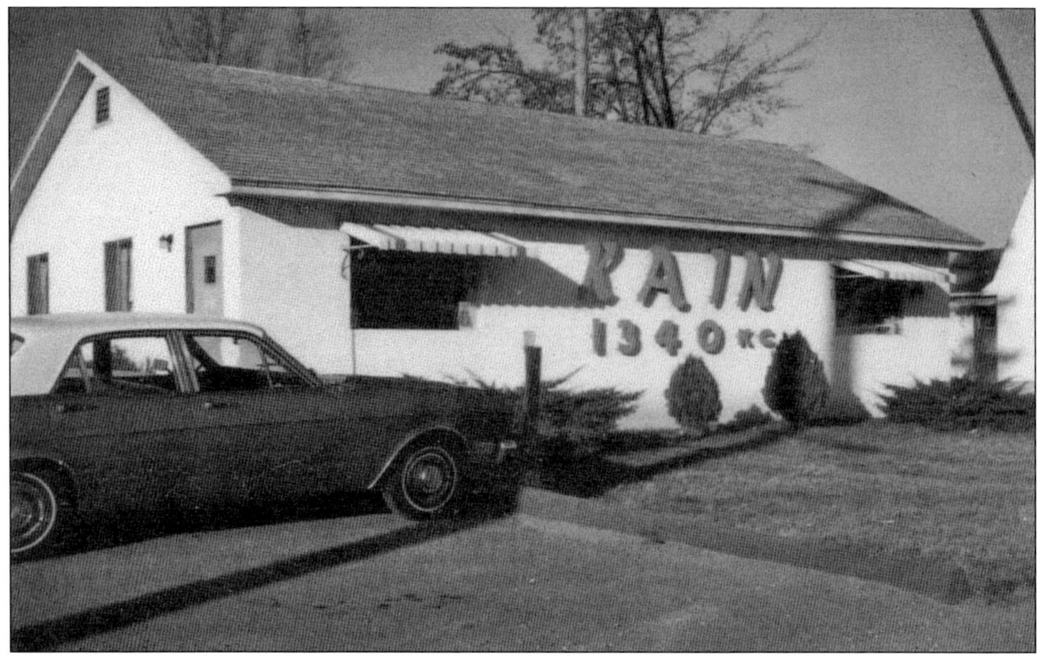

In 1962, Howard Nafziger and Doyle Cain partnered to open KAIN radio on Third Street South in Nampa. They had bought out KWLW and changed the format and call letters. The format was middle-of-the-road music, news, weather, and an abundance of sports, with programs and play-by-play.

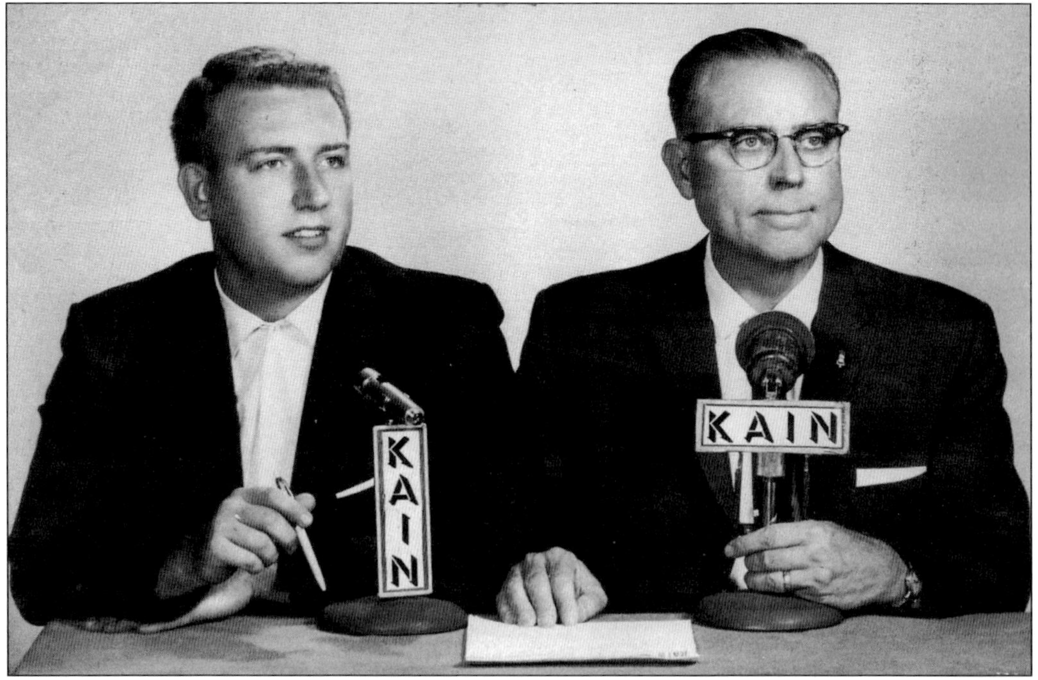

The first sports play-by-play team on KAIN was Doyle Cain and his son Larry. Larry had broadcast his first game in 1954 over KFXD, giving a verbal description of the College of Idaho–Seattle Ramblers game. Hal Denson later became a member of the team.

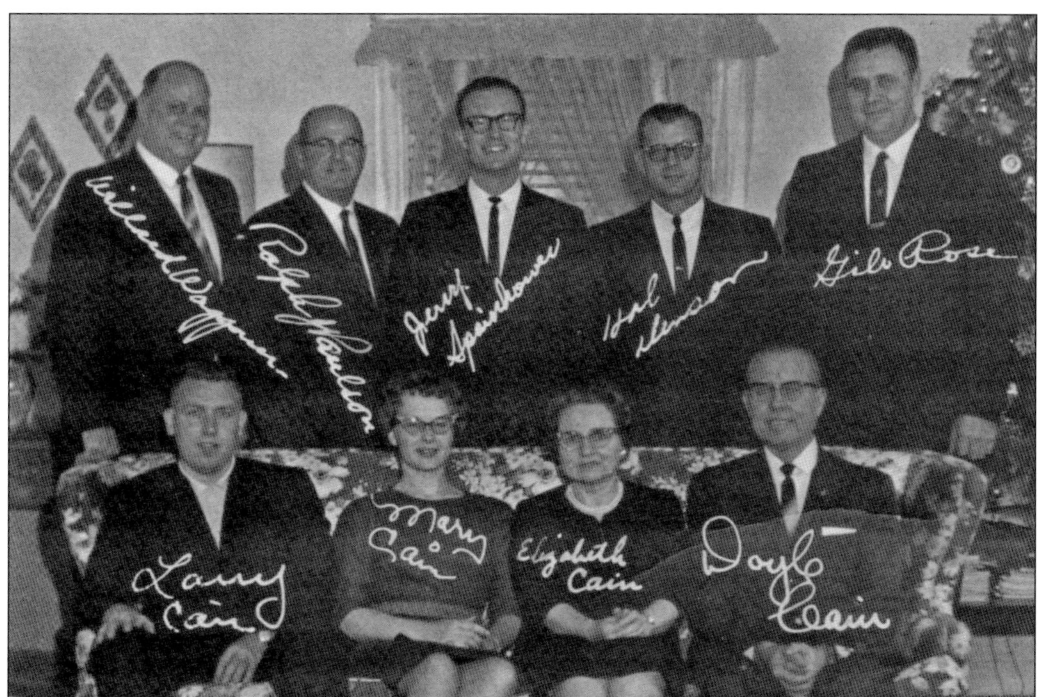

The KAIN radio staff included their signatures on this 1963 photograph. From left to right are (first row) Larry Cain, sports and sales; Mary Cain, receptionist; Elizabeth Cain, accounts receivable and payable; and Doyle Cain, president; (second row); Willard Waggoner, announcer; Ralph Paulson, program director; Jerry Spainhower, announcer; Hal Denson, sports and sales; and Gilbert Rose, chief engineer.

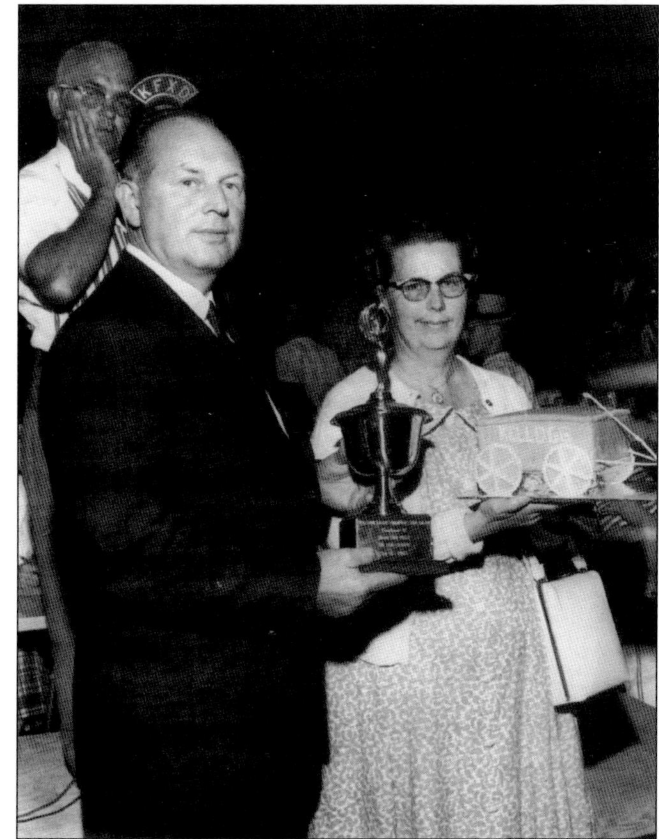

Adam Kalb, publisher of the *Idaho Free Press*, presents an award for the best cake in the Treasure Valley. Note the KFXD microphone behind him. Kalb was very civic-minded and participated in these kinds of ceremonies. The newspaper and the radio station got along well and pooled their efforts in supporting the community.

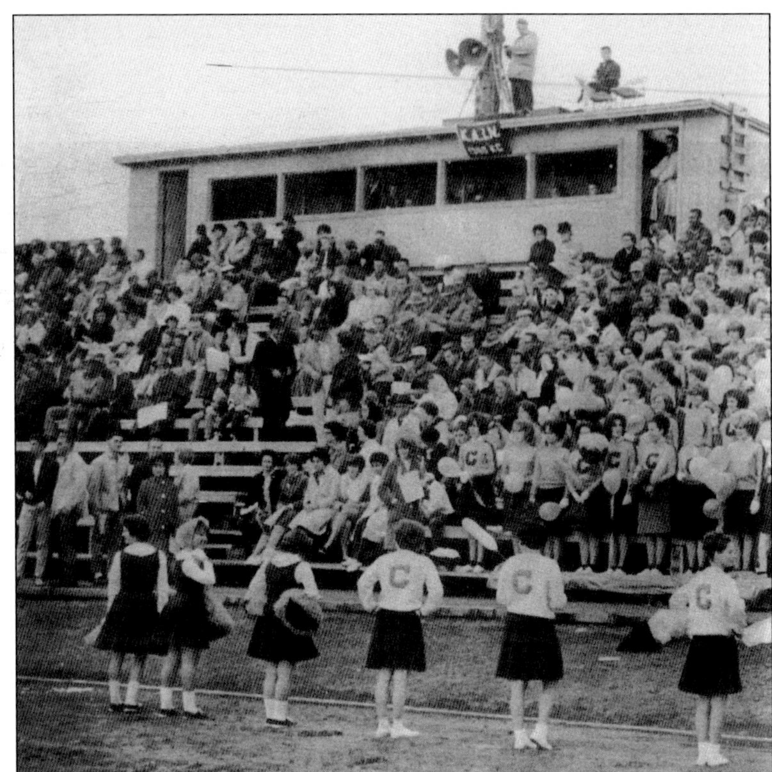

This is the 1960s Nampa-Caldwell football game at Bulldog Bowl in Nampa. The Caldwell section and cheerleaders are pictured. KAIN was doing the play-by-play of the game, and the station's banner can be seen hanging from the booth. The presence of a KAIN sports crew at a Nampa High School game was as familiar as the bleachers.

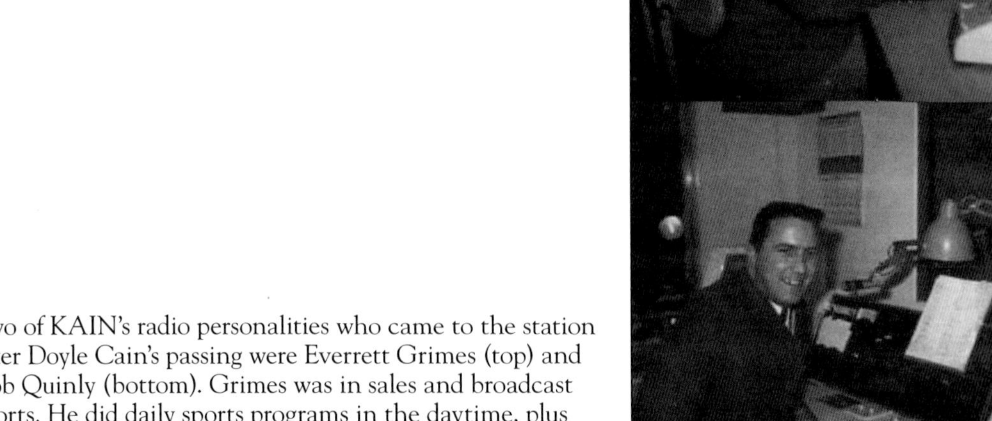

Two of KAIN's radio personalities who came to the station after Doyle Cain's passing were Everrett Grimes (top) and Bob Quinly (bottom). Grimes was in sales and broadcast sports. He did daily sports programs in the daytime, plus play-by-play. Quinly was a disc jockey in the evenings.

Seven

EVENTS

An event may refer to anything and everything different that happened in Nampa. This also includes annual events, but not the day-to-day, mundane type of happenings. Such annual events include the Miss Nampa contest, the Harvest Festival that grew into the Snake River Stampede, and the old Lettuce Bowl. Charlotte Berg's visit to Nampa with the Chautauqua was a huge event. Berg had graduated from Nampa High School and gone on to nationwide singing fame.

There were many promotions by businessmen during the years, but the event that lasted the longest was Pathfinder Week in 1946. *Pathfinder* was a weekly magazine, and its staff went in search of a typical small town to show the impact that the 16,430 towns with a population of under 25,000 had on the nation's economy. The winner would be dubbed "the Capital of Main Street America." They picked Nampa, which had a population of 13,800 at the time. Every big promotion had to have a queen, so one was chosen: Bonnie Lou Rodwell. People came by car, bus, train, and even airplane to the weeklong celebration. There were dances, barbecues, concerts, fashion shows, and a Hollywood premiere of *The Well Groomed Bride*, starring Ray Milland and Olivia de Havilland. The Mutual Broadcasting Network performed its show *The Better Half* from Central Auditorium's stage for the week. Merchants tripled their normal business for the week, so everyone was happy.

Not all events were happy ones. There were disasters, such as the great fire of 1909, the Drake Drug fire in the 1930s, the explosion of the Forbidden Palace in the 1940s, and numerous fires over the ensuing years.

The photographs in this chapter illustrate the big times in Nampa over the years and will hopefully bring back memories for the old folks and educate the young on their hometown.

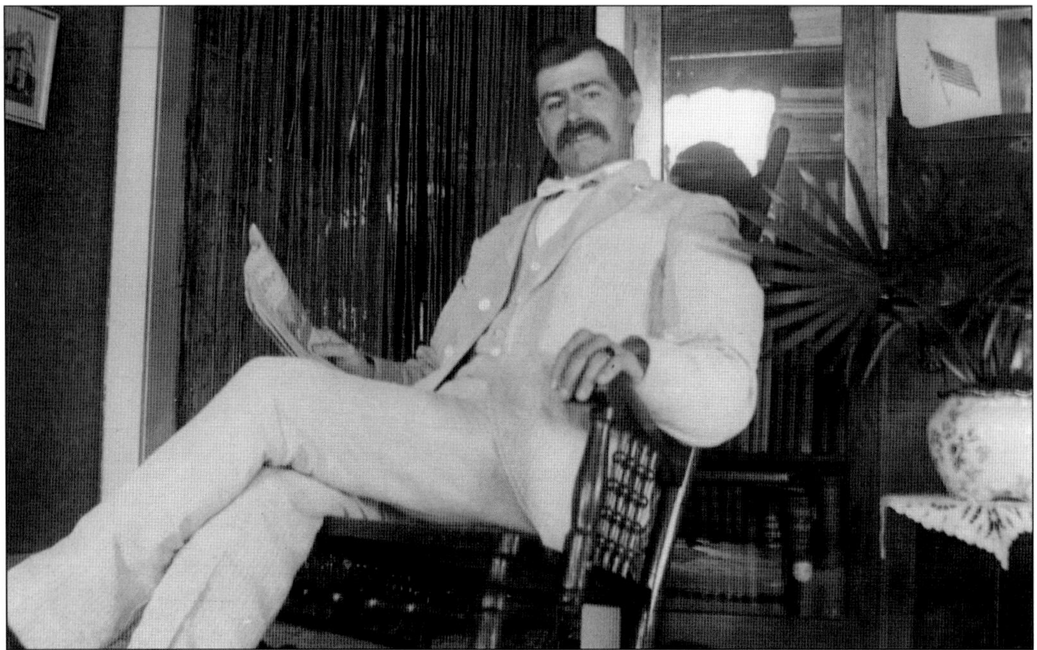

Fred Mock, pictured here in 1896, wrote two novels—*The Romance of the Sawtooth* and *Blue Eye*—under the name Ogal Alla. The *New York Times* said *Blue Eye* was the best book ever written by an Indian woman. Mock's lectures on travel were always an event because of his speaking ability and fantastic sense of humor.

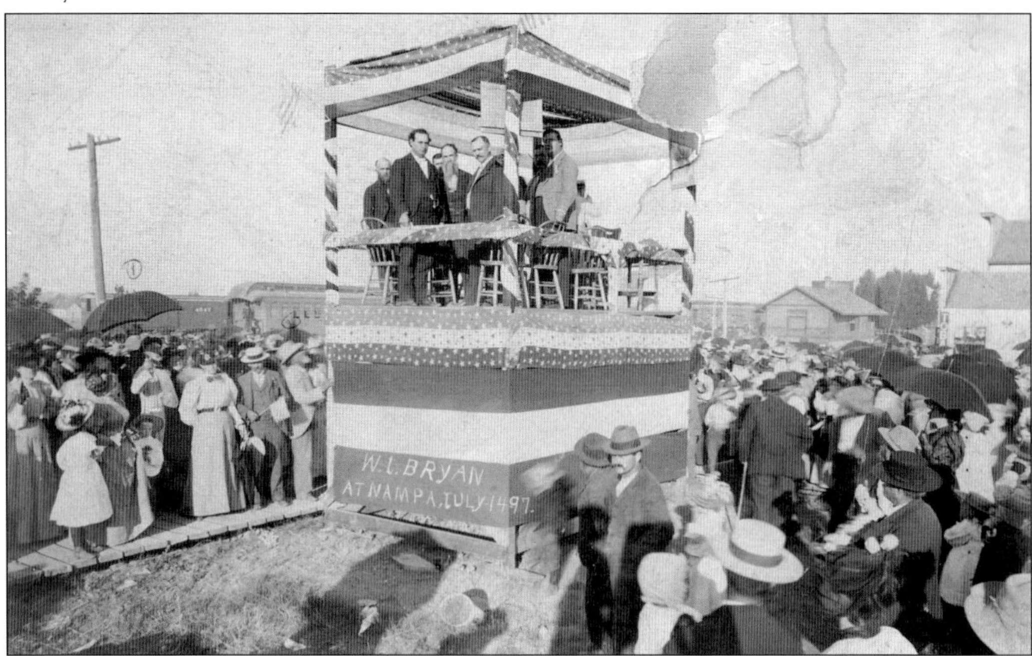

William Jennings Bryan looks down at the crowd in 1897 before his speech promoting silver and degrading gold. The Democratic candidate for president of the United States in 1896, 1900, and 1908 is probably best known as the prosecutor in the 1920s Scopes Trial in Tennessee, where he faced Clarence Darrow.

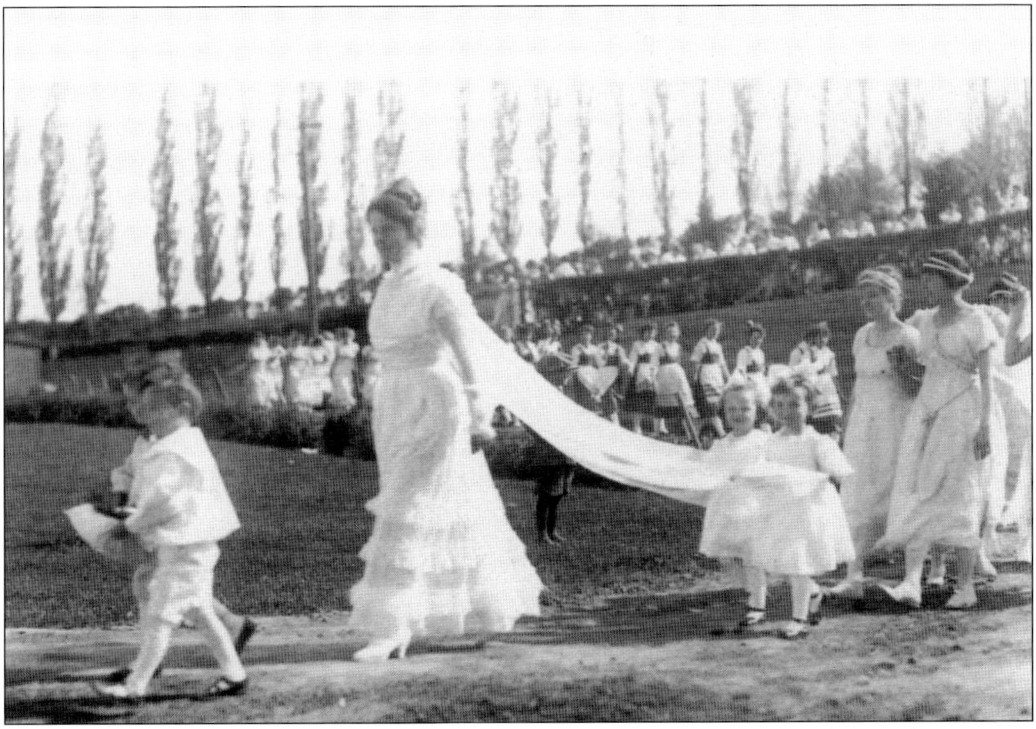

The May Day queen and her retinue are pictured in 1907. May Day was celebrated in Nampa annually until the 1950s. The schools were brought into the celebration, and the participants numbered in the hundreds some years. This photograph reveals a certain insight into the dress and pomp associated with the event.

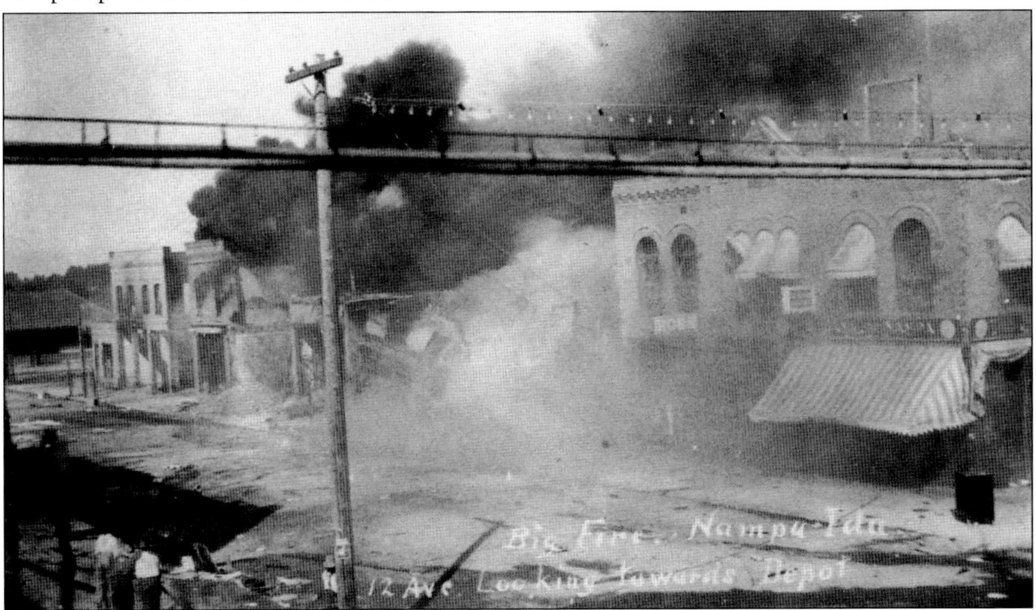

The great fire of 1909 destroyed an entire city block in Nampa. It was started when a man, never identified, threw a match into a fireworks display. Fire departments from Boise and Caldwell came to help fight the blaze. The Boise firemen came by train on the Idaho Central.

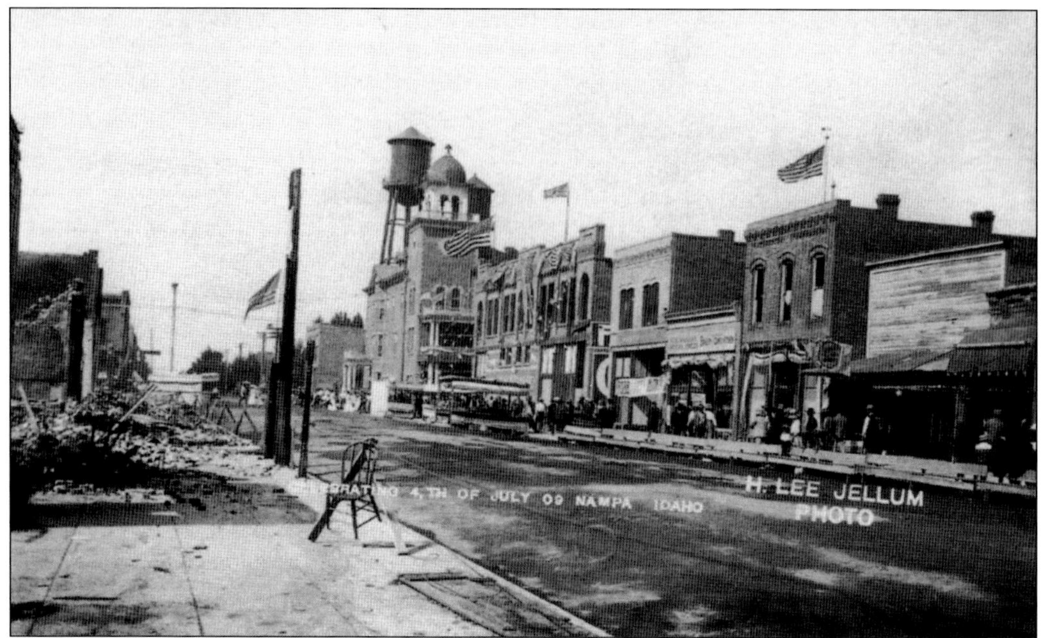

The fire was stopped at Twelfth Avenue, and people lined the opposite side of the street to view the fire. H. Lee Jellum was a photographer in Nampa until about 1912, when he moved to Colorado. His superimposed caption, "Celebrating the 4th of July 09 Nampa Idaho," is interesting. The "fireworks" were not exactly the celebration that the townspeople were expecting.

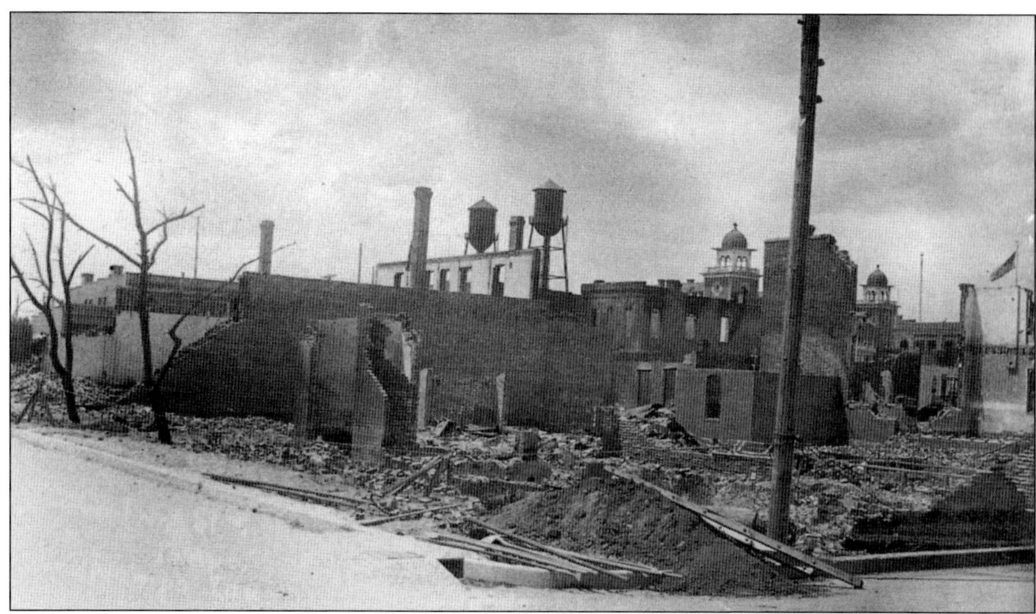

After the fire was out, this is what was left of the block. One building on the corner of Thirteenth Avenue and First Street was the Blue Eye building. He took the original plans and rebuilt the building again. The name is still visible at the top of the building today.

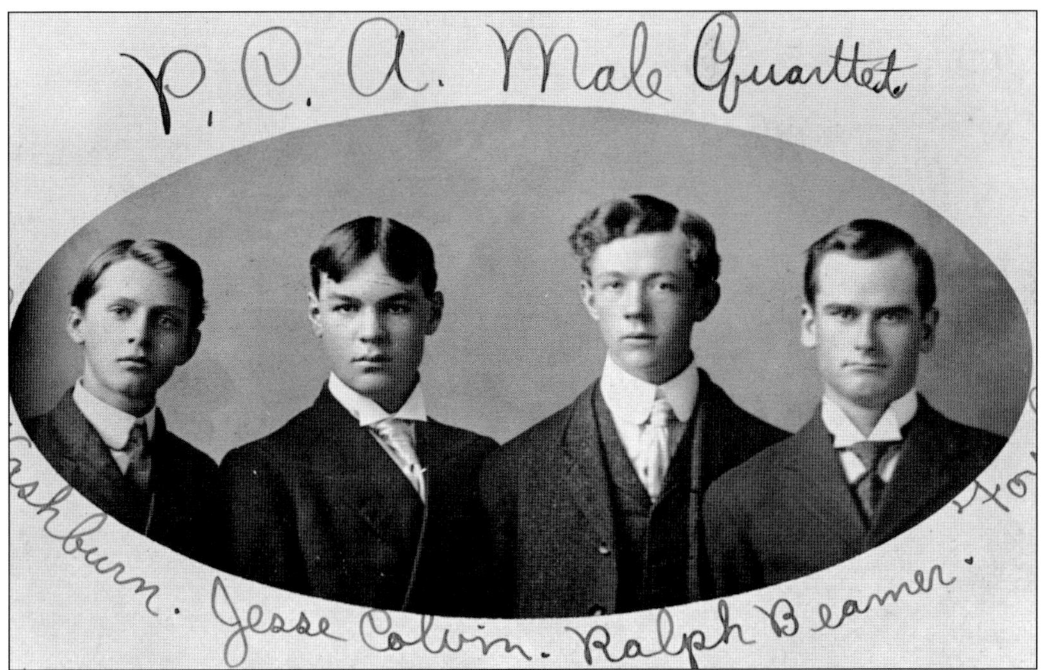

The Presbyterian Male Quartet of 1910 entertained all over the valley. The group consisted of Carl Washburn, Jesse Colvin, Ralph Beamer, and Foy Carter. Local, live entertainment was the favorite form of diversion in the early years of the 20th century. There were no radio, movies, CD players, or television.

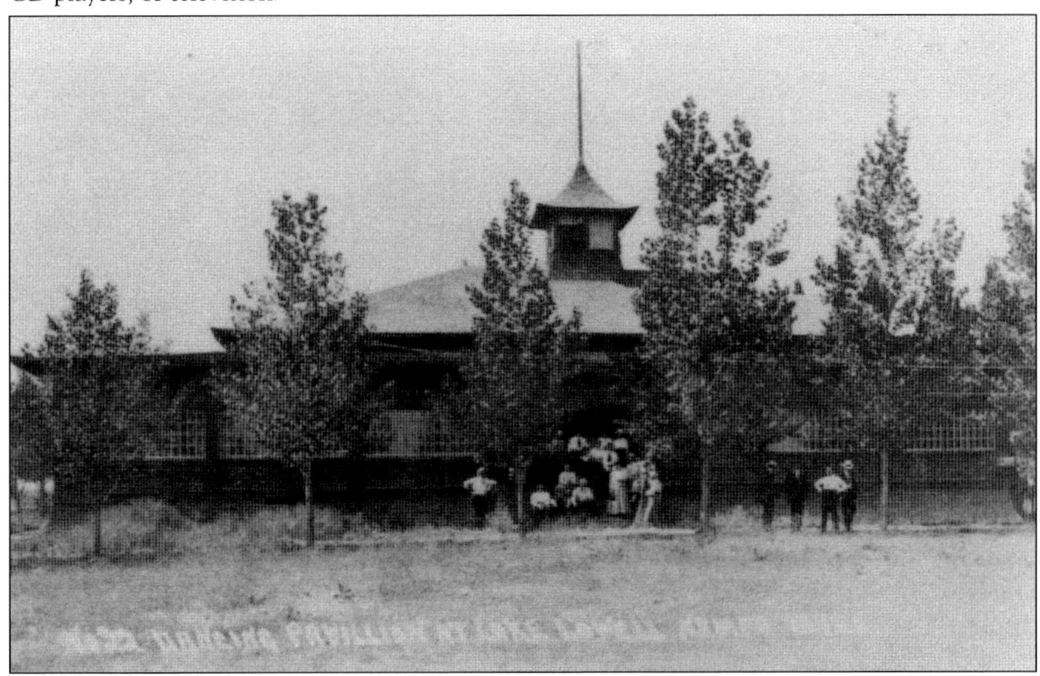

This photograph is not an event, but a place where events were held. It was the dance pavilion at Lake Lowell in 1917 and was used by many clubs and organizations as well as the regular dances held there during the summer. It could be reached by interurban, car, or horseback.

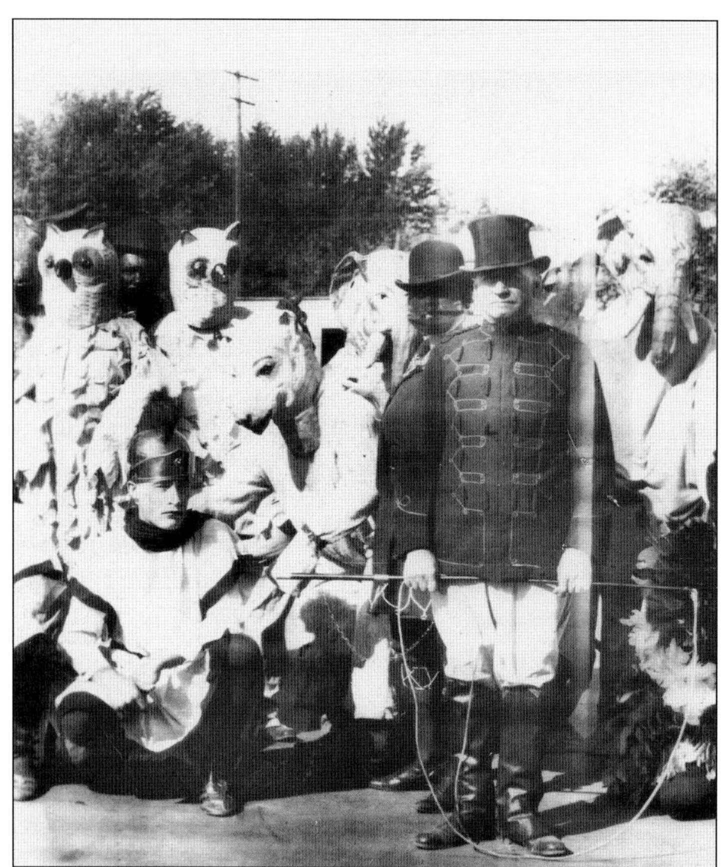

Pictured here are some of the participants in the annual Animal Parade, held each year during the 1920s. Many of the other participants were real animals, although these men do justice to our furry and feathered friends. Everyone loves a parade, and Nampa held multiple parades every year.

The Farm and Fireside Parade goes down Main Street in Nampa around 1929. They were very patriotic in those days. The turnout on the sidewalks speaks to the popularity of a parade in those days. Businesses pictured here include, from left to right, Blake's, McClain Hardware Co., a restaurant, Walker Electric Co., and a meat market.

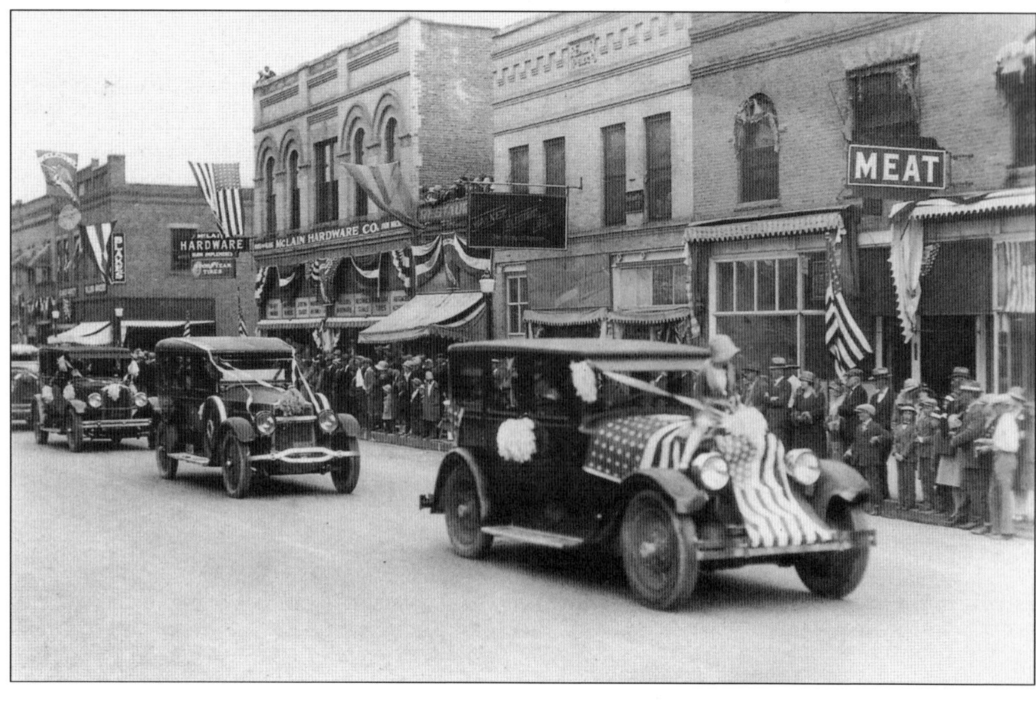

Miss Nampa of 1934, Charlotte Togstad, and her court are looking regal in this photograph. Beauty contests were big in Nampa for both men and women. The first was in 1927, with Irene Auger taking the crown. A week later, she was chosen Miss Idaho.

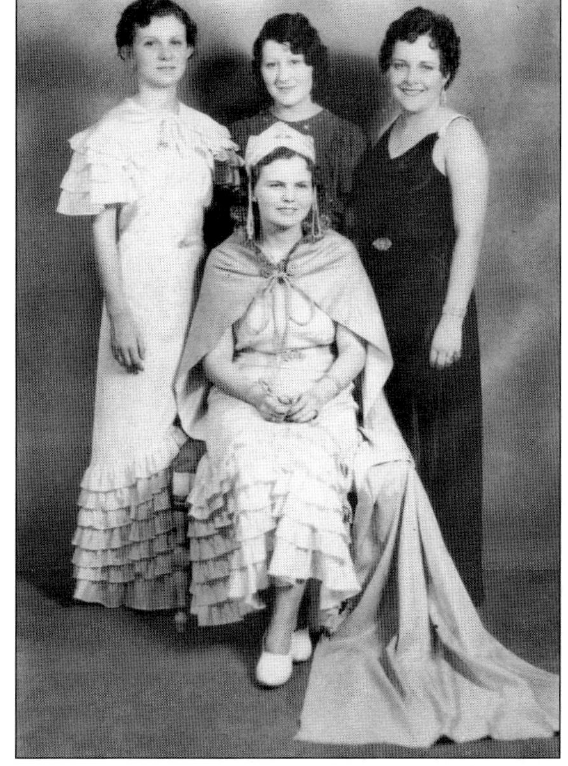

Winette Lockman is pictured taking the Office of Price Administration pledge to not overpay for goods during World War II. The OPA, as it was known, controlled prices as part of the war effort. What the men's ties had to do with it has been lost. Winette had a B-17 bomber named after her that saw action.

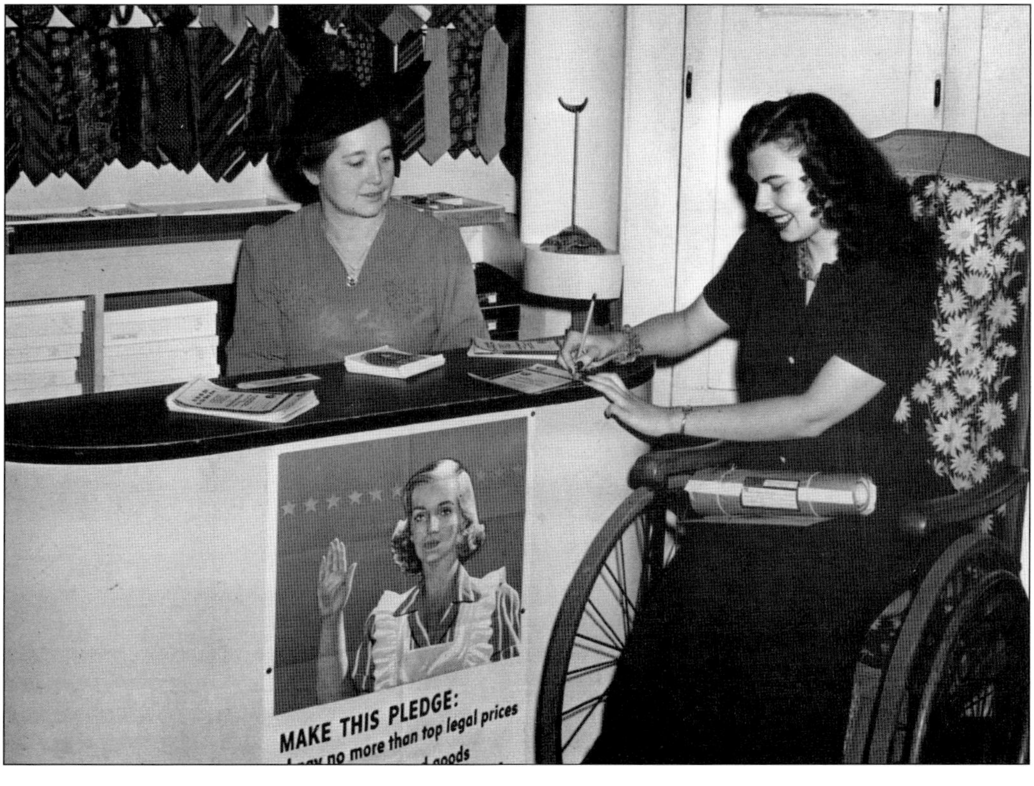

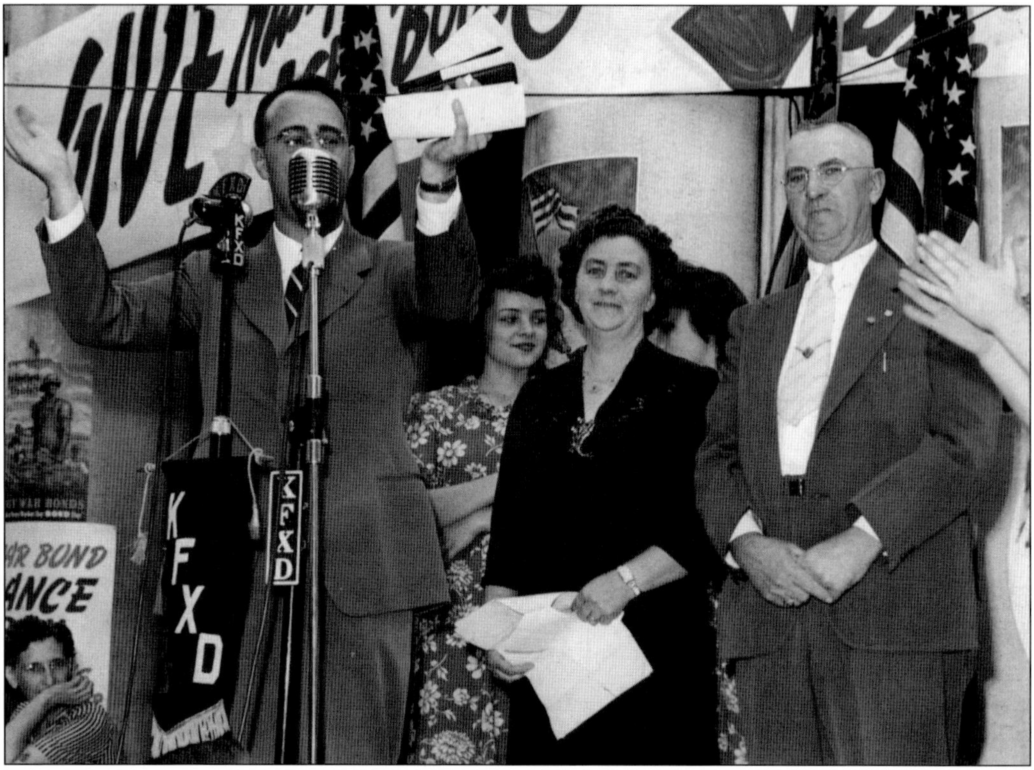

Mr. and Mrs. Henry Huter do their bit at a war bond rally during World War II. KFXD was broadcasting the event to urge people to come down and buy bonds or stamps. Many Nampa locals remember buying war stamps at school during the war.

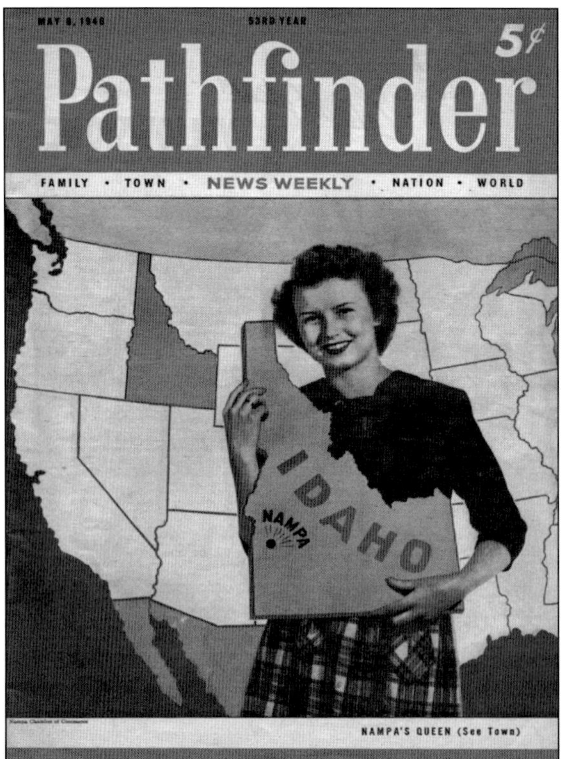

Bonnie Lou Rodwell graces the cover of *Pathfinder* magazine. The queen of the event, she was 18 years old and a student at the University of Washington. She was the daughter of Dr. and Mrs. R.L. Rodwell of Nampa. Nampa's own Sen. Charles Gossett came from Washington to place the crown on her head.

Van Moad was the president of the chamber of commerce in 1946 and was instrumental in getting Nampa chosen as "Main Street America" for Pathfinder Week. He was in the real estate business. The chamber of commerce was promoting Nampa at all times, as is evident in the photographs to come in this chapter.

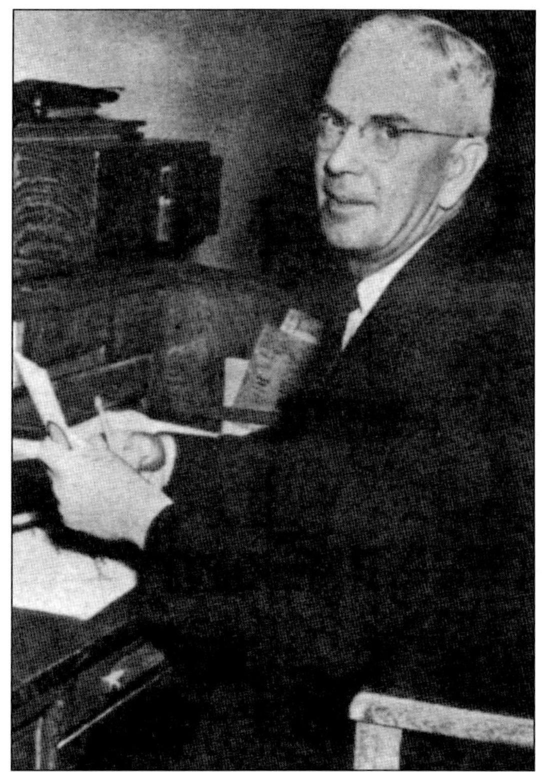

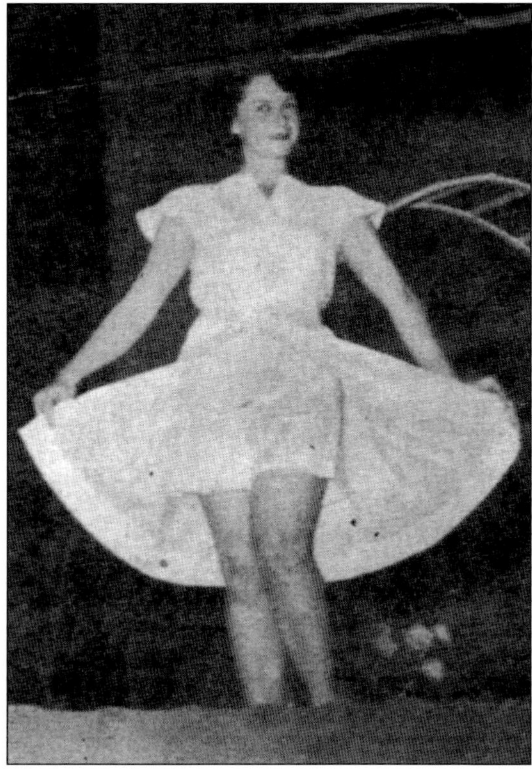

At a fashion show during Pathfinder Week, Loma Lou Buck models what the young woman of 1946 wore. The show was just one of the attractions for the crowds during the event. Barbara Lessinger was photographed with Bonnie Lou Rodwell promoting the fashion show. Nampa school musicians supplied the music.

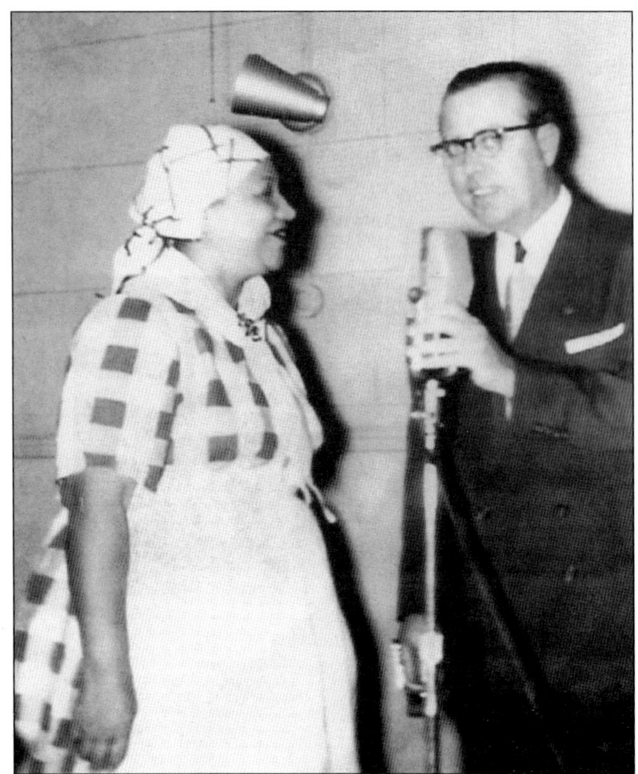

Doyle Cain is pictured during Pathfinder Week at Wall and Rawlings interviewing "Aunt Jemima" for broadcast over KFXD. Many companies sent representatives to push their goods, but none were as well known as Aunt Jemima. KFXD was everywhere promoting the week in the previous month. The *Free Press* ran daily stories for a month leading up to the week.

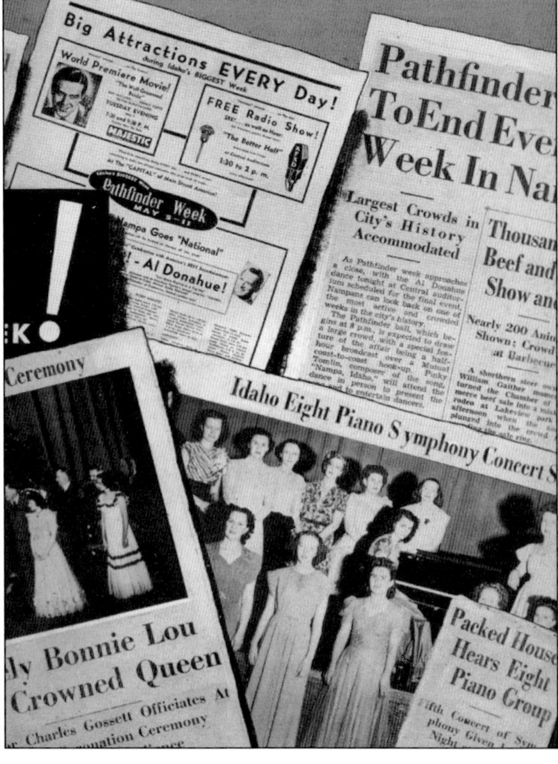

This collage of stories and pamphlets during Pathfinder Week includes one about the Eight Piano Symphony. The group was led by Fern Nolte Davidson, who performed on her own at Carnegie Hall in New York. Quite versatile, she was city tennis champion as well.

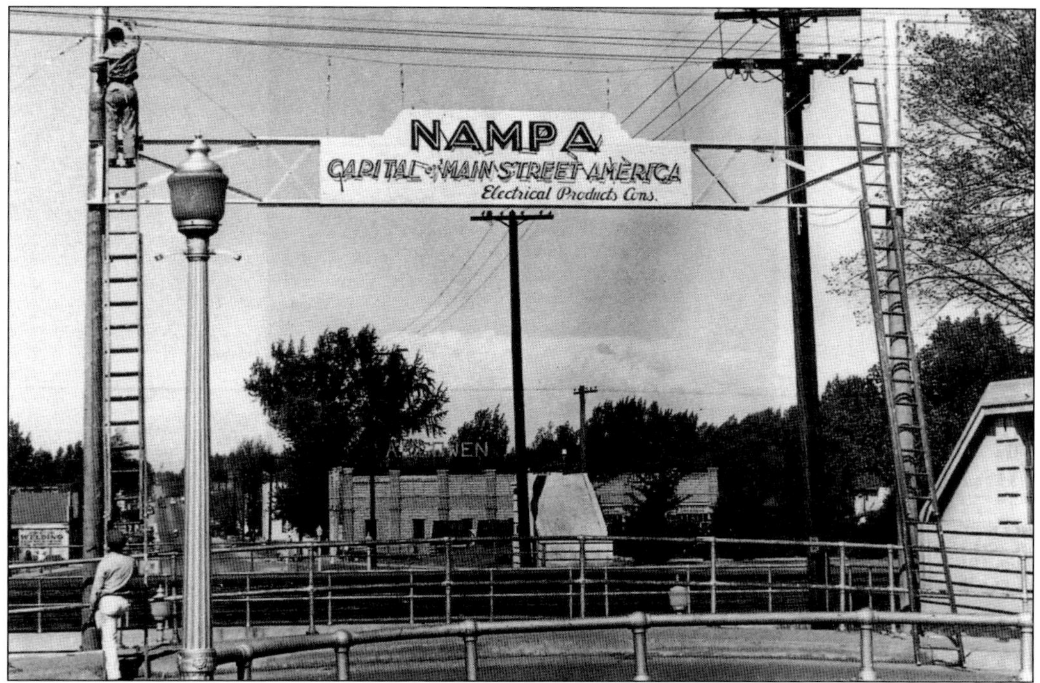

Employees of the Electrical Products Construction Company are pictured installing the sign over the Eleventh Avenue subway. They donated this neon sign, trumpeting Nampa as Main Street America. The fate of the sign is lost in the mists of time.

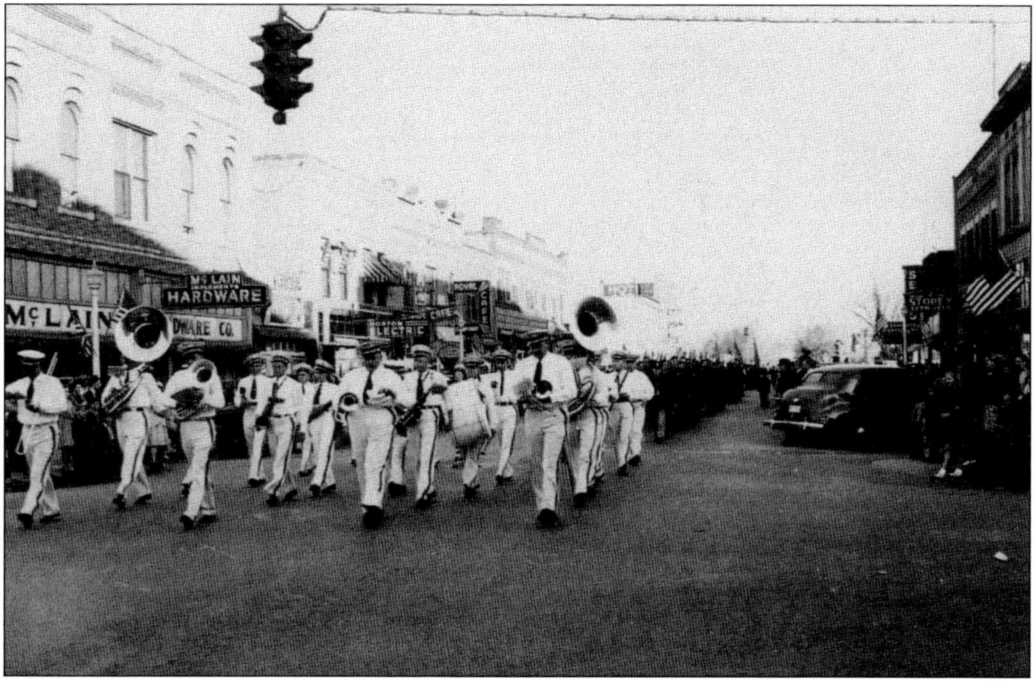

Another parade travels down Nampa's Main Street at Thirteenth Avenue South. The band is leading, and the military is right behind. As pointed out in an earlier depiction of a parade, the turnout was overflowing into the street, proving the event's popularity.

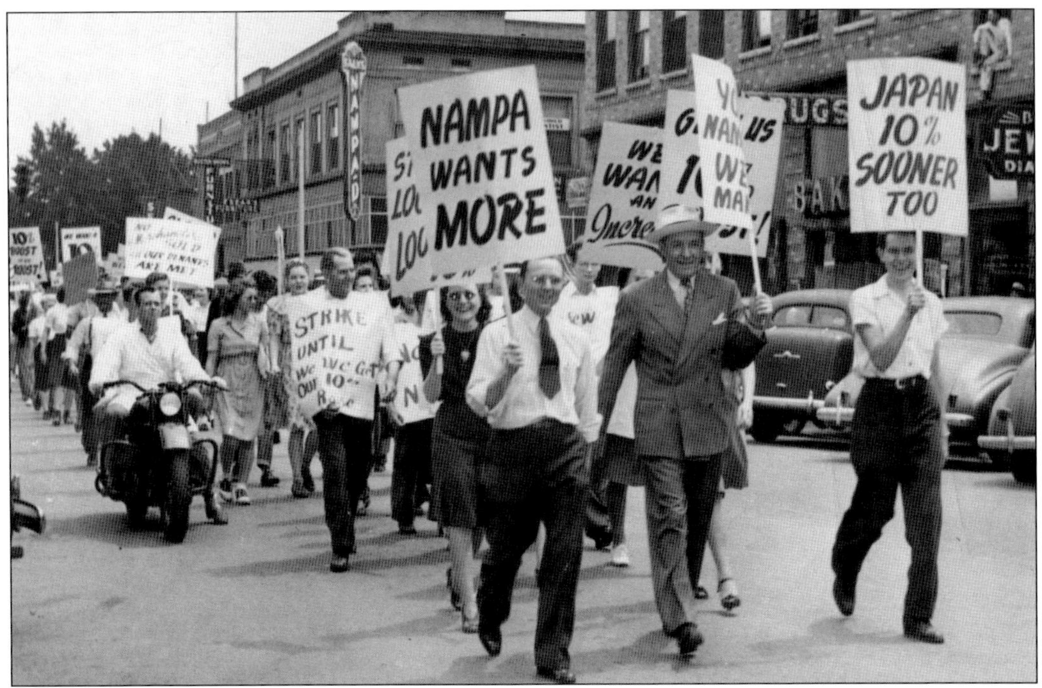

Some parades did not capture the crowds, even though they traveled down the center of Main Street. The turnout for this parade was minimal, although one fellow has a bird's-eye view from his perch in a second-story window. The telephone workers were on strike in 1946.

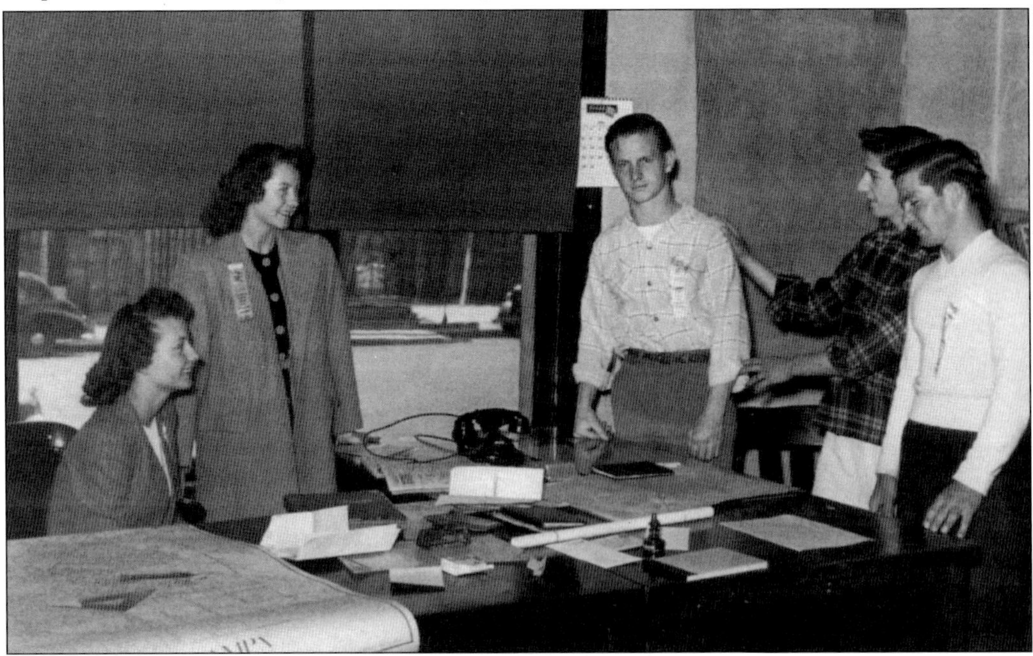

This event was held annually during the 1940s and early 1950s. It was "Mayor for a Day," where high school students took a position in city government for a day. Pictured from left to right are Irene Richards, Loma Lou Buck, Keith Biowin, Angel Mallea, and an unidentified student. The photograph was taken in the mayor's office.

Petite Mary Jean Price was Lettuce Bowl Queen in 1947, when the Nampa Bulldogs defeated Albany, Oregon, 7-6. The Lettuce Bowl started out as a college game featuring the College of Idaho. The first game was in 1941 between College of Idaho and Gonzaga. The game was changed in 1943 to feature Nampa High School.

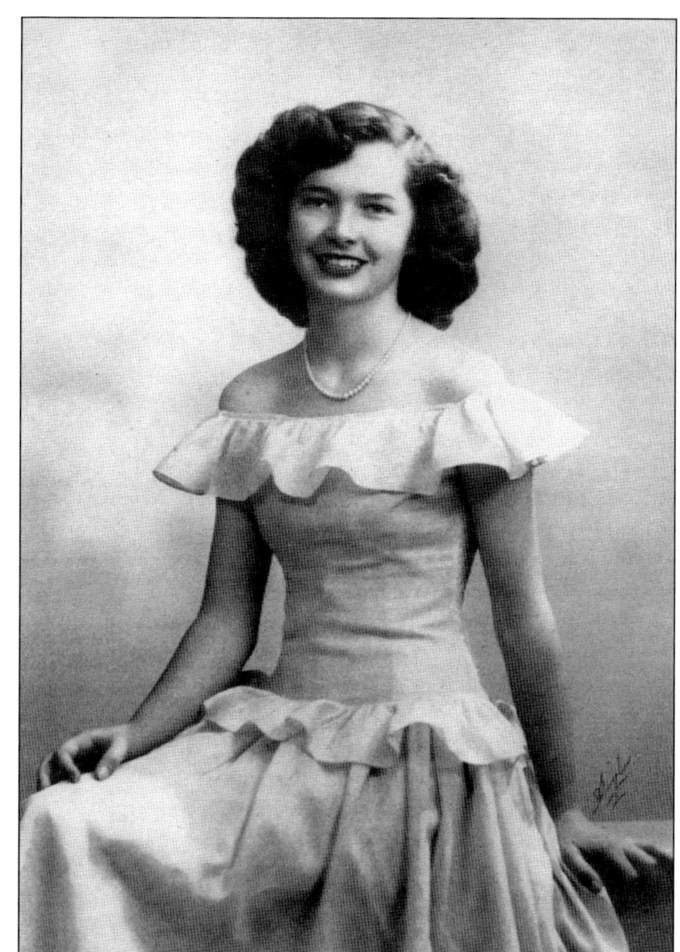

The boat races at Lake Lowell were a must-see for a large number of people, as evident in this 1947 photograph. High-powered boats raced on a course laid out so that everyone on the dam could see the action. The races are no longer held.

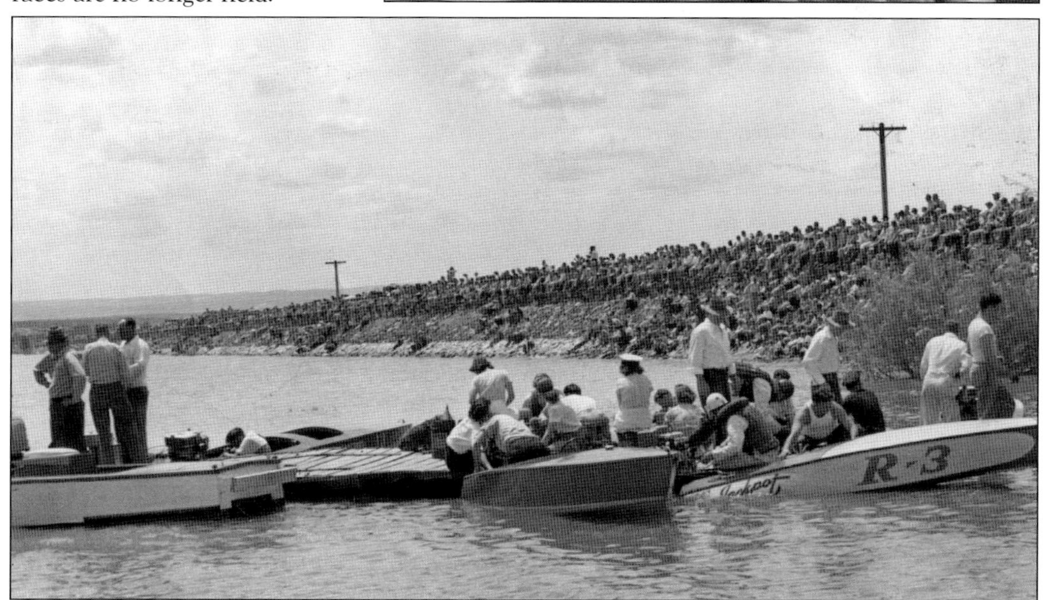

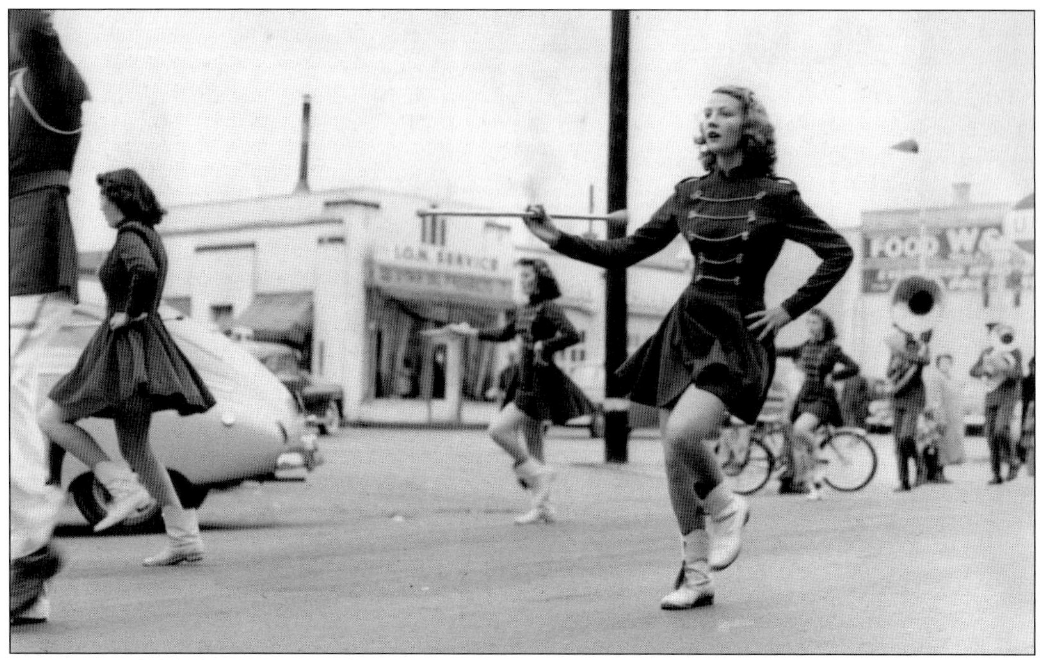

Mary Jo Holmes struts her stuff down Second Street between Thirteenth and Twelfth Avenues, with the Nampa High School Band in 1947. Wall and Rawlings and the Vico Pep 88 service station are in the background. The high school bands seemed to have more opportunities to perform in those days.

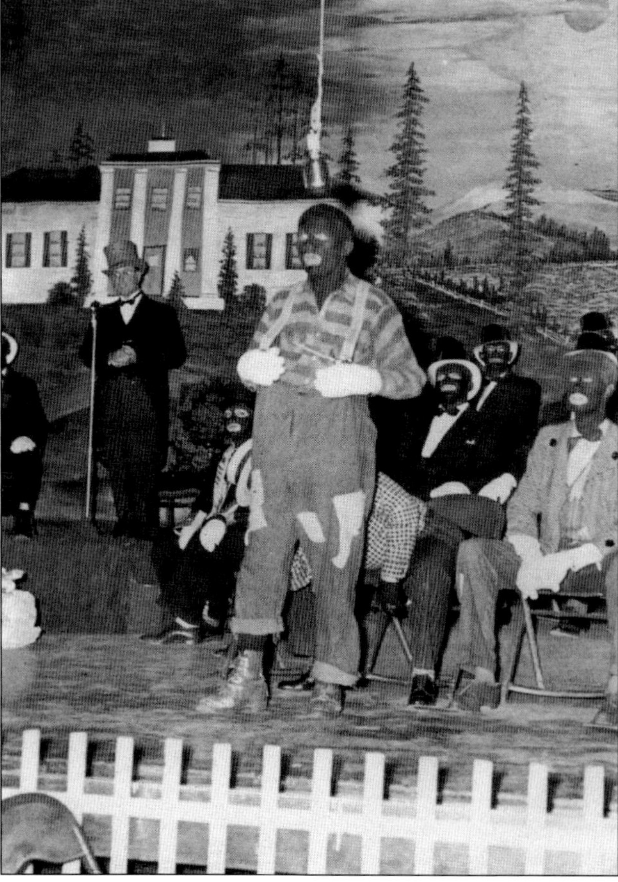

Vic Budell performs as Mushmouth in the Lions Club presentation of an old-time minstrel show in 1948 at the Central Assembly Building. A.B. Ellis, as Gluefoot, is seated at right. Doyle Cain (in the top hat) was the interlocutor, and Donna Montague was the director. This was a Lions Club event to raise money for glasses for the needy.

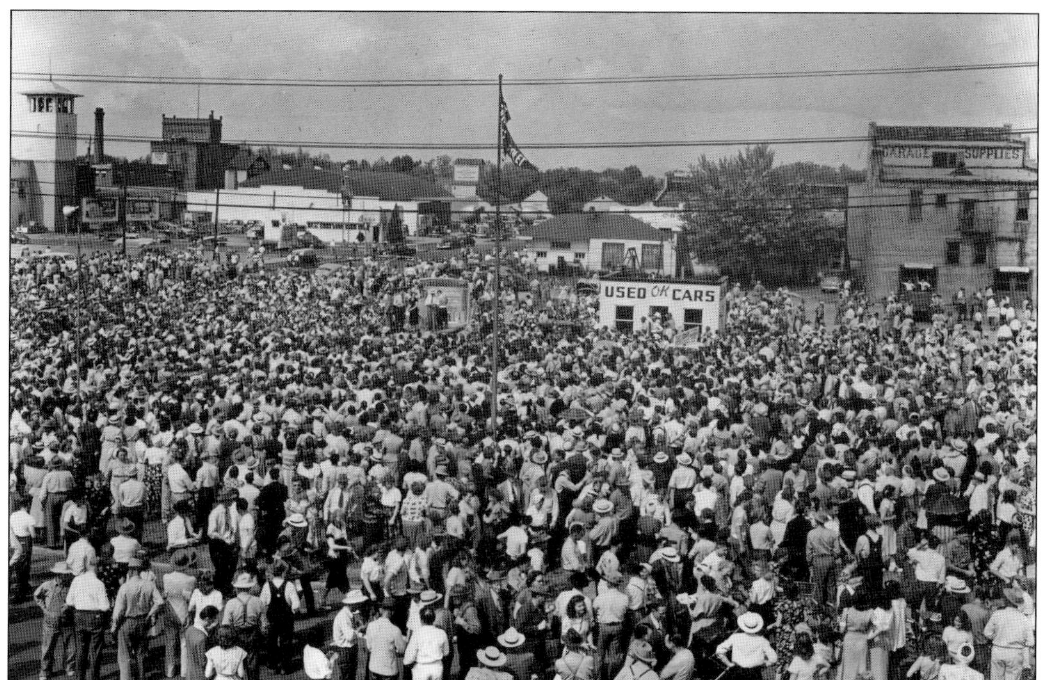

The Nampa Merchants Association held "Trade Days" each year to promote sales. In 1949, the association raffled off a new Studebaker on Showalter's used car lot. It drew quite the crowd. The tower in the background was the fire department.

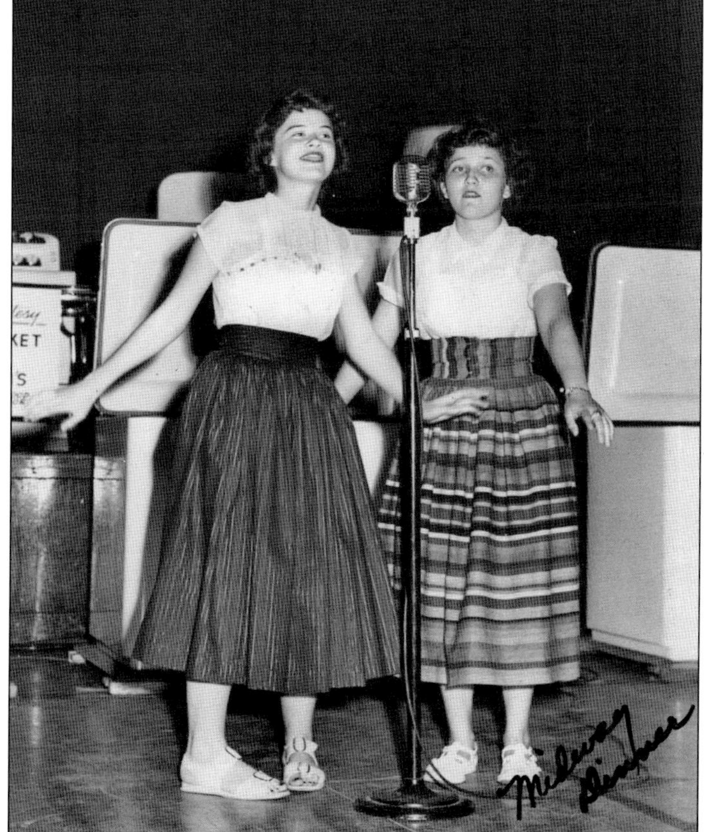

Diane Wade and Barbara Goodwin sing their hearts out for a Midway dinner in 1956. Both girls graduated from Nampa High School that year. Even though television was available in Nampa in 1956, live local talent was still in demand.

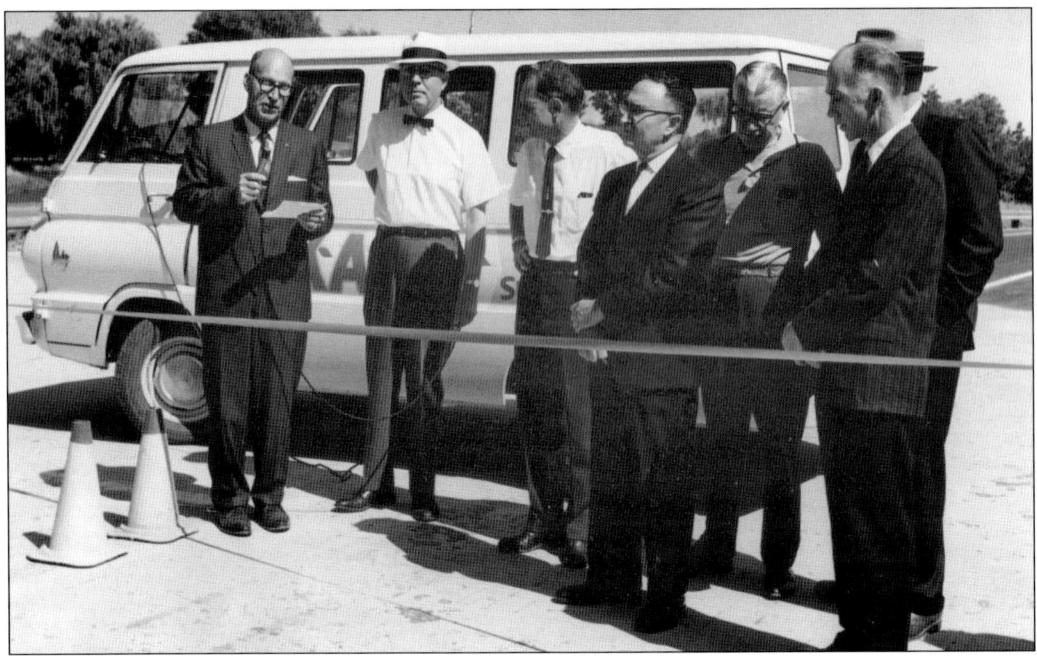

The year 1965 marked the opening of the new Franklin Overpass at Franklin Road and the Interstate. Presiding over the ceremonies is Doyle Symms with the microphone. The others, from left to right, are Doyle Cain, Mayor Ernie Starr, Ellis Mathis, Red Wade, and Bill Sacht. The ever-present KAIN van was there to broadcast the event.

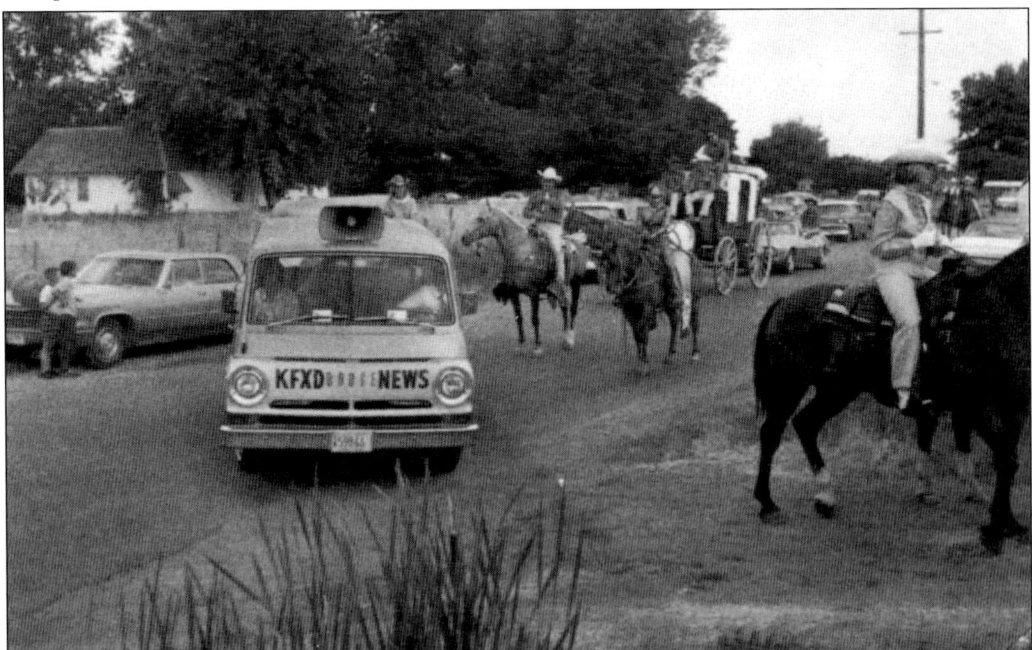

The Snake River Stampede was an annual event and still is. Each year before the show, a caravan is sent out to neighboring towns to promote attendance to the rodeo. This photograph documents one of those recruiting excursions in 1967. KFXD and KAIN both always sent their vans and broadcast events on the tours.

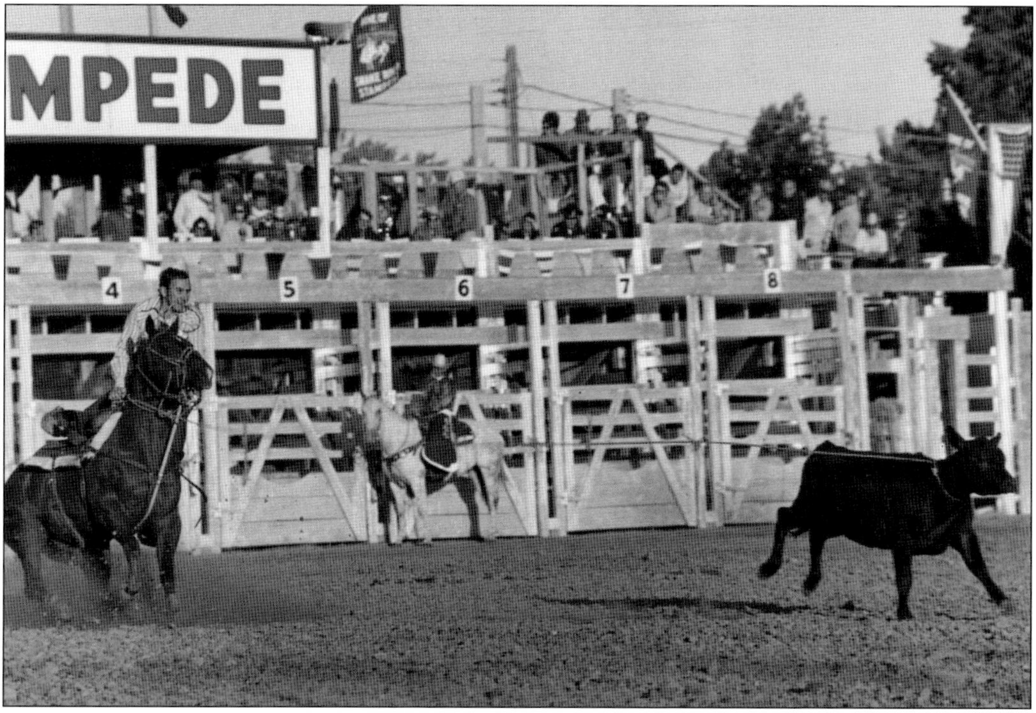

The Snake River Stampede is always packed with cowboy action. The calf-roping event is pictured underway in the arena. Nampa boasted the world's calf roping champion, Dean Oliver, who won the trophy numerous times. Both radio stations considered this an event worth airtime, both before and during the show.

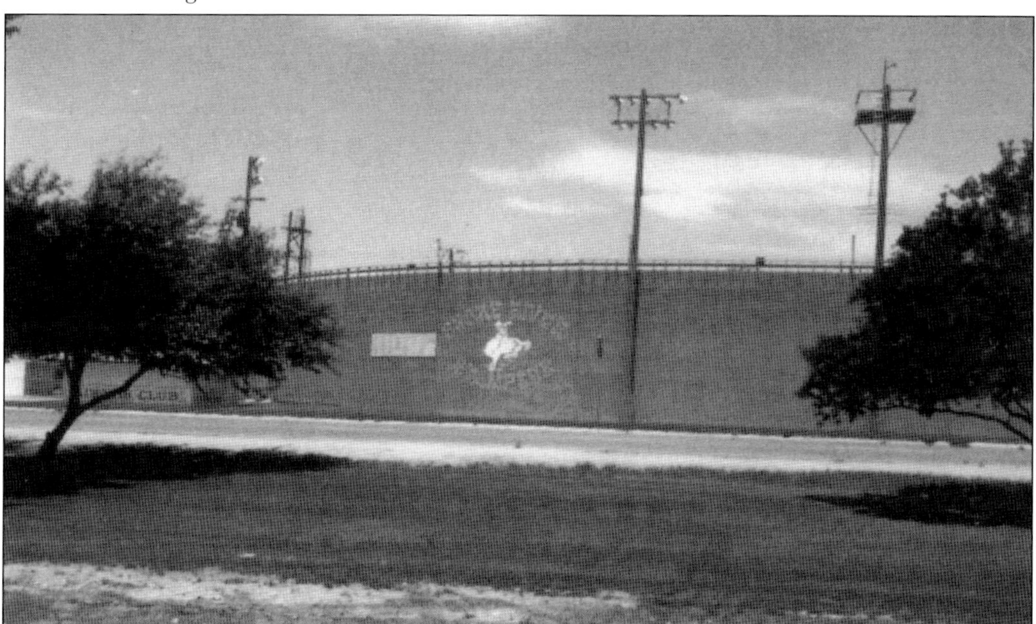

The old Stampede arena is pictured here around 1967. It was built in 1950 and served as the venue for the show for many years. It has since been torn down, and the rodeo is now held indoors at the Idaho Center. The photograph was taken from Lakeview Park across Garrity Boulevard.

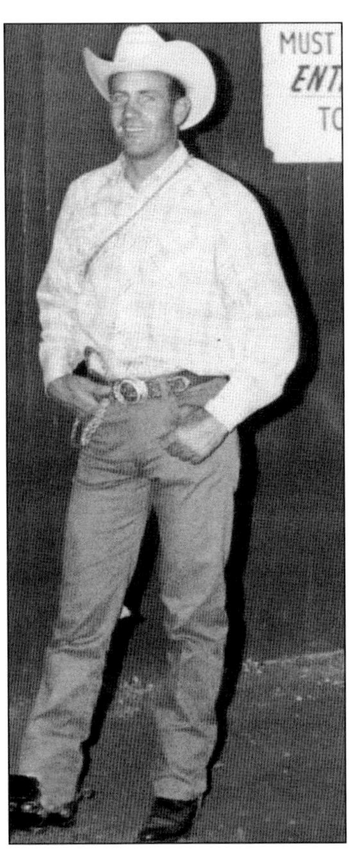

Harry Charters of Melba was another local rodeo world champion. He held the crown in the bulldogging event. He was rookie of the year when he was in his early thirties at an age when most competitors are veterans. He was a native of Melba, Idaho. Harry was also an excellent basketball player.

Pictured in 1969 wearing his cowboy garb, Ken Bort stands in front of the sign listing the sponsors of the free Buckaroo Breakfast held in conjunction with the rodeo each year. Ken was involved with the Snake River Stampede for many years. Both locals and out-of-towners came to this event.

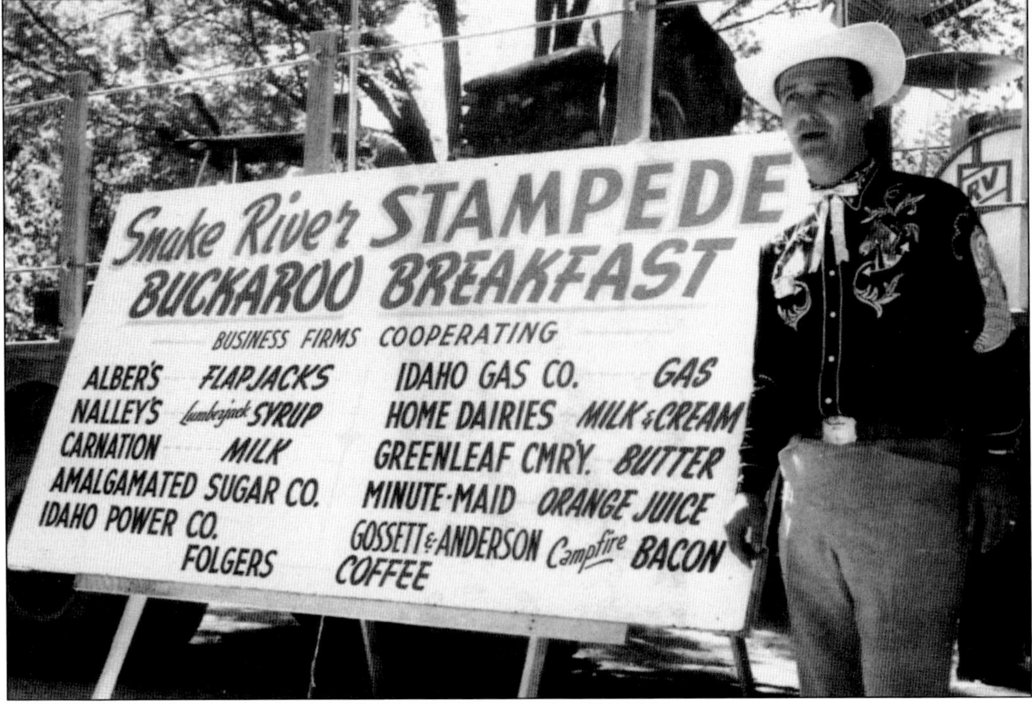

Eight

Sports

Sports have been an important part of Nampa life since the beginning. A town baseball team was formed in the 1890s, and Nampa won its first league championship in 1902. Town baseball was almost a religion from then until the 1950s. Town basketball came on the scene in the 1920s. World War II put a stop to almost all athletics, because of gas rationing and travel restrictions, but they reemerged after the conflict.

Team sports reached their height of popularity with the Nampa High School teams. The first sports team at the school was girls' basketball in 1905. They lost to Weiser 36-0 on the outdoor court at Kenwood School. There was no gym then, and this fact would plague both boys' and girls' teams for many years. They played in hotel basements, second floor storerooms, outdoors, and in Yorgasons Dance Hall. They had their own gym in the early 1930s, but it lacked seating for the fans. It was not until Central Assembly Building was completed in 1937 that Nampa had the floor and seating needed for its program.

The school fielded football and boys' basketball teams for the first time in 1909. The football program was more successful than basketball and won the state championship in 1925, 1930, and 1949. The basketball team won its only state title in 1950. The golf team won the Idaho state title from 1945 through 1948.

Nampa had a comprehensive grade school and Little League program starting before 1910. By the 1930s, a boy could play football, basketball, or baseball on junior teams. Alas, there were no programs for the girls other than the swim teams. These teams were sponsored by the schools or the city. Many treasure their memories of that time along with the knowledge of the game they acquired.

Outdoor sports were enjoyed by individuals and families in the mountains, lakes, rivers, and streams of Southwest Idaho. Fishing, bird hunting, and big game hunting not only were perceived as sport and recreation, but also put meat on the table.

This chapter presents a sense of the sporting life enjoyed by Nampans for over 100 years.

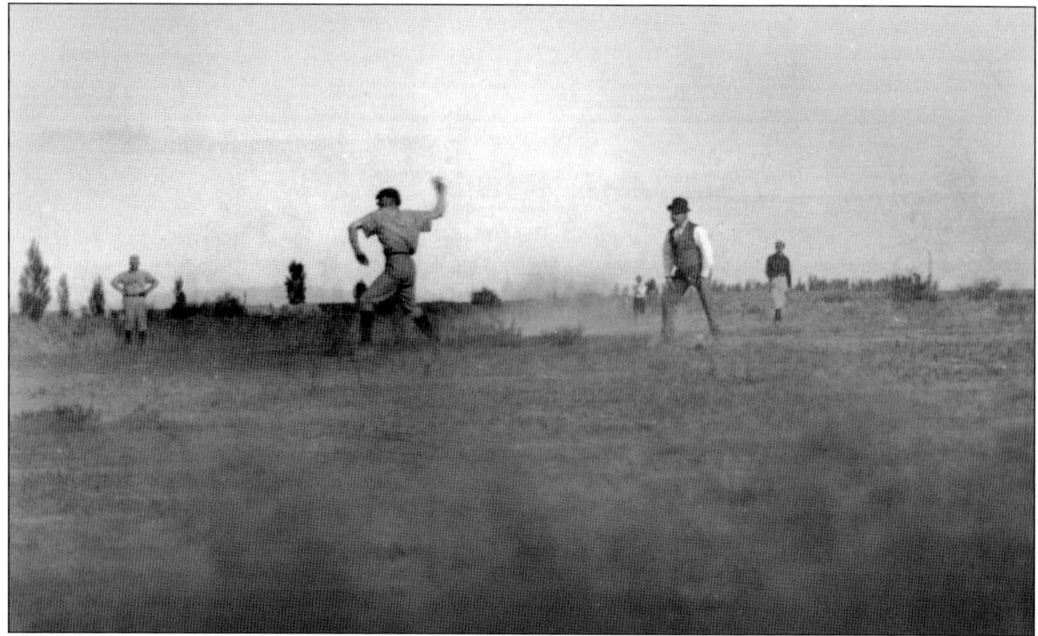

This 1896 baseball photograph came from a glass negative. The game was played in the sagebrush then, with no stands or fences. They were enthusiastic, though, and the umpire standing behind the pitcher is very nobby in his derby. From this early beginning, Nampa town teams drew numerous fans over the years.

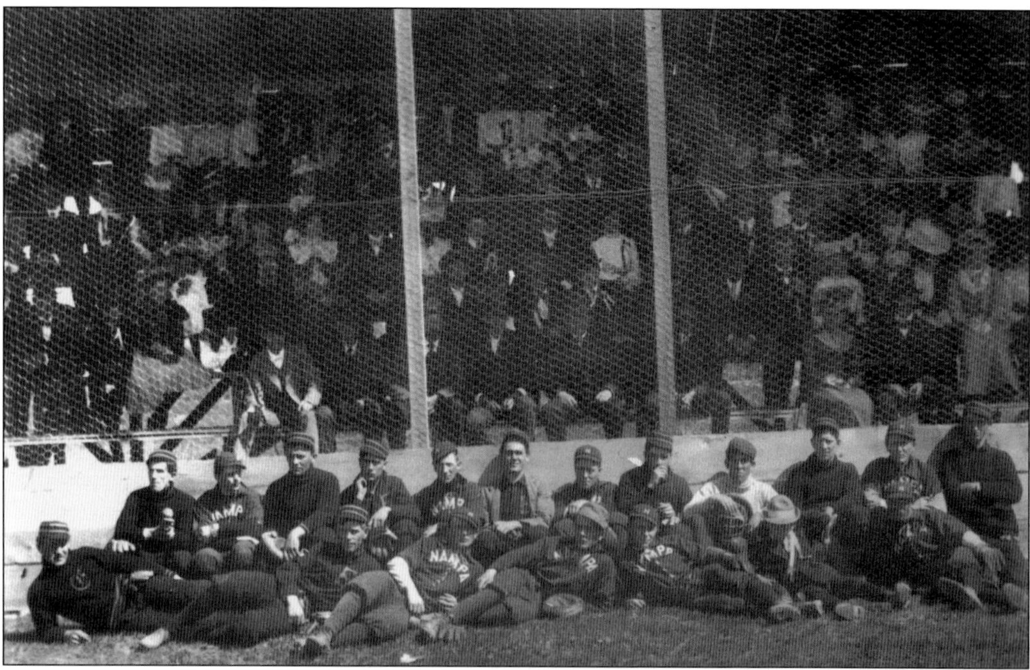

This photograph shows the grandstand at Nampa in 1907. The players lounging in front of the backstop are wearing Nampa, Caldwell, and Boise uniforms. The teams of that time did not pay attention to rosters in games where money was on the line. Players from other teams filled in as ringers. The spectators' clothes are representative of the fashions of the times.

The 1909 Nampa pennant winners are pictured here. From left to right are (first row) Clint Ford, mascot Howard Lore, and Eddy Corbin; (second row) Eddie McMahan, Bert Kinnear, Ed Ford, and Carl King; (third row) manager Vic Elver, Fred McLin, John Herwig, Ted Geelan, and secretary Oscar Pierce. Vic Elver was in the clothing business and ordered the uniforms. The newspaper reporter called them *knobby* when he saw them. It was a term used at the time to mean classy.

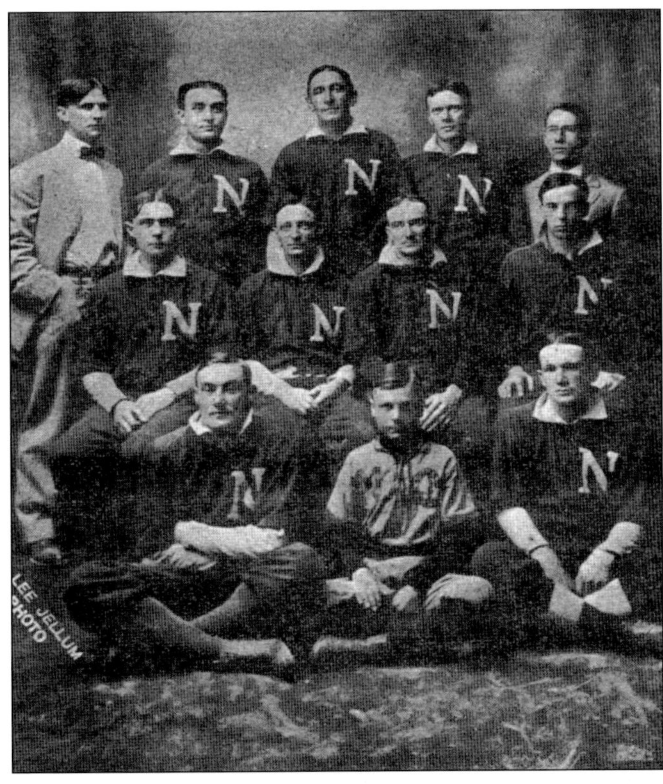

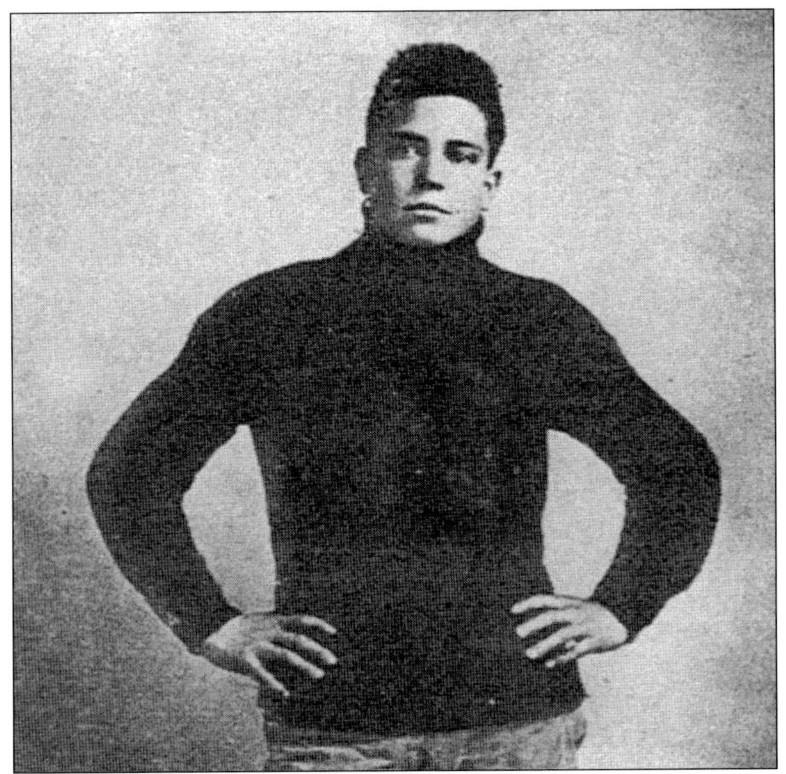

Nampa High School football and baseball star Sumner Rodriguez is pictured in his football togs. He graduated in 1912 from Nampa High School and then graduated from the University of Wisconsin in engineering. He rose to serve in many upper management positions with Standard Oil Company. He also rose through the Army ranks from private to lieutenant, receiving a battlefield commission in World War I.

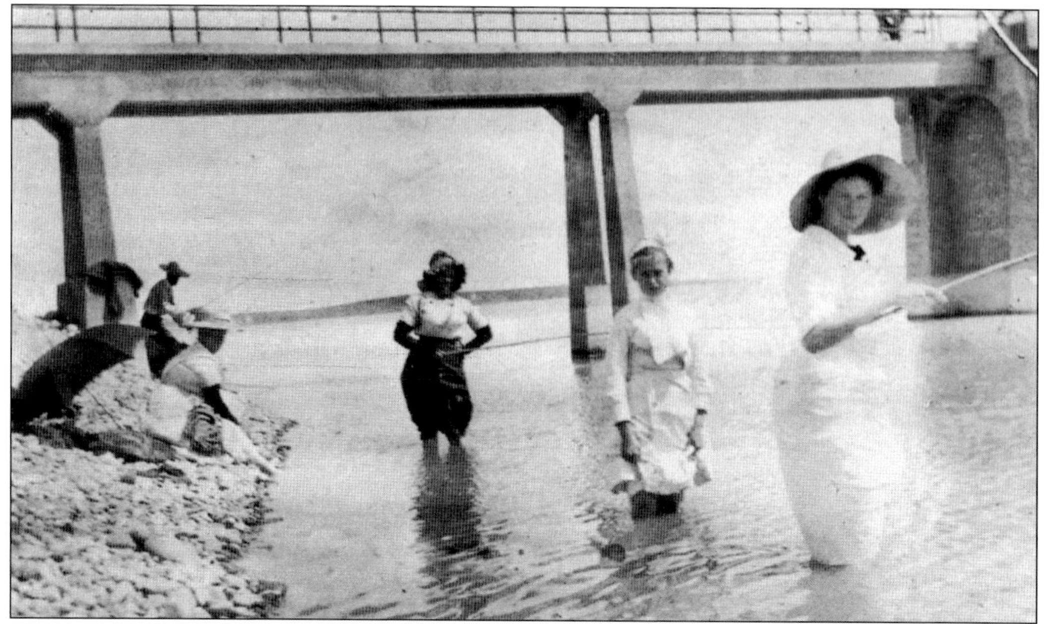

Members of the Colvin family are pictured enjoying the sunshine and fishing under the headgate for the dam at Lake Lowell in 1913. The Canyon County Historical Society received a whole box of Colvin family photographs, and this fishing trip was just one of many taken by the family.

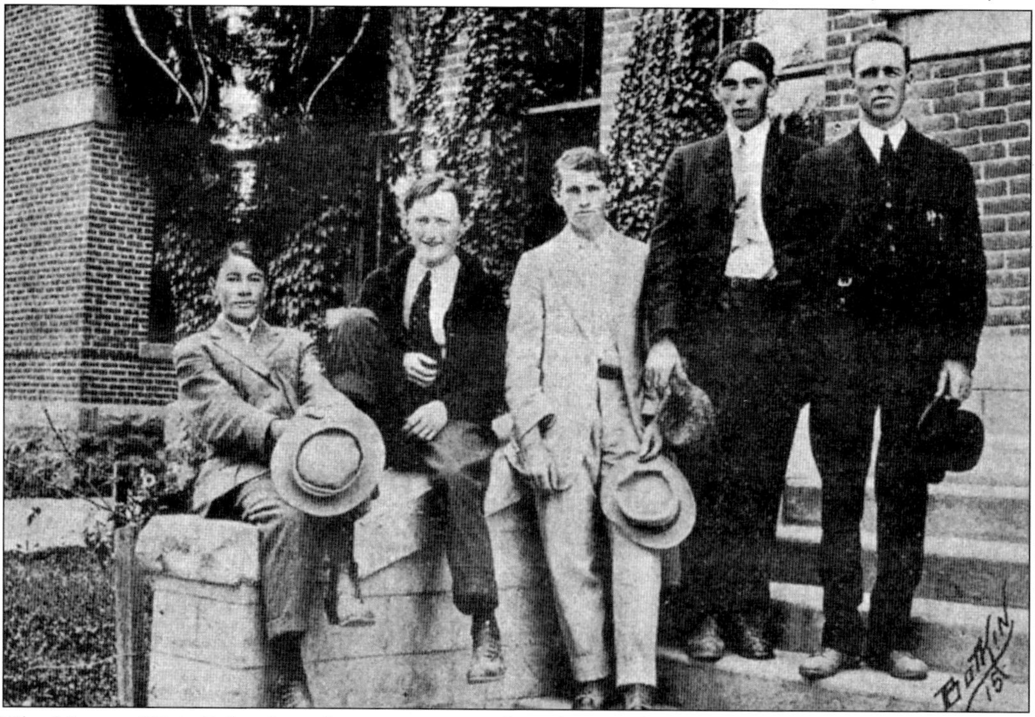

The Nampa High School track team competed at the 1915 Harvest Festival. From left to right are Dewitt Hasbrouck, Tip Pendleton, Harold Hasbrouck, Dale Peterson, and their unidentified coach. The photograph was taken by Lafe Botkin (class of 1916), the first Idaho soldier to give his life in World War I.

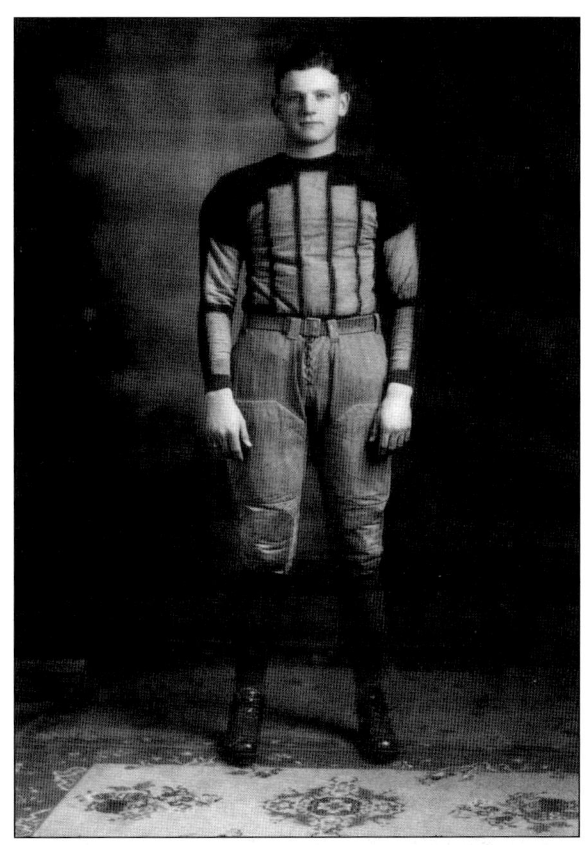

This c. 1925 photograph of Charles Graybill wearing his red and blue Nampa High School football uniform shows the equipment of that day. The pants contained kneepads and thigh pads that were sewn into them. His shoulder pads were quite small compared to the ones used by players today. His shiny new shoes have wooden cleats. The rug on the floor makes it clear that this is a studio photograph.

The 1922 Nampa High basketball team were the Southwest Idaho champions. From left to right are (first row) Harold Hamilton, Orval Hostettler, George Bass, and Leon Compton; (second row) Thomas Smith, Wendell Spriggs, coach A.J. Werrell, Warren Grothe, and John Armitage. The team won 10 and lost 2. Their two losses came in the state tournament.

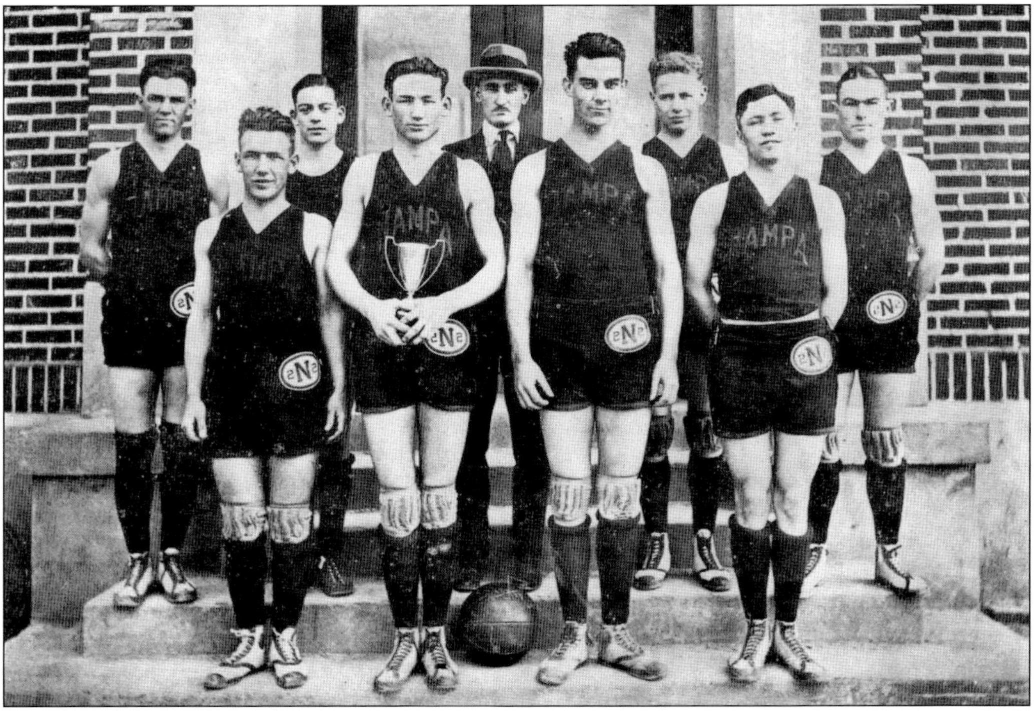

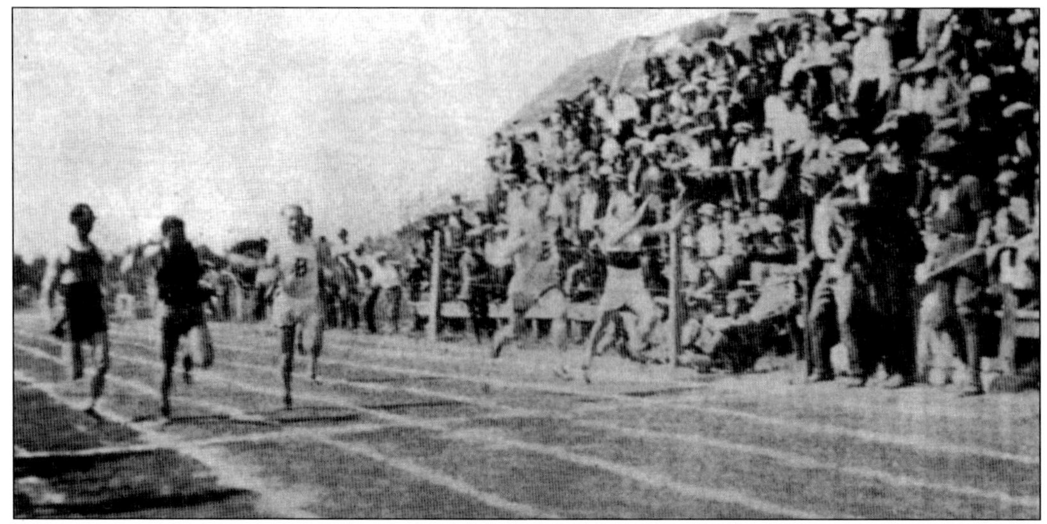

This photograph documents the finish of the 100-yard dash at the 1924 district track meet. At the far right is Art Ord of Nampa being edged out by McCormack of Boise in 10.4 seconds. Ingelsby of Boise finished third. Ord was also a football star at Nampa and went on to an outstanding career at the University of Oregon.

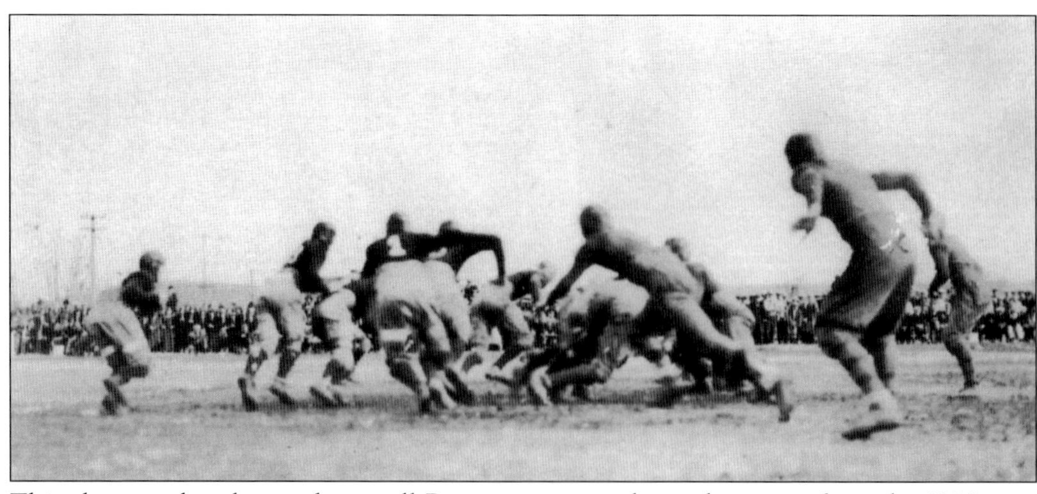

This photograph, taken with a small Brownie camera, shows the action from the 1924 state championship game at Lewiston. Art Ord of Nampa on the far left is beginning an end run for a large gain against the Bengals. The Bulldogs won a thriller, 21-15, to cap an undefeated season. The coach was H.F. "Zip" Harrington.

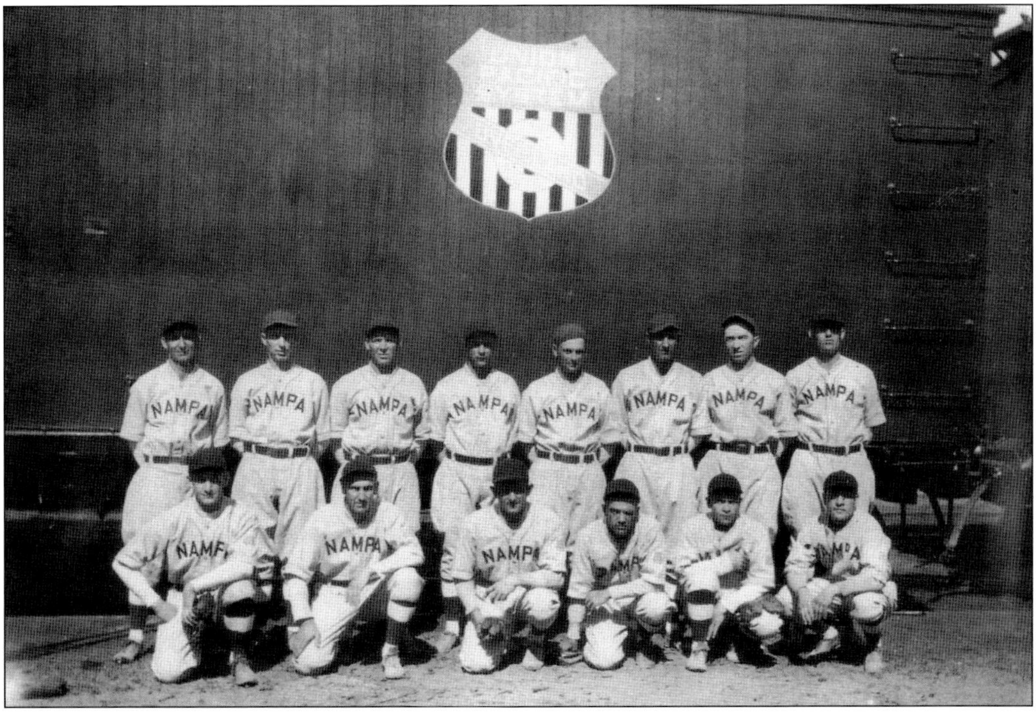

Nampa's Union Pacific baseball team is pictured in 1928. In the 1920s, Union Pacific started an intensive employee sports program. Nampa, with the railroad and Pacific Fruit Express, was well represented. The Nampa team shown here had only four players from Junction City. Included in this photograph are George Gilpin (third from left), John Amen (next to him in back row), Orton Kelly (first on the left), and James Bruce (third from left). The others were from Pocatello and Salt Lake City.

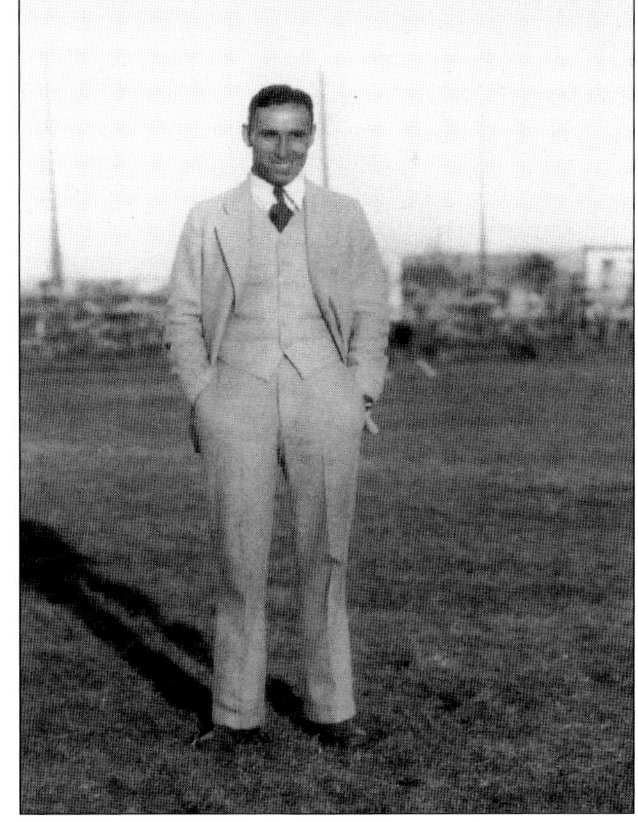

Vernon "Skip" Stivers was one of Nampa's top-five winning football coaches. His record was 29-9 during his tenure. His 1930 team won the Idaho state championship. Stivers ran a successful sporting goods store in Nampa for a number of years after his coaching career. The other four top coaches were Zip Harrington, Lefty Marineau, Harold White, and Babe Brown.

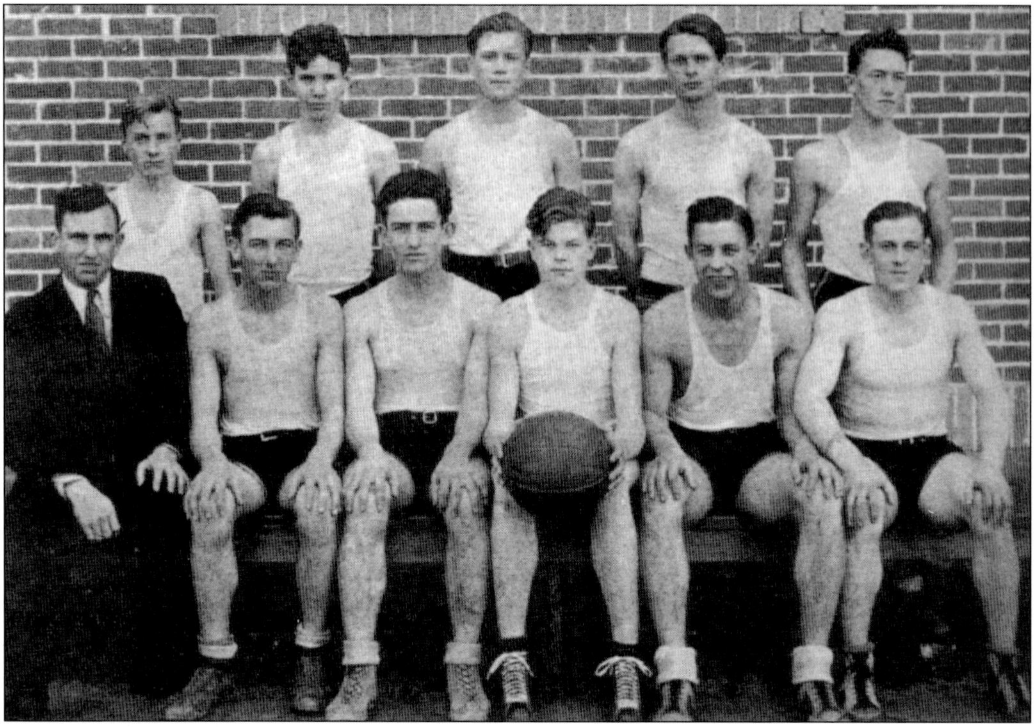

Members of the 1934 Northwest Nazarene Academy basketball team included, from left to right, (first row) Coach Brown, Quilling, Nees, Fifer, Cline, and Pounds; (second row) Nolte, Harper, Spencer, Winans, and Tate. Not pictured are Eastly and Schemelzenbach, who were the only seniors. They played games against small school and town teams. The academy has evolved into today's Nampa Christian High School.

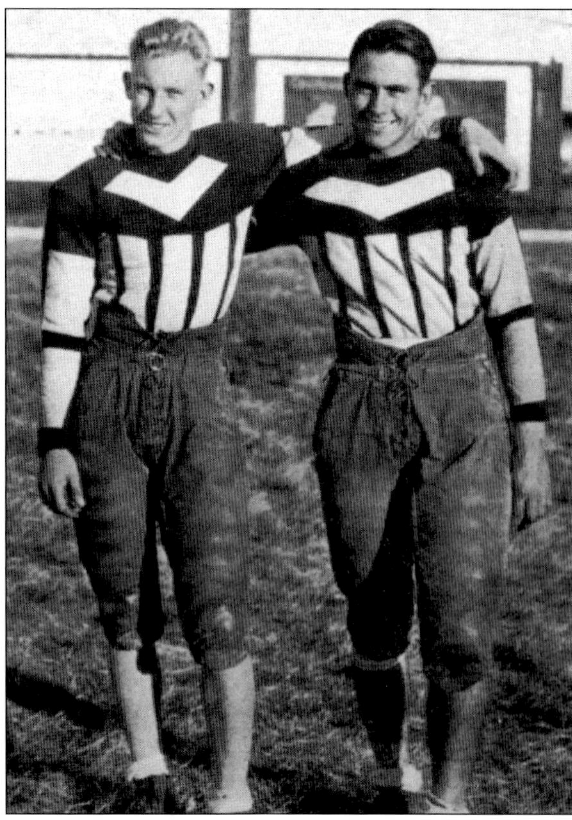

Howard Schmidt and J.D. Michael were two Bulldog stalwarts on the 1933 football team, which chalked up a 10-0 season under the direction of Lefty Marineau. They were the Big 10 conference champions. Only 22 points were scored against them: 13 by Rupert, 7 by Boise, and 2 by American Falls.

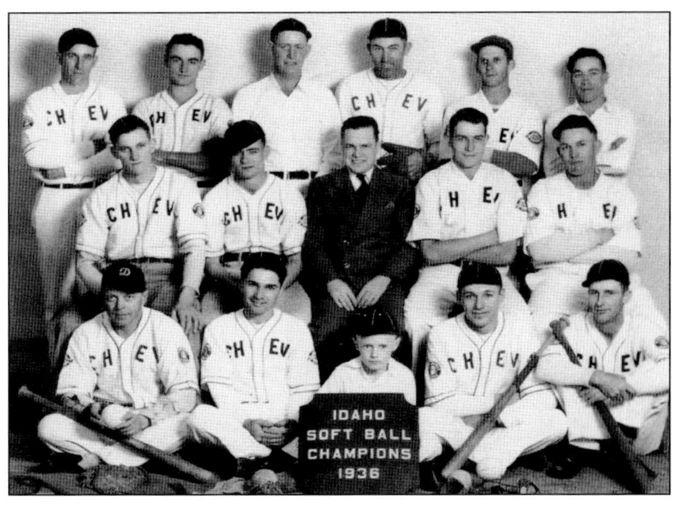

The Showalter Chevrolet 1936 state champion softball team included, from left to right, (first row) Chuck Pilant, Harold Nihart, Guy Taylor, Jack Simmons, Ted Sheehotz, and Ray Brimhall; (second row) Marvin Trask, Jud Brimhall, Bill Showalter, Millard Faylor, and Landes Dutro; (third row) Ed Robb, Dick Rhodes, Milo Shimanek, Frank Huntsman, unidentified, and Emit DeCoursey. The batboy was Marvin Taylor.

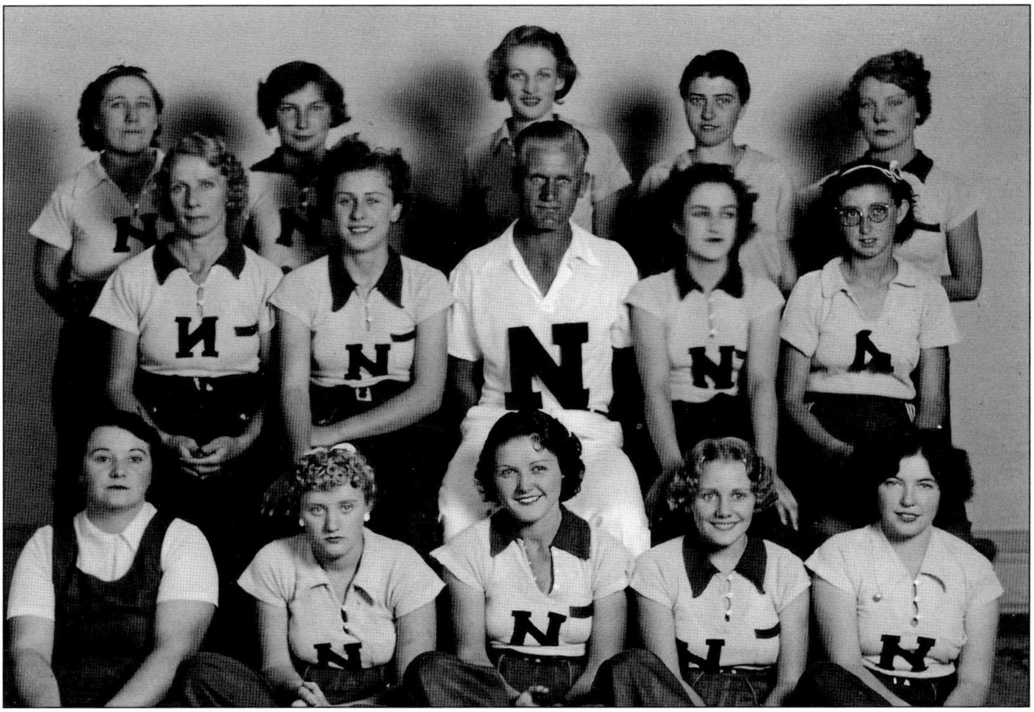

The 1936 Yellow Jackets girls' softball team is pictured here. In no particular order are Bader, Harms, Mervin, Brannon, Tucker, C. Lockwood, I. Lockwood, Carlow, Robinson, and Tullis. They only lost one game, but it was in the district tournament, which was a single elimination affair. They did beat Payette, the district champions, in an exhibition.

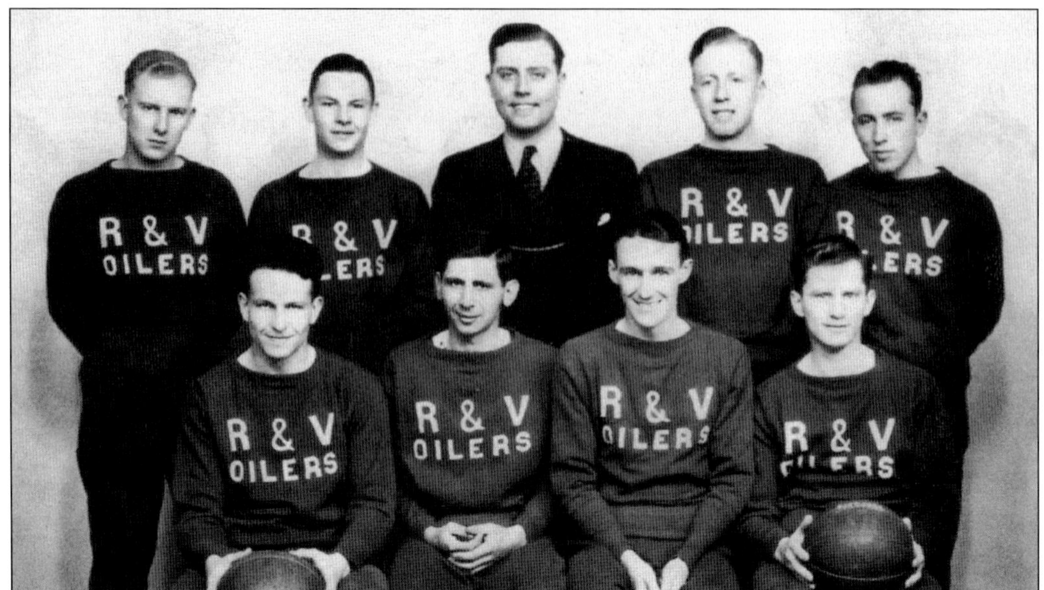

The 1937 R&V Oilers were the Commercial League champs for the third consecutive year and posted a 24-11 record. From left to right are (first row) Bob Tidwell, Ed "Fat" Daniels, Howard Nafziger, and Bob Wilson; (second row) Howard Schmidt, Orville Carver, Doyle Cain, Elvis Cain, and Claude Cain. The Oilers were one of the top teams in the state in the 1930s and 1940s.

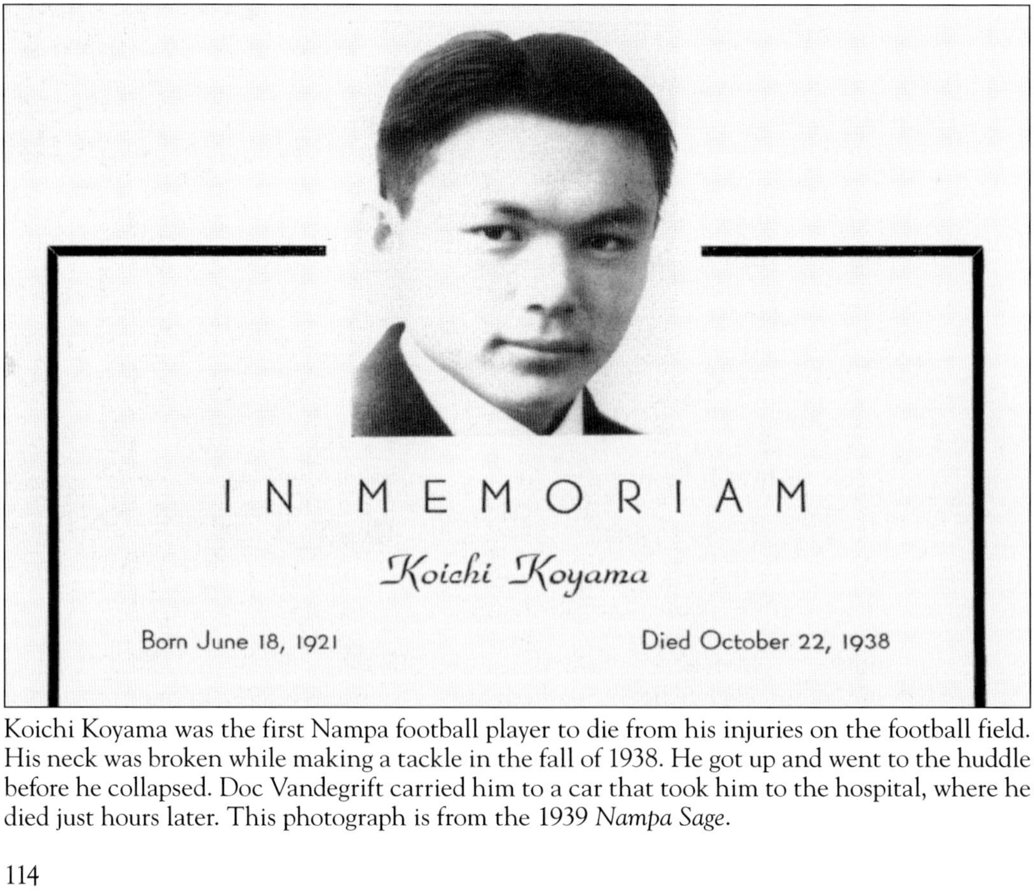

IN MEMORIAM

Koichi Koyama

Born June 18, 1921 Died October 22, 1938

Koichi Koyama was the first Nampa football player to die from his injuries on the football field. His neck was broken while making a tackle in the fall of 1938. He got up and went to the huddle before he collapsed. Doc Vandegrift carried him to a car that took him to the hospital, where he died just hours later. This photograph is from the 1939 *Nampa Sage*.

Pictured here are the 1936 Idaho State tennis champions. From left to right are Grant Evans (men's doubles), Evelyn Hagelin (singles), Esther Hicks (dethroned singles champ, doubles), Helen Martin (doubles), and Gordon Giles (singles and doubles). Hagelin and Evans were mixed doubles champs. Hagelin taught French and coached tennis at Nampa High School for many years.

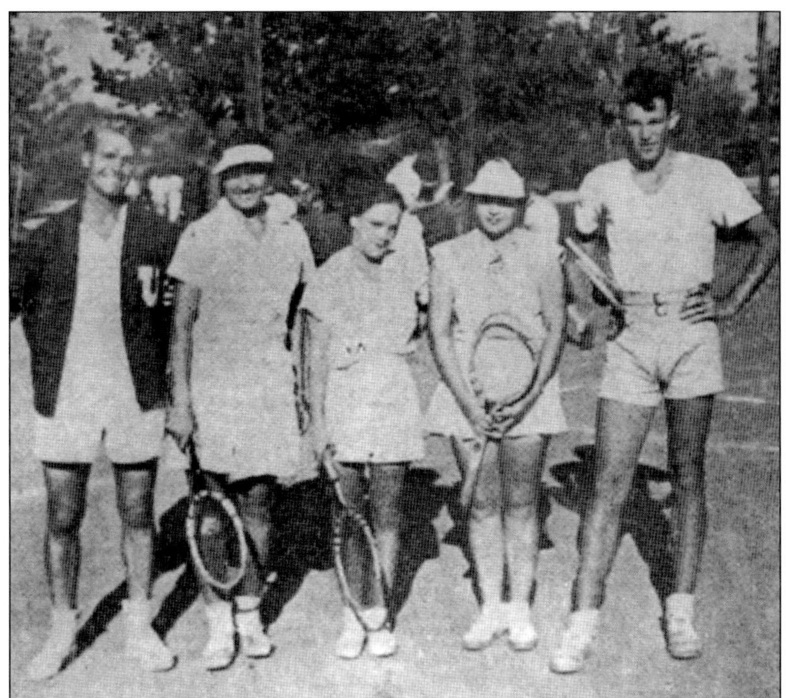

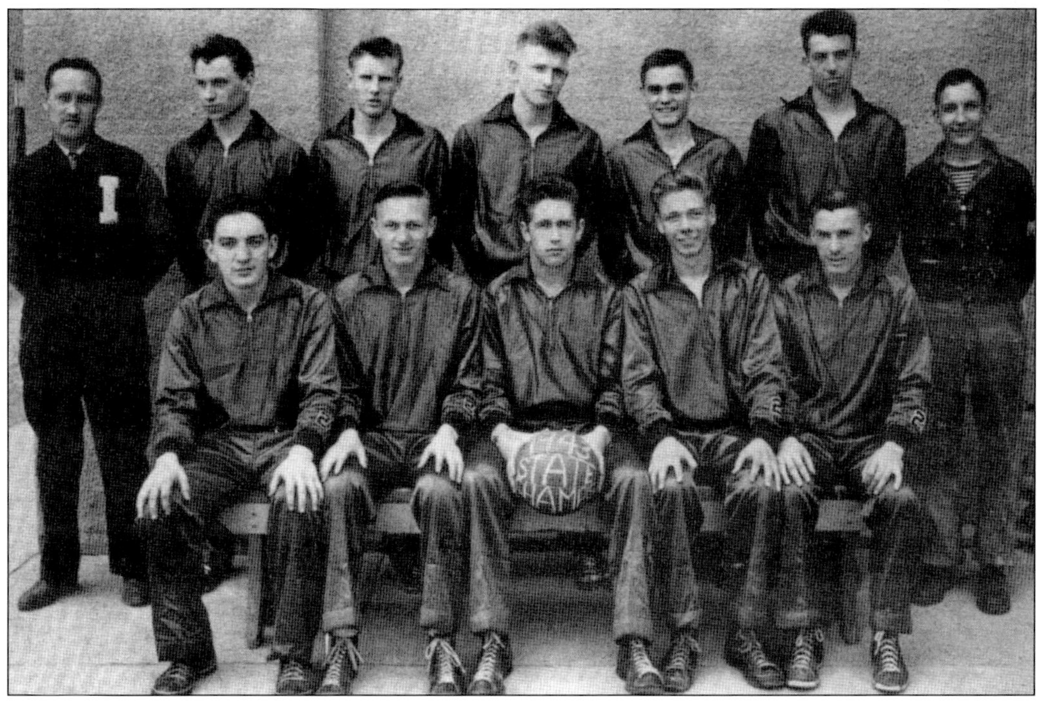

Pictured here are Nampa High School's Southern Idaho champions of 1943. Because of wartime travel restrictions, two tournaments were held, one in the south and one in the north. From left to right are (first row) Glen Montague, Howard Neil, Gene Rodwell, Bob Tullis, and Eugene Shepard; (second row) coach Jerry Dellinger, E. Steele, Warren Wheeler, Bob Pritchett, Burke Schindal, Dave Schas, and G. Purdy.

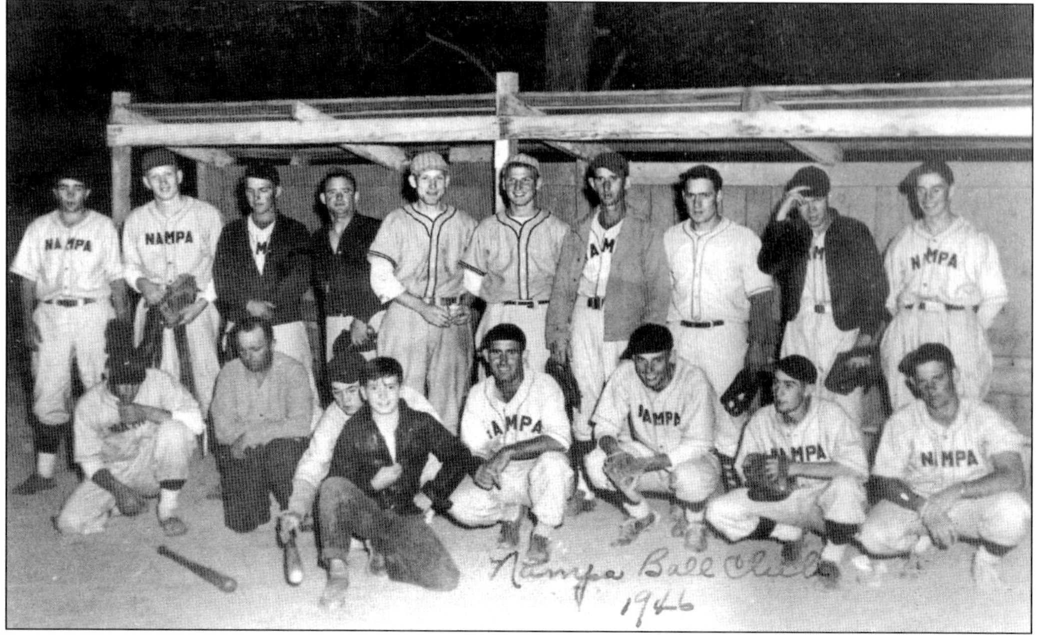

The Nampa Clippers are pictured in 1946. From left to right are (first row) unidentified, Hank Zink, Pat Robb, two unidentified, Bob Wilkerson, and unidentified; (second row) Bob De Coursey, Bob Pritchett, Del Lampe, unidentified, Ed Bonham, Bud Lyda, three unidentified, and R. Newton. The Clippers in the following five years dominated the league. Players not shown were Emit DeCoursey, Bill Moad, John Kuroda, Tommy Gibson, and Sumner Johnson.

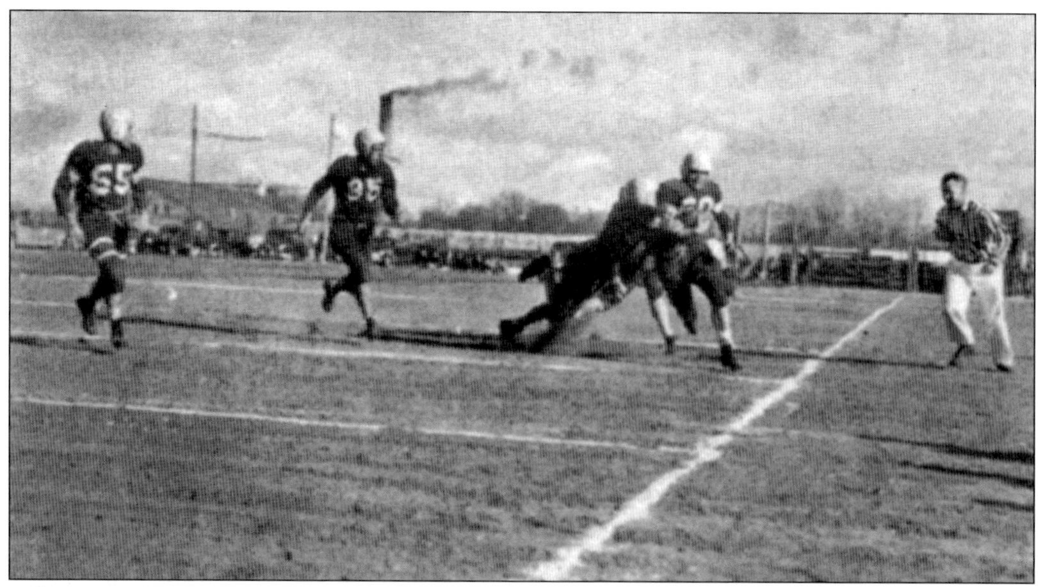

Bill Moore packs the mail against Caldwell in 1947 at Rodeo Park in Nampa. No. 55 is Bud Jones of Nampa, and No. 95 is Ray Dillon of Caldwell. The Bulldogs won the game 25-7. This was Babe Brown's first year at the helm. Moore was a four-year starter for the Bulldogs and went on to star at Boise Junior College.

J.A. "Babe" Brown took over the Nampa athletic program in the fall of 1947. His football teams went 61-21-2, while his basketball teams won eight district titles and one state championship. He also served as head baseball coach for one season. He brought Dean Lewis to Nampa with him. Lewis would follow Brown as head football coach in the fall of 1956.

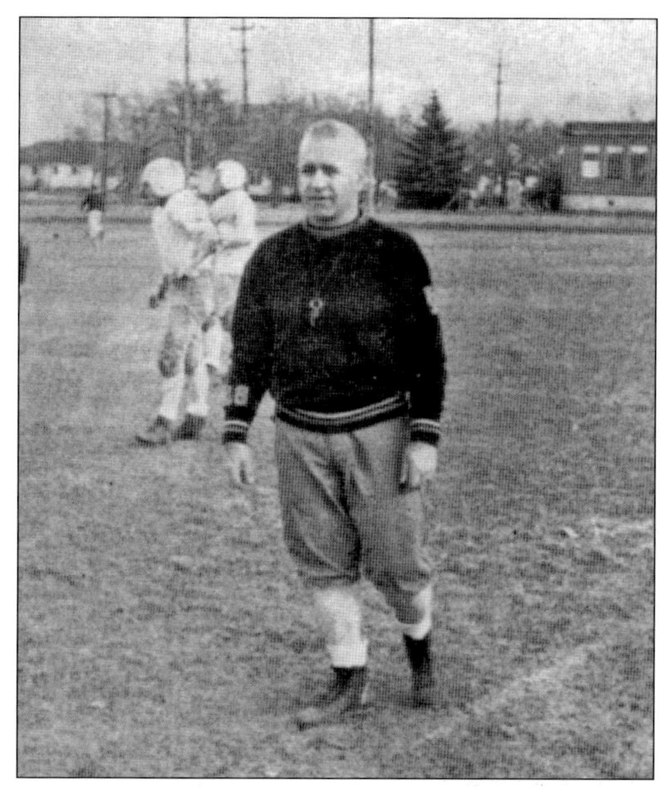

Dale Huss gains yardage against Boise at Rodeo Park in 1948. Other Nampa players are John Salove (No. 53) and George Keim (No. 71). Nampa won the game 6-0, breaking a six-year Braves streak. The Bulldogs tied for the Big Six championship with Pocatello. They had an 8-2 record, losing by one point to Pocatello and Missoula, Montana.

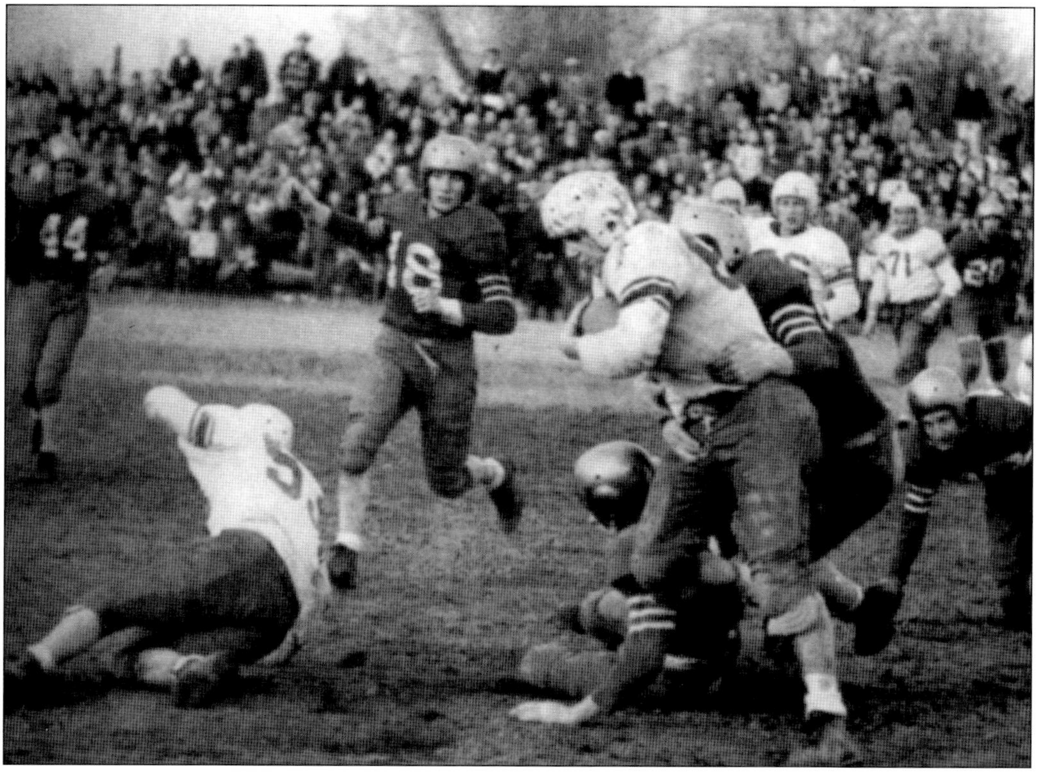

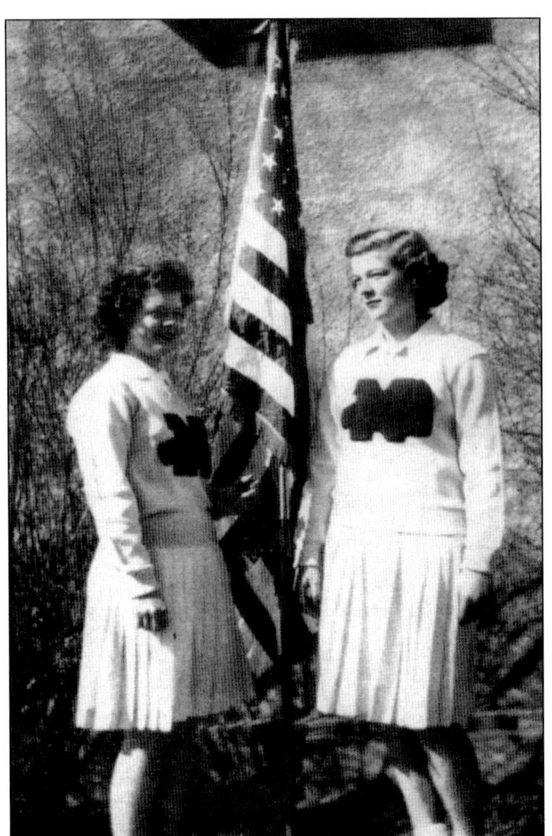

Nampa cheerleaders Patricia McFarland and Sally Robb proudly display Nampa's Sportsmanship Award, given to the student body at the 1948 District Tournament. The award was coveted by all of the high schools in the district. It was the only recognition received by the fans. Nampa won the district championship and went one-and-one at the state championship. They had a 22-5 record.

The 1949 Roosevelt Grade School basketball team included, from left to right, (first row) Larry Cain, Gerry Behunin, Bob Martindale, Dorlen Hammon, and George Betts; (second row) John Alsip, Dennis Baker, Buck McGillvary, and Weldon Wood. Nampa had sports for boys in the grade schools then that included football, basketball, and softball. They also held an all-school track meet most years.

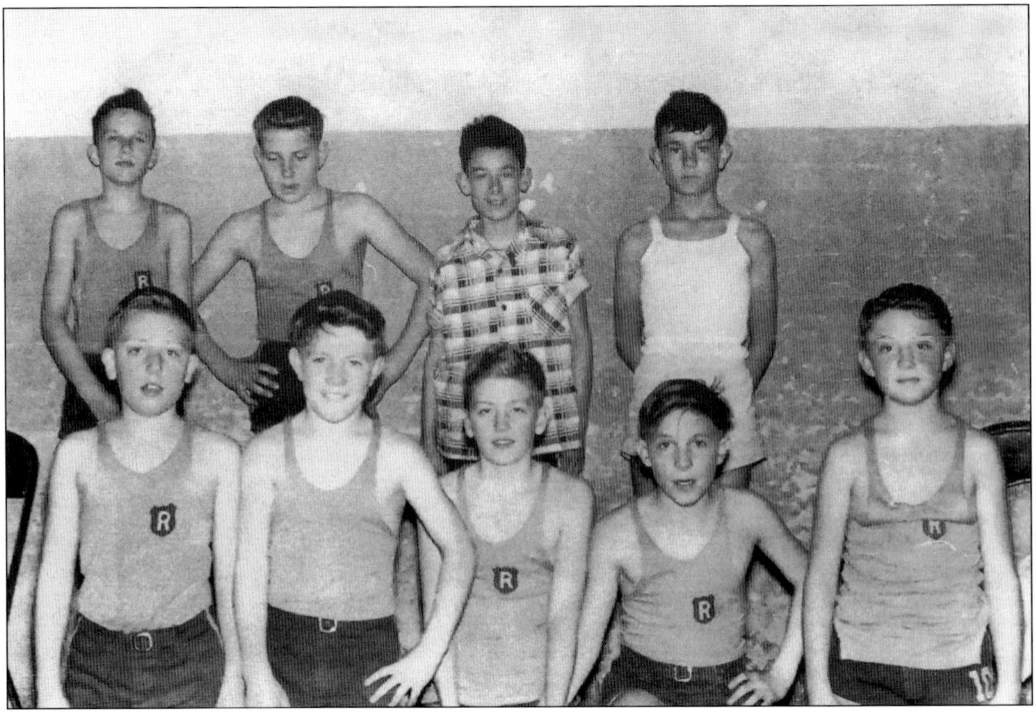

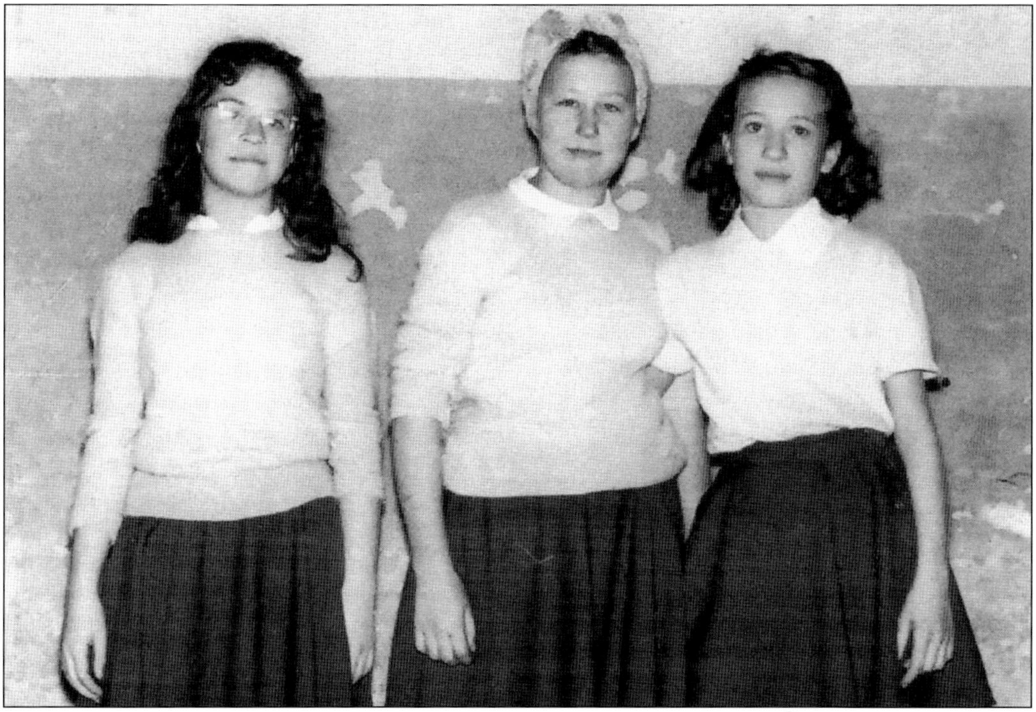

The boys from Roosevelt Elementary had to be cheered on to victory, and this is the crew that did it. From left to right are Dorothy Montgomery, Pat Nelson, and Dorlene Hammon. This was really the only participation for girls in organized sports. Times have changed, and girls have many sports to compete in now.

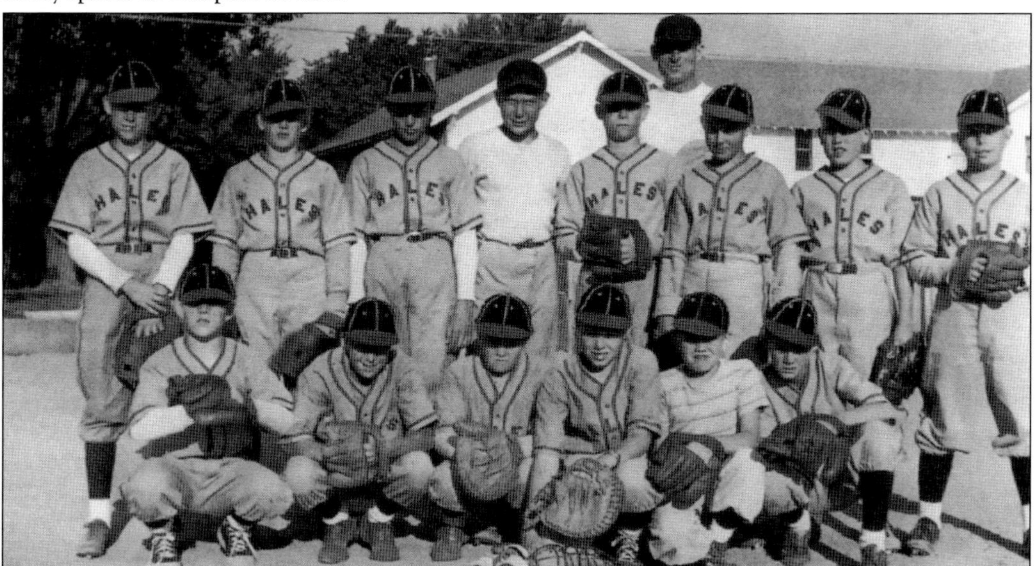

The 1949 Hales Furniture midget baseball team included, from left to right, (first row) Gerry Behunin, J.E. Morris, Jerry Hilton, Lee Hales, unidentified, and Tommy Lytle; (second row) Bucky McGillvary, Bob Martindale, Dewayne McClung, Dennis Baker, Ron Zarbnisky, George Betts, Larry Cain, and Bruce Harmon. The city put on the Little League program under longtime city recreation director Wendell Christensen.

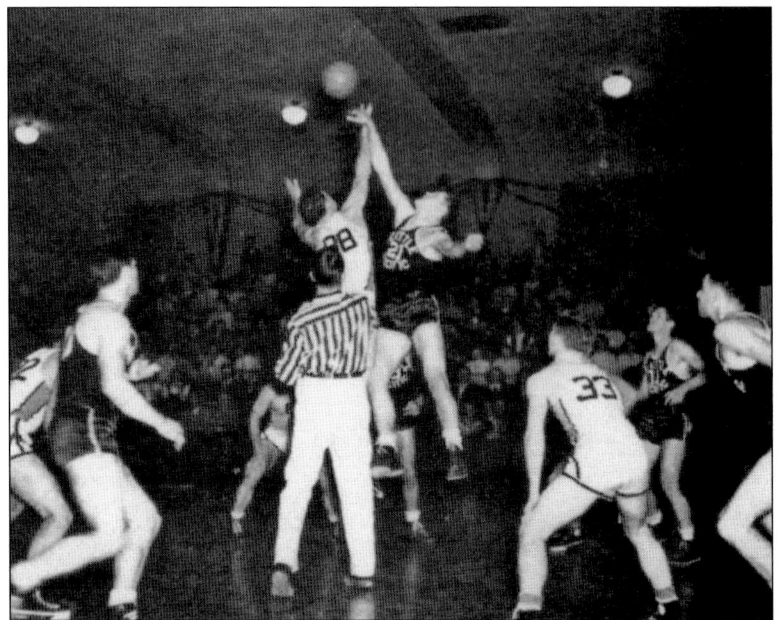

This photograph shows a moment from the Northwest Nazarene College vs. Seattle Pacific game at Central Auditorium in 1950. NNC players are Ralph Unger (No. 22) and Woody Beukelman (No. 33). The Crusaders played their games at the Central Assembly Building on the Nampa Junior High campus. Their own gym was not big enough to handle the crowds that attended their games.

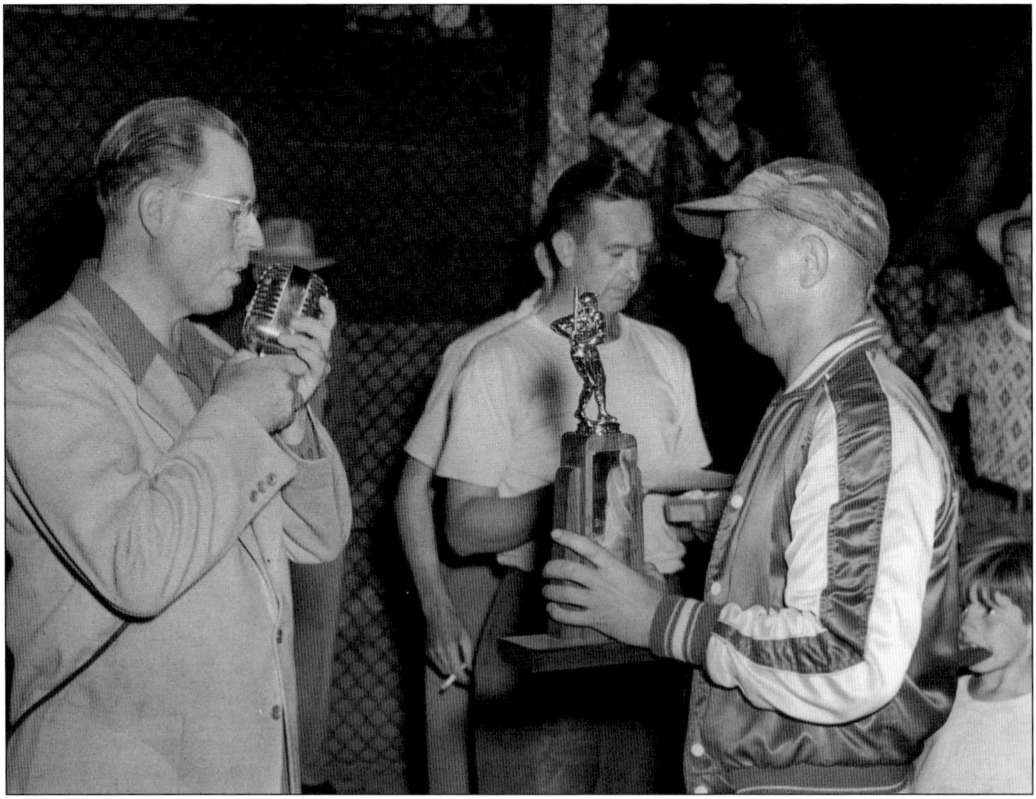

Doyle Cain is presenting the 1950 city softball championship trophy to Connie Schaefer, captain of the Warden's Super Service team. Mebs Thompson is in the background. The games were played at the Lakeview Park Diamond, right next to the municipal swimming pool. The park served the softball teams of Nampa for many years.

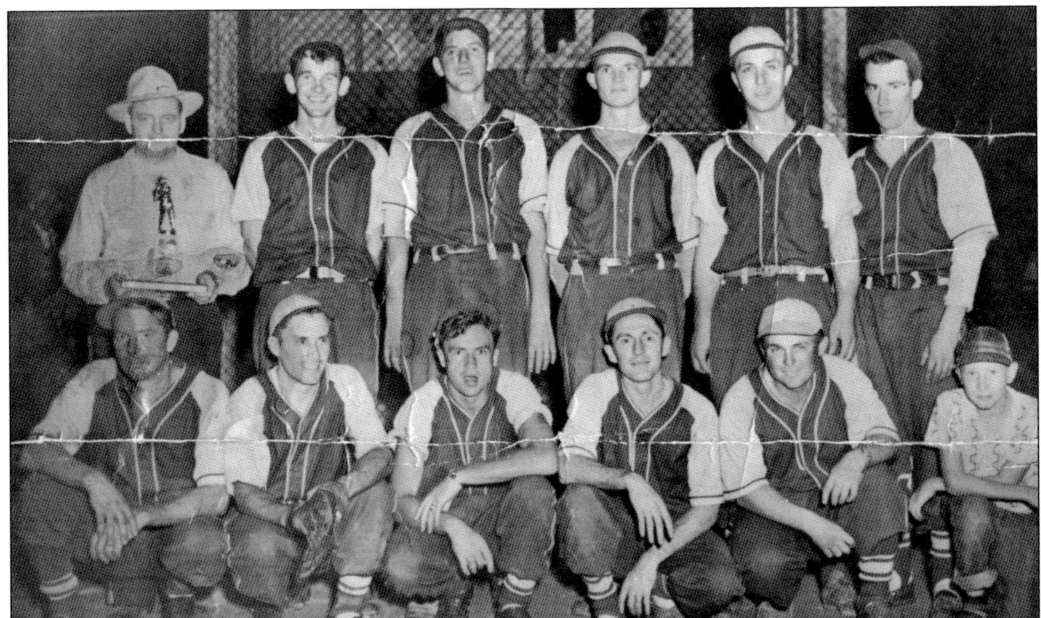

The 1952 Moose softball team is pictured here. From left to right are (first row) unidentified, Gene Shepard, unidentified, Jerry Epperly, unidentified, and Everrett Grimes (batboy); (second row) unidentified, John Cramer, Merle Iles, Herb Day, Ken Bort, and Howard Miller. Softball was originally called kittenball and was played with 10 players. Softball constantly drew big crowds to Lakeview Park on warm summer evenings.

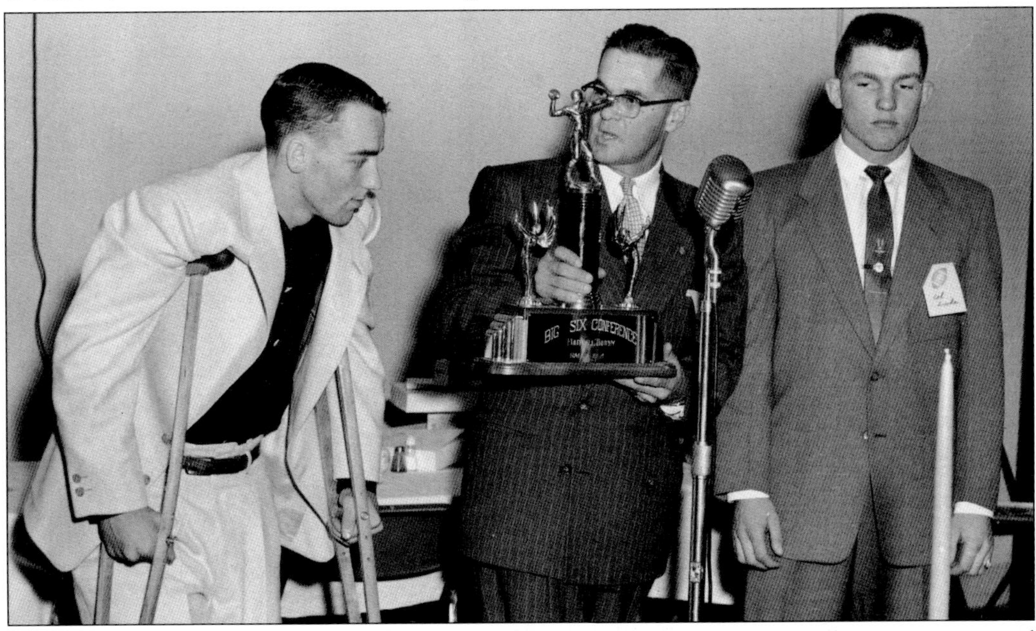

Jack Acree and Calvin Linde, co-captains of the 1954 Nampa Bulldog football team, are pictured receiving the Big Six conference championship trophy from Harry Mills. Along with the 1949 aggregation, they were the only Nampa teams to take the crown undefeated in league play. Babe Brown's team lost only to Great Falls, Montana, on their home field. The Bisons were Montana's state champions that year.

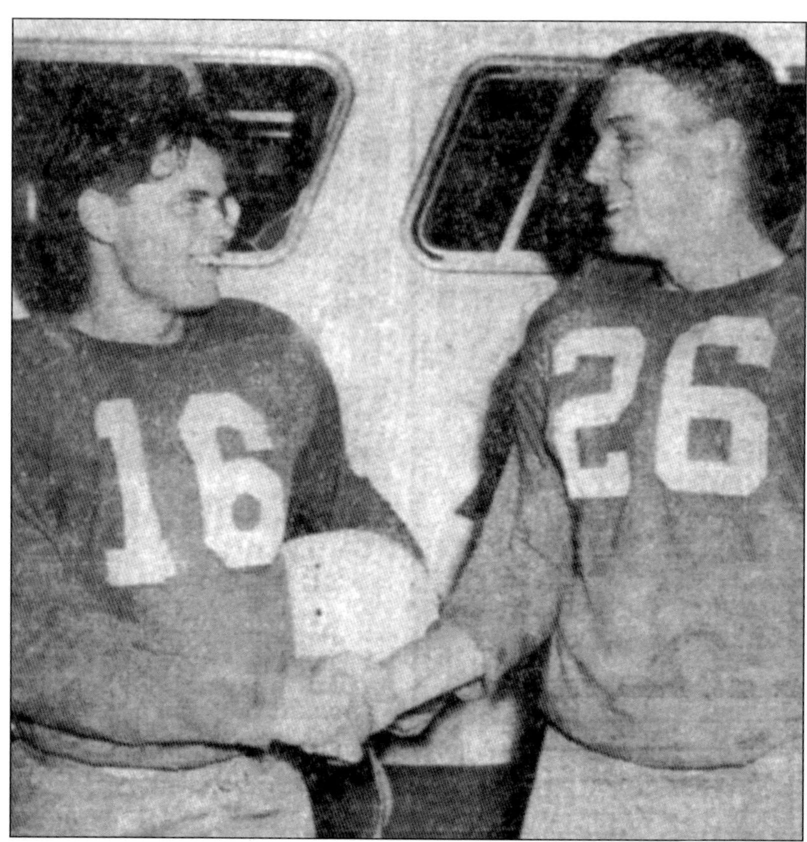

Fred Corey (left) congratulates Fred Towery on their win in the All Star game. The Boise Valley All Stars defeated the Snake River Valley All Stars 14-0 in the summer of 1955. The former Nampa Bulldogs scored the only touchdowns. Other former Bulldogs who saw action in the game were Dick Skinner, Gerry Behunin, Larry Cain, Gene Brock, and Calvin Linde.

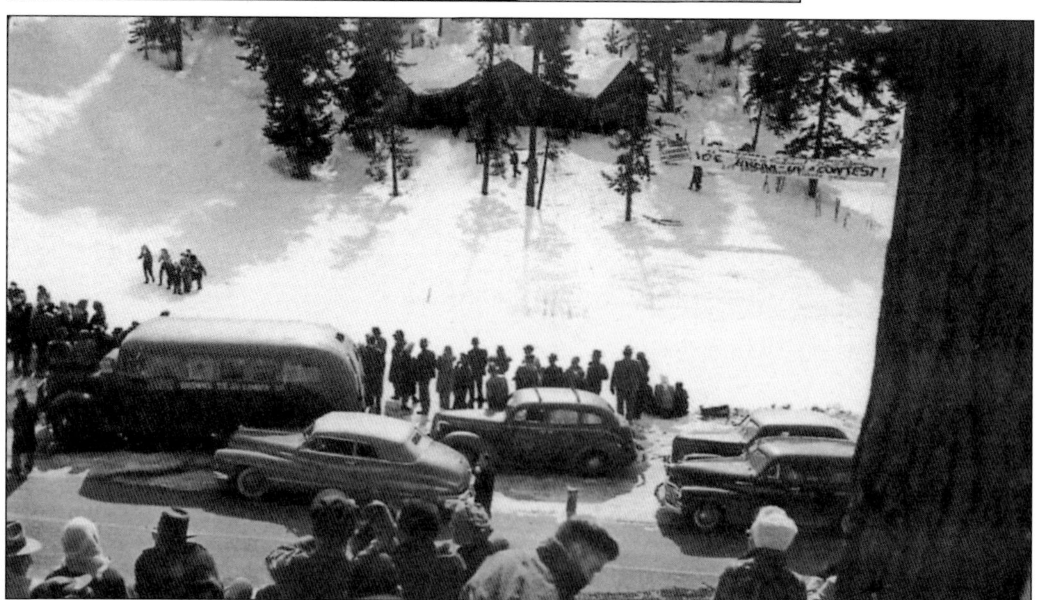

Many Nampans spent winter days hurtling down the mountain and enjoying other winter sports at the ski lodge near McCall, Idaho. The Brundage Mountain Ski Resort near McCall was and is a very popular winter playground. The Bogus Basin ski area above Boise is the closest to Nampa's skiers and snowboarders.

This was a Church League game in 1958 between Christian and First Church Nazarene. Val Toolson puts up a shot for Christians as Wesche tries to stop him. Donavan Omstead, First Church, looks on. Gary Knudson and Bill Wallis are the other Christian players. The Christian team was the only one to win both the Church League and the City League the same year in Nampa.

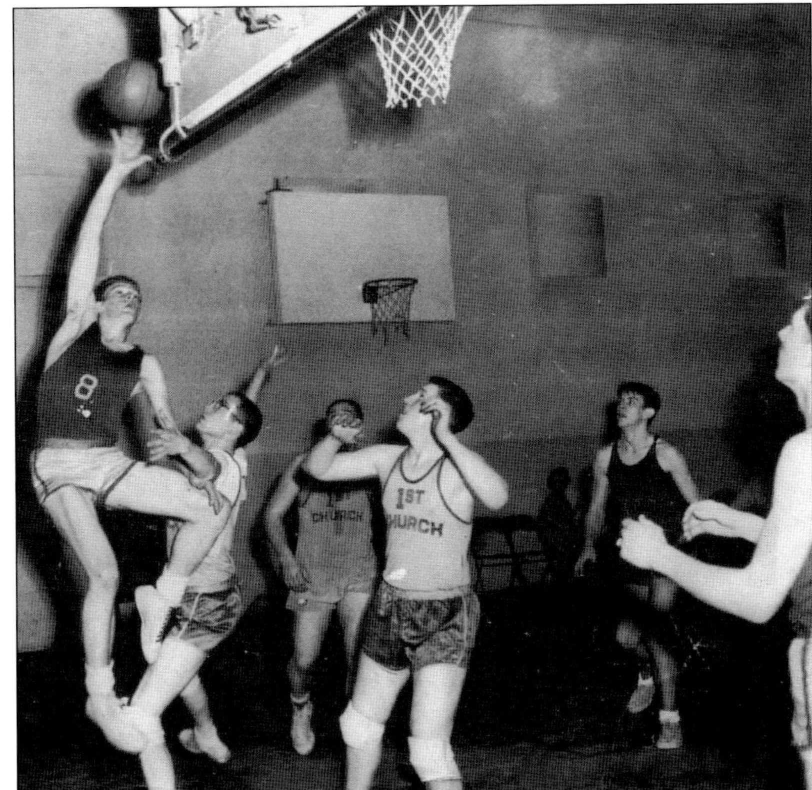

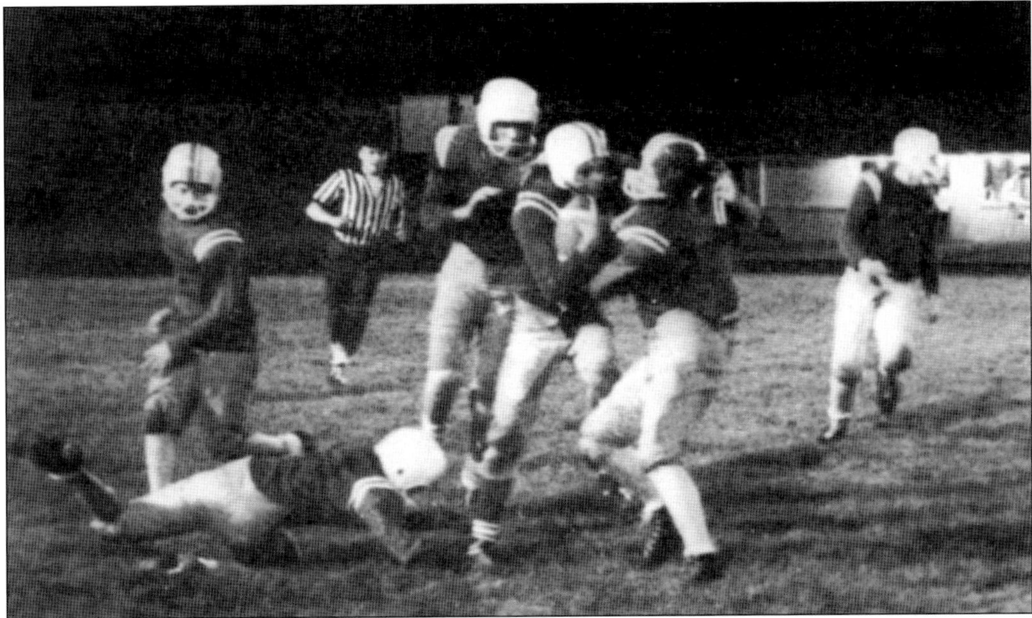

Bob Shepard, packing the pigskin for West Junior High, is tackled by Gary Gilbert of Central in an Exchange Club Little League game in 1958. Nampa had an extensive Little League football program. The games were played under the lights at the Rodeo Park baseball field. The program was sponsored by the Exchange Club.

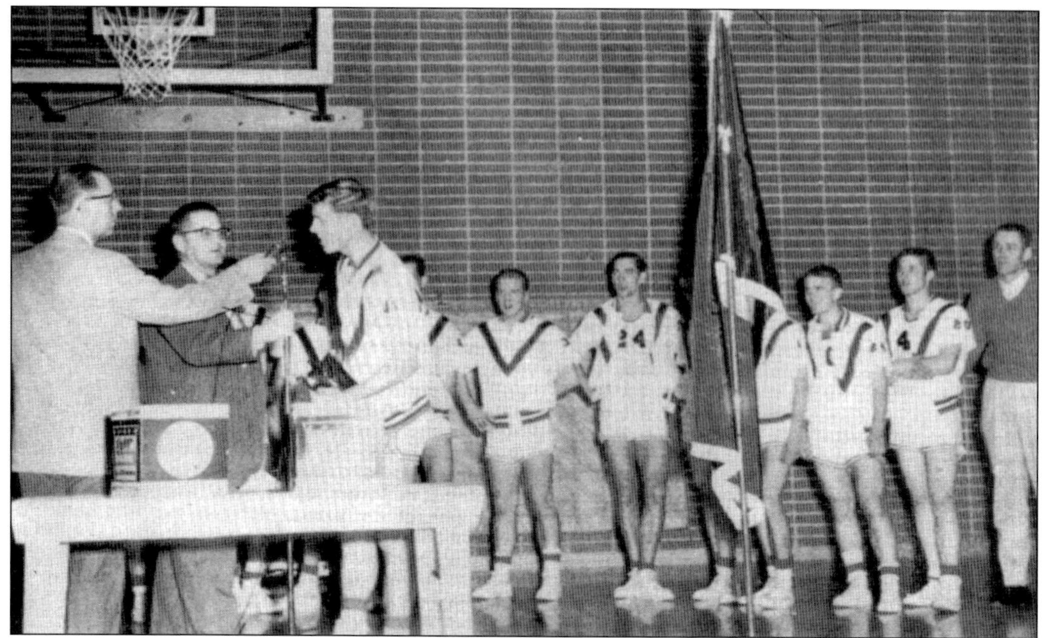

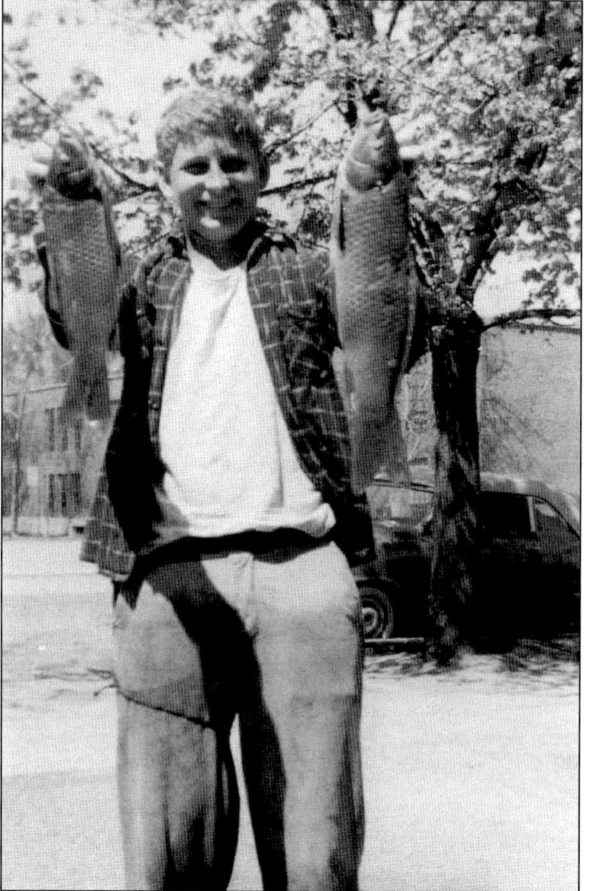

Harry Mills presents the 1958 District Trophy to team captain Jim Lynch, as Doyle Cain captures the ceremony for the radio audience. Bulldog coach George Keil is at far right. To his left are Ron Dike, Dick Davies, Ron Robinson, and Hal Murray. The tournament game was played in the Nampa High School gym on Lake Lowell Avenue next to Bulldog Bowl.

Larry Fowble proudly holds up his catch of the day in front of his home at 520 Fifteenth Avenue South in Nampa in 1959. Larry was an avid sportsman, as were his five brothers and one sister. He was a licensed pilot and Nampa City policeman in later years. He was the son of Steven and Matilda Fowble.

These two Little League players celebrating their newly won championship are cousins Jay Griffin and Kevin Cain of Eastside Grade School. Under the direction of the Exchange Club's Larry Higgs and the city's Wendell Christensen, Nampa's Little League football program was highly successful. This book is dedicated to Kevin.

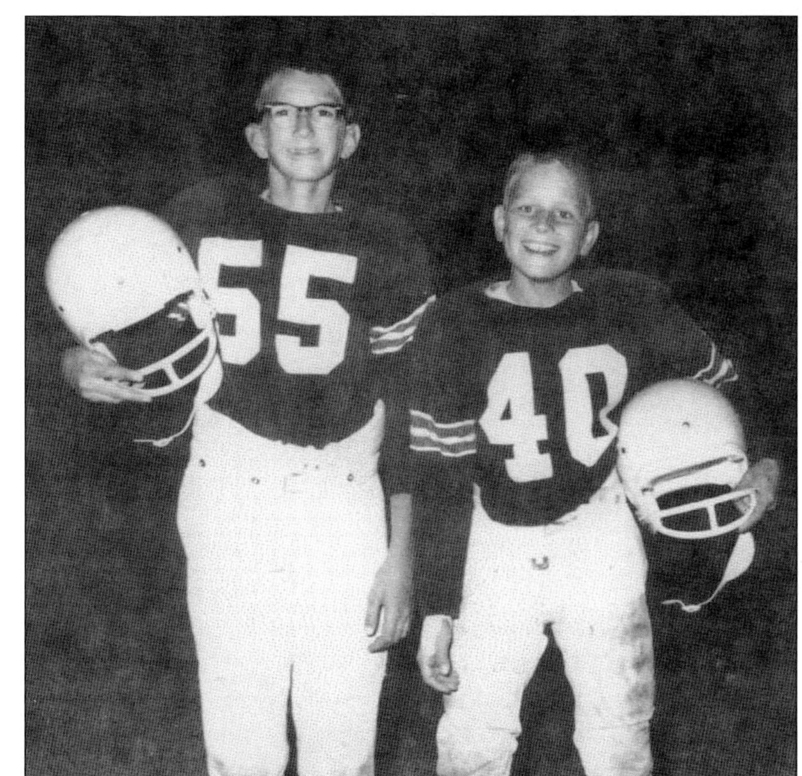

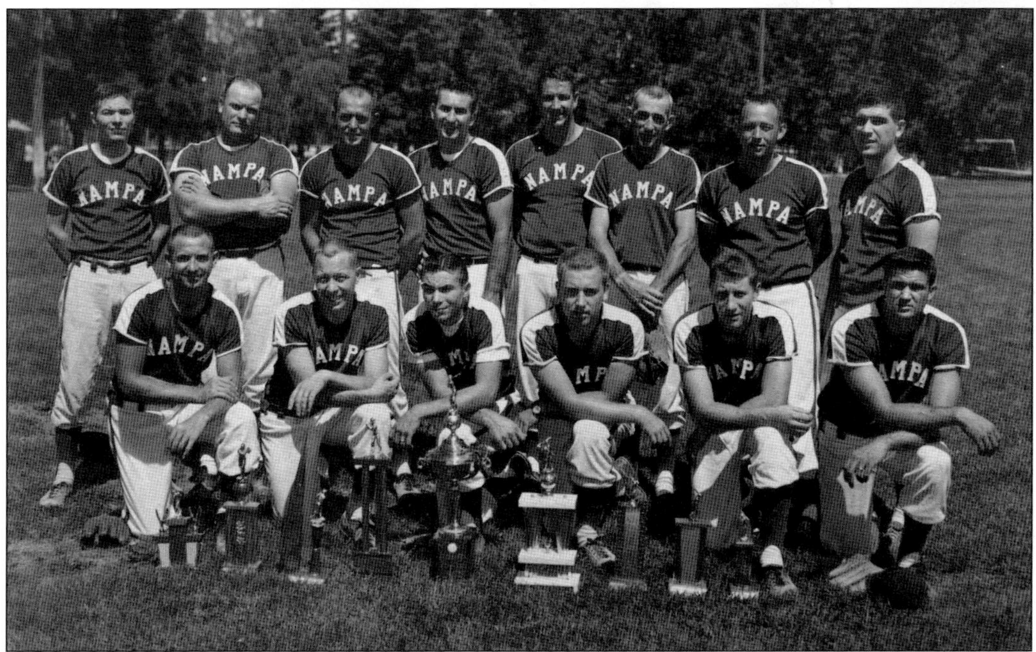

The 1966 KAIN Radio softball team were league champions, district champions, and runnerup at the state tournament. From left to right are (first row) Ben Kerfoot, Gary McMahan, Ron Romer, Larry Cain, Everrett Grimes, and Don Freeman; (second row) Don Romer, Carl Padour, Ron Ostrom, Frank Needs, Kenny Wilkens, Dud Mausling Sr., Bob Pickett, and Dud Mausling Jr.

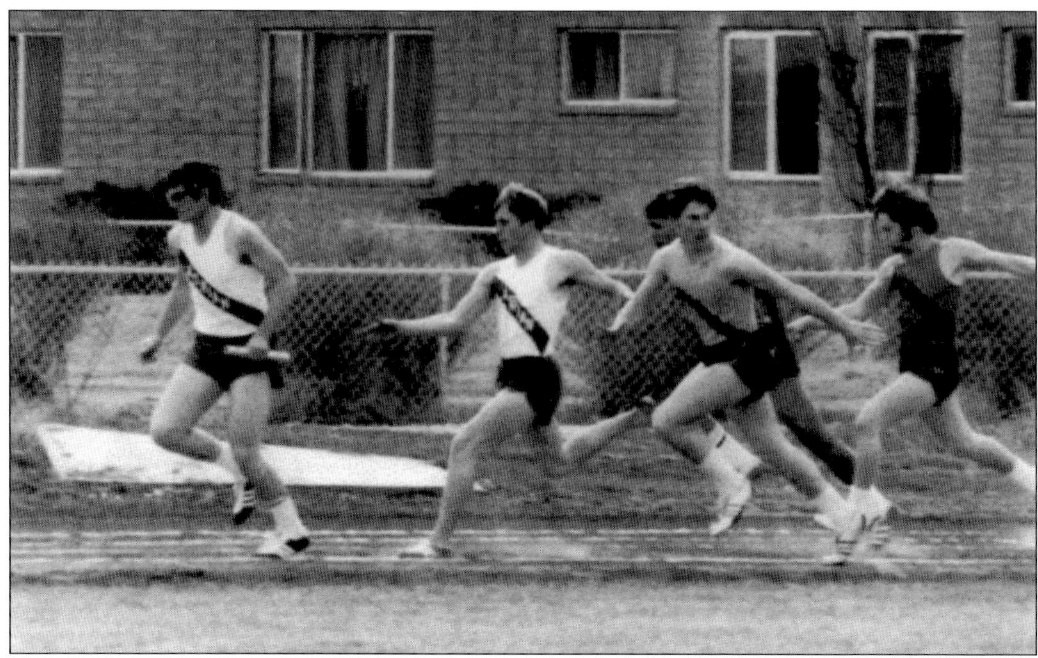

This 1974 photograph shows the 440-yard relay at Nampa between Adrian, Oregon, Rimrock, and Nampa Christian High Schools on the Nampa Christian track. From left to right are Dennis Bebee and Bob Martin from Adrian, Doug Elmore from Nampa Christian, and Todd Agenbroad from Rimrock. The three teams, along with Melba, Wilder, Notus, and Marsing, were in the same league.

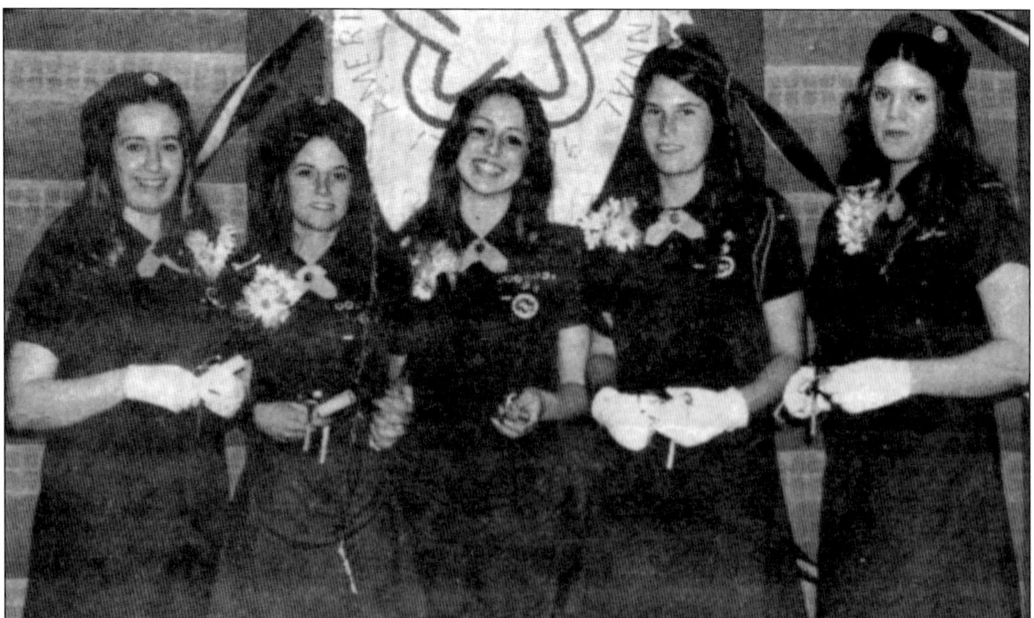

Senior Girl Scouts participated in outdoor activities and sports for merit badges. Here, five girls are graduating. From left to right are Dorothy Gano, Lynn Were, Tracy Brownfield, Laura Fergusson, and Ronda Stiehl. The 1975 ceremonies were held in the Four Seasons Room at the Mercy Medical Center.

Rain or shine, track meets go on as in this 1975 photograph of a quadrangular meet at Hayman Field in Caldwell. Participants were with Nampa, Caldwell, Boise, and Vallivue. Lori Martin hands off to Staci Cain as the Nampa team takes the 880 relay. Jeanette Ford was the Nampa coach.

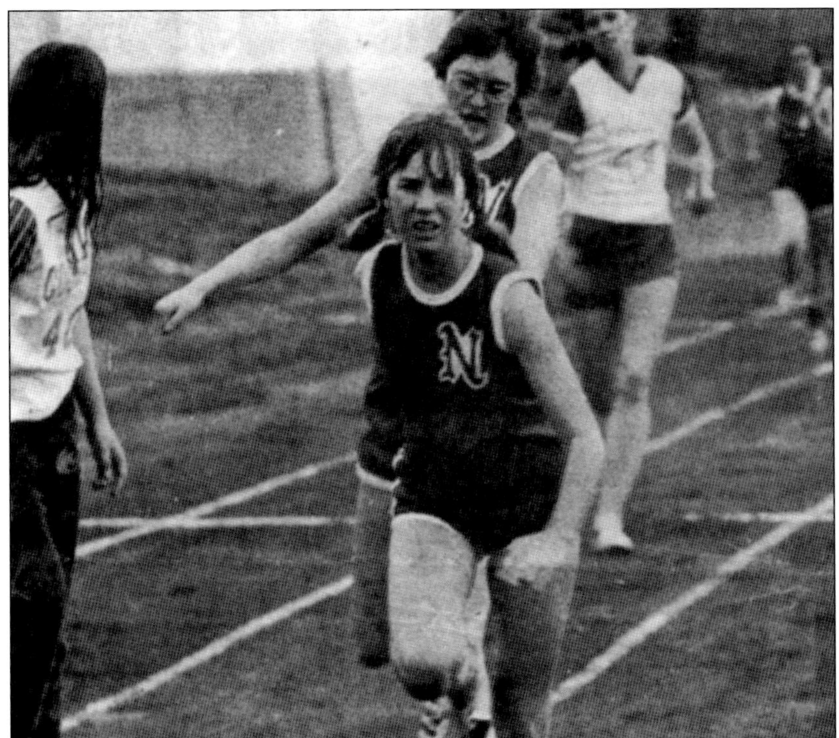

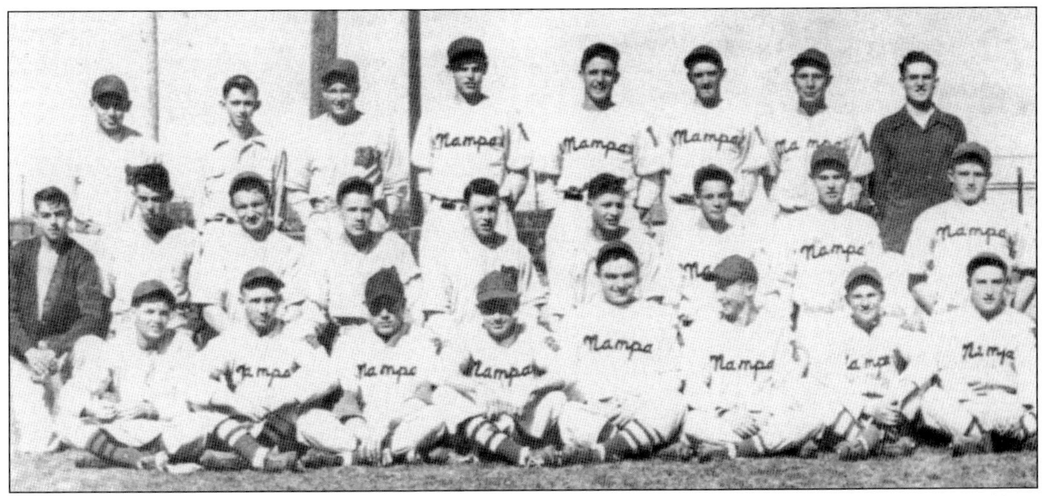

The Nampa High School baseball team of 1950 lost only one game. From left to right are (first row) Nephi Donahue, Bill Shannon, Gary Johnson, B. Evans, Dick King, Ike Thomas, Ted Hallberg, and Happy Lyda; (second row) B. Rode, D. Howard, LeRoy Crill, Myron Finkbeiner, J. Flitton, J. Conner, M. Nunenkamp, Mickey Dean, and Bob Rodwell; (third row) Coach White, H. Forshey, Jack Newman, Jay Dean, Wayne Blickenstaff, Neil Stephens, Wayne McFarland, and B. Perkins.